Arts Marketing

Arts Marketing

Finola Kerrigan
Peter Fraser
Mustafa Özbilgin

ELSEVIER
BUTTERWORTH
HEINEMANN

AMSTERDAM BOSTON HEIDELBERG LONDON NEW YORK OXFORD
PARIS SAN DIEGO SAN FRANCISCO SINGAPORE SYDNEY TOKYO

Elsevier Butterworth-Heinemann
Linacre House, Jordan Hill, Oxford OX2 8DP
200 Wheeler Road, Burlington, MA 01803

First published 2004

British Library Cataloguing in Publication Data
A catalogue record for this book is available from the British Library

Library of Congress Cataloguing in Publication Data
A catalogue record for this book is available from the Library of Congress

ISBN   0 7506 5968 8

For information on all Elsevier Butterworth-Heinemann publications
visit our website at http://books.elsevier.com

Typeset by Charon Tec Pvt Ltd., Chennai, India
Printed and bound in Great Britain by Biddles Ltd, King's Lynn, Norfolk

Contents

Biographical notes

Dr Ian Fillis is a Lecturer in Marketing in the Department of Marketing at the University of Stirling, Scotland. He holds a BSc in Civil Engineering from the University of Glasgow, an MA in Marketing from the University of Ulster and a PhD on the internationalisation process of the smaller firm from the University of Stirling. His main research interests focus on issues at the Marketing, Entrepreneurship and Art interfaces such as creativity and innovation, in addition to exploring international marketing and export related phenomena. He is an active member of the Academy of Marketing/ University of Illinois at Chicago Marketing and Entrepreneurship Special Interest Group, and the Academy of Marketing Arts and Heritage Special Interest Group. Since investigating the link between marketing and art is also his hobby as well as one of his research interests, he spends much of his spare time visiting art galleries around the world.

Iain Fraser is a Lecturer in Marketing at Dundee Business School, in the University of Abertay, Scotland. He holds an honours degree in Building Technology from the University of Manchester Institute of Science and Technology and an MSc in Business Studies from London Business School. His early career was spent in London, working as a quantity surveyor on building sites during the day and attending performing arts events at night. Now he combines work with pleasure by researching theatre, opera and other performing arts from a marketing perspective. His other research interests involve the development of economic infrastructure, entrepreneurship and small businesses in Eastern Europe. In this respect he currently makes regular visits to Lithuania in fulfilment of a Department of Trade and Industry contract. He is a member of the Chartered Institute of Marketing, an active member of the Arts Marketing Association and is currently chair of the Whitehall Theatre in Dundee.

Dr Peter Fraser is a Senior Lecturer in Marketing at the University of Hertfordshire. He gained an MA degree in English Literature and Language from the University of Edinburgh followed by an MSc in Business Studies from London Business School. Before moving into academic life he obtained a wide range of management and marketing experience in both public and private sector organisations, working in sectors ranging from health services to arts video distribution. His PhD thesis, adopting a complexity perspective, highlighted some ways in which business schools currently fail to address many important aspects of how people survive financially and lead a life outside the organisation. Peter is a member of the Complexity and Management Centre at the University of Hertfordshire Business School. Currently Secretary of the Academy of Marketing, he is also an active member of the Academy's Special Interest Group in Entrepreneurial and Small Business Marketing.

Finola Kerrigan is a Lecturer in Marketing at King's College London. She is currently completing a PhD in marketing in the European film industry at the University of Hertfordshire Business School where she is a member of the Film Industry Research Group. She is also a visiting lecturer on the MA in Film and Television Production at Royal Holloway, The University of London. Her research focuses on marketing of the arts, specifically film, and she has published and presented at national and international conferences in this area. She is a member of the Academy of Marketing and the Arts and Heritage Special Interest Group of the Academy of Marketing, The International Arts Marketing Association and the British Academy of Management.

Nil Şişmanyazıcı Navaie is an artist, development advocate, and the founder of the '*Arts For Global Development Network (www.art4development.net)*'. The network is an online initiative where worldwide arts and development advocates share their ideas, experiences, works, and concentrate on developing tangible policies and projects collaboratively. Nil S. Navaie does consulting in institutional strengthening, organisational development, and works with national and international organisations that focus on arts, youth, education, social and economic empowerment issues. Prior to becoming an independent consultant, she worked in the marketing/advertising sector (Ogilvy and Mather) and led projects in management consulting and telecommunications fields for fortune 500 companies. After attending Mimar Sinan Fine Arts Academy in Turkey Nil S. Navaie continued her studies in International Relations and Economics at the University of Maryland and received her master's degree in Development Management from the London School of Economics and Political Science in the UK. Her research interests lie in creative development, societal enterprises and responsibility.

Dr Dorothea Noble is a Principal Lecturer in Strategic Management at the Business School of the University of Hertfordshire and has been a member of the Complexity and Management Centre at the University since it was established in 1995. The strand of complexity theory developed by the members of that Centre encourages research into one's own practice, which influenced the work she chose to contribute for this book. She was Chairman of the Board of Trustees of a jazz development trust during recent years, an experience she has explored here. She had been a fan of jazz since her teens, and was a member of a thriving jazz club for many years. Before becoming an academic, Dorothea held a range of international marketing roles in two small international companies, finally as Marketing Director and board member. Her research activity has focused on the exploration of complexity theory through her professional experiences and roles.

Daragh O'Reilly is a Lecturer in Marketing at Leeds University Business School. Originally a modern languages graduate of Trinity College, Dublin, he spent much of his early career in inward investment promotion in Ireland, followed by a number of years working in West Africa on handcraft development and marketing. He subsequently did an MBA at Bradford University School of Management, following which he spent 3 years as a marketing advisor to organisations selling a wide variety of products into the UK. He then joined the academic staff at Bradford, where he lectured in marketing and in research methods, before moving to Leeds. His research interest lies in the relationship between business and culture, including issues such as the marketing and consumption of cultural offerings, cultural brand identity, product placement, and advertising. He is currently writing up a doctoral project at Sheffield Hallam School of Cultural Studies on the production and consumption of popular music. Daragh is a member of the Chartered Institute of Marketing.

Dr Mustafa Özbilgin is a Lecturer in Human Resource Management and Industrial Relations at the University of Surrey, School of Management. His research is in the field of cross-national and comparative employment relations, with specific focus on equal opportunities, diversity, ethics and change. With particular reference to this book, he researches in the field of ethics in arts management. He is currently the co-chair of the Diversity Action Research Group, funded by the Chartered Institute of Personnel and Development. The group has 10 institutional members, all large and complex organisations, from public, private and voluntary sectors in the UK. He is the co-author of a monograph titled, *Banking and Gender: Sex Equality in the Financial Services Sector in Britain and Turkey* (published by IB Tauris, Palgrave).

Dr Ruth Rentschler (BA Hons Fine Arts and Germanic Studies, Melbourne, PhD, Monash) is acting executive director of the Centre for Leisure Management Research in the Bowater School of Management & Marketing, Faculty of Business & Law, Deakin University. Ruth has published widely in the cultural field including the *Cultural and Entertainment Industries Handbook*, *Shaping Culture*, *Innovative Arts Marketing* and *The Entrepreneurial Arts Leader*. In 2003, her book *Shaping Culture* was published in Chinese (Five Senses Arts Management, Taiwan). She has guest edited a special issue of *Corporate Reputation Review* (with Professor Roger Bennett in Britain) on nonprofit organisations (Autumn 2003) and a special issue of the *Journal of Arts Management, Law and Society* on 'Culture and Entrepreneurship' (Fall 2003). Ruth has a special interest in art, marketing, creativity and entrepreneurship. She maintains a strong interest in the visual arts and art museums in her work and private life. Ruth has held various government appointments to panels such as the Arts Marketing Task Force and Arts Victoria Professional Development Panel.

Elif Shafak is a novelist. She was born in France in 1971. She spent her teenage years in Spain, before returning to Turkey. Her first novel, Pinhan-The Sufi, which she published at age 27, was awarded the Rumi Prize – a recognition given to best works in mystical/transcendental literature. Her third novel Mahrem (Hide-and-Seek), received the Turkish Novel Award. While on a fellowship at the Women's Studies Center in Mount Holyoke College, Elif Shafak wrote her new novel in English, The Saint of Incipient Insanities, which will be published in Fall 2004. Elif Shafak is also a social scientist, holding a Masters Degree in Gender and Women Studies from the Middle Eastern Technical University, and continuing her PhD in The Department of Political Science working on State, Secularism and Masculinities in Turkey: Male Gender Roles in the Secularist–Islamist Power Frame. Shafak has taught Ottoman History From the Margins', 'Turkey & Cultural Identities' and 'Women and Writing' in Istanbul Bilgi University and is currently teaching at Ann Arbor, University of Michigan. Shafak also writes for various dailies, weeklies and monthlies in Turkey. Contesting the dominant and manipulative discourse of religious orthodoxy and nationalist ideologies, as well as the established gender patterns and roles, has been a central theme in her writings, fiction and nonfiction alike.

Chapter 1

Introduction

Finola Kerrigan, Peter Fraser and Mustafa Özbilgin

This volume has emerged from connections formed at a series of symposia and meetings which took place from 1999 onwards. The symposia were organised in order to encourage discussion and development of research in the area of arts marketing. Although arts marketing as an area of academic research has been developing for a number of years, literature in the area is still limited to a relatively narrow range of books and journal articles. This book is an attempt to build on existing literature by focusing on a number of areas of the arts and examining the development of marketing activity in these areas. There are many similarities as well as peculiarities between the organisation of marketing in these various art forms. These activities are informed by the requirement to address the needs of a variety of stakeholders including artists, funders, shareholders, policy makers and the general public. Although this volume is not exhaustive, we have tried to include a range of art forms in order to present a broad picture of the development of marketing within the arts.

In Chapter 2, existing research within marketing and consumer studies in the area of popular music is examined, and contrasted with views from popular music studies. A gap between the literatures is identified. Then the structure and environment of the popular music industry is dealt with, mapping out the popular music business domain, identifying the key categories of 'player', their inter-relationships and business-environmental issues. The focus then moves to brand identity in the popular music business, the different kinds of brands to be found there, including performer brands, venue brands and content provider brands. A music brand web is offered as a model for analysing musical brand identity. Following on from this, the question of the marketing mix is explored and an adapted mix developed for popular music acts. Finally, five directions for future interdisciplinary research are suggested: music brand identity, online music fan communities, major label marketing practices and live performance. A bibliography is provided which is intended to help the reader make the journey from marketing/consumer behaviour into popular music with the best guides available.

Chapter 3 considers the development of marketing within the film industry by setting film marketing within the wider context of the film industry. It maps out the historical development of the industrial formations which exist in the contemporary film industry and examines early forms of marketing which were used. The chapter also examines the development of market research in the film industry, showing how early research used film as a tool in order to research society, only later moving on to actually research audience tastes and use this information in order to satisfy them. The chapter also examines the roles of policy in the film industry and identifies the marketing tools used in today's film industry by proposing a framework of analysis for the marketing of films. Examples will be derived mainly from the American and European industry, although other industries are also drawn upon. The marketing of film differs from the marketing of the majority of art forms included in this book in that the most films which we see in the cinema do not receive public funding. Like rock music, those in the film industry can only afford to nurture new talent and take risks by achieving a level of commercial success with others. In saying this, the chapter acknowledges the importance of public funding in developing and sustaining the film industry.

Drawing on historical, critical and practitioner insights, Chapter 4 examines theatre marketing. The growing body of academic management literature dealing with theatre marketing often describes the application of techniques that are beyond the resources of the majority of theatres to implement. Even when relatively sophisticated techniques have proven their worth one wonders at the ability of organisations to finance repeat assessments. In real life, practitioners of theatre marketing are often poorly trained and must work with far fewer resources than their private sector counterparts. Despite this, the best practitioners have developed intuitive skills of a high order. Marketing is now a discipline requiring the sound operation of certain mechanical functions yet little has been written about the importance of the impresario or showman. Theatre is about excitement, and requires hullabaloo or razzmatazz in its promotion. In this chapter, attention has been paid to some key themes such as the role of amateur theatre and distinctions between amateur and professional, and the role of the impresario. Government policy is critical here in forming not so much the agenda as the constraints within which marketing practitioners have to work.

Chapter 5 addresses some of the particular issues in the promotion, presentation and marketing of opera and the ways in which the marketing of opera has developed in the UK and elsewhere. With the most expensive and exotic of the high status arts in the western world, opera is described from the perspective of a consumer and now as a researcher in the field. Threads from marketing theory and practice include the nature of the product or service itself and its evolution; barriers to consumption and appreciation; audience development; education and outreach; location and accessibility; government subsidy and political processes; the role of the marketing department, and word of mouth. The centrality of social or group processes, so critical to experience goods, is highlighted.

Chapter 6 offers a narrative account of the experience of being involved in the setting up, and running, of a jazz development agency funded by the Lottery and various local public bodies. The author of this section, Dorothea Noble, was Chairman of the Board of Trustees for most of the life of the organisation, a role that drew her into the management of the agency itself, and the management of the relationships with the various funders. The theme of marketing runs through the account in this chapter, not only as a relevant activity for the promotion of their activities – gigs, workshops, master classes and the like – but also in its representation of what could not be said. The chapter highlights that there are notable contradictions inherent in bringing together bureaucracies and creative groups. The first demand accountability for every pound spent in terms of their own strategic aims as imposed by government policy; yet the arts organisations, and particularly jazz-related ones, are also required to stimulate creative activity among diverse groups in the community. This chapter explores this situation as it was experienced in one small, publicly funded jazz agency.

Chapter 7 is concerned with the marketing of visual arts. This chapter provides an overview of visual arts marketing from critical, theoretical and practitioner perspectives. To date, little attention has been paid to the philosophical clashes of art for art's sake versus art for business' sake when constructing visual arts marketing theory. Unlike the majority of other industry sectors, non-pecuniary factors often outweigh any financial benefits as the artist seeks to develop the artwork. By understanding how visual arts practitioners creatively combine artistic and business expertise, the marketing researcher can then construct a more appropriate form of marketing theory. The existing theory versus practice gap is in line with other areas within marketing where what is actually carried out does not match the formulated, theorised version. Art has been used to describe the representation of the underlying nature of reality, the manifestation of pleasure or emotion and direct intuitive vision. This last interpretation mirrors the thinking of the author in terms of the importance of understanding how the artist uses sets of creative competencies to develop and market the artwork. The artist is essentially a risk taking entrepreneur and, as such, creative entrepreneurial marketing factors must be incorporated into visual arts marketing theory if this theory is to be relevant to industry practice. Instead of continually following customer demand as per the marketing concept, the successful visual artist often creates marketplace demand from within the self, in the same way that successful entrepreneurs have a belief in an idea or a feel for a product which will sell. This chapter emphasises the need for visual arts marketing theory to incorporate product/artist centred factors rather than continue to solely pre-scribe regurgitations of the now dated marketing concept where the customer dictates demand. If artists always responded to the wishes of the marketplace, there would never be any meaningful progression of artistic thinking, new schools of thought, movements and development of theory.

Chapter 8 considers the museum sector and examines the competing pres-sures faced by museums. For the last two decades there have been a number of changes in government policy towards the arts. Specifically, governments have tried to introduce a creative industries approach while at the same time levelling public funding, hence pushing non-profit arts organisations further towards reliance on the tripartite funding model. In this more competitive environment, it becomes important for museums to invest in the visitor experience, while also seeking to broaden their audience base by reaching out to marginal groups who are infrequent visitors. Hence, there is an oppor-tunity to explore the importance of understanding the relative values of dif-ferent types of audiences. Traditionally, museums have operated with an emphasis on the object, with little prominence given to the needs of audi-ences. This chapter examines the origins of museum marketing, its current status in museums and its relationship to different types of audiences. It is important for museums to pitch to multiple markets, where traditionally they have served one market. The chapter identifies the value of museum marketing to customer retention and greater representation in a post-modern world, presenting a concept that service organisations can use to assess their response to changing demographic and psychographic conditions.

Chapter 9 provides an insight into societal arts marketing, supplementing the emphasis of earlier chapters on conventional marketing approaches. The chapter achieves this through an overview of the arts in the development field and examines how the arts can contribute to enhancing development on a global scale through social marketing. Since the early ages, humankind has been using their creativity to generate individual prosperity and build up social capital. Along with the 'globalisation' and recently 'localisation' phe-nomena (together 'glocalisation'), the current trend has led decision makers to value the 'human' aspect of development, such as the Millennium Development Goals that were formulated by the world leaders at the UN Millennium Summit (2000), and management themes such as good govern-ance and social responsibility. The goal at micro and macro levels, besides cre-ating competitive advantage and individual benefit, is mainly to overcome societal challenges and alleviate the cycles of underdevelopment, through societal marketing. In our interdependent world setting, where sectoral syn-ergies progressively emerge and individual wealth and societal gain have become ever more interlocked, it is difficult to address developmental issues with a single discipline. Therefore, an interdisciplinary approach is essential in finding the optimum way for helping people and their surroundings. By using a series of case studies as illustration, this chapter illustrates how the arts, combined with the social sciences, have been an effective medium in development, significantly in educating and assisting on issues such as human development and rehabilitation, the empowerment of women and micro-enterprising, conflict resolution, health and sustainable development. There are hundreds of projects that prove the positive impact of arts' involvement in building capacities and fostering communities worldwide. In order to further develop this approach more research needs to be conducted and also supportive policies are required to shape the suitable environment for arts to maximise its potential in the development process. The chapter also includes a debate piece by Elif Shafak, a novelist from Turkey, exploring the social position of the artist in the international context and the discussion questions seek to examine why the international context described in this piece is important for arts marketing.

Finally, Chapter 10 summarises the key issues addressed in the text and identifies areas for future research. This chapter also highlights some of the key themes common or particular to marketing in all the art, which the book covers.

Chapter 2

The marketing of popular music

Daragh O'Reilly

Introduction

Music has a wide range of social functions (Crozier, 1997; Gregory, 1997), including healing, the accompaniment of dancing, the creation of a group or ethnic identity, the relieving of work through the use of rhythmic singing, storytelling, religious worship (Rouget, 1985), salesmanship, the entertainment of oneself and others, and the communication and arousing of emotions. The performance of music is essentially a social experience (Crozier, 1997; Frith, 1996; Hargreaves and North, 1997). From a social-psychological viewpoint, Hargreaves and North (op. cit.) argue that for the individual consumer the social functions of music create a context in which three issues are key: the management of self-identity, of interpersonal relationships and of mood. They find that musical preference acts as a mark of identity during adolescence in particular. Again, DeNora (1999) conducted more than 50 in-depth interviews with female consumers and found that respondents used music as a resource for doing emotional work, a mood-changer, a way of doing identity work and to help build life stories or self-narratives.

But what is popular music? Shuker (1998) says the term defies a precise, straightforward definition, and characterises it as commercially made, mass distributed music which is popular with many people, and as a product with political or ideological meaning. For the purposes of this chapter, the term popular music is intended to cover musical genres such as chart pop music, rock, rap, hip hop, soul, R&B, dance, metal, punk, reggae, garage, blues and so on. In other words, the focus is on the kind of music that people currently listen to in the home, car, bus, train or plane, or while out jogging; the music that is played at festivals like Glastonbury or Lollapalooza; the music that we see and/or hear on rotation on MTV or radio and the music played at live concert or club venues.

The view from marketing

Despite marketing's confident onward march into an ever widening number of commercial and public sectors of economic activity, neither marketing-managerial nor consumer behaviour research has engaged specifically with popular music in any systematic or prolonged way. This is surprising when one considers the size of the popular music business, its strong brand identities, the amounts of money which can be made in it, its heavily mediated links with popular culture, the intensity of the relationships which popular music fans (in particular adolescents) form with their favourite musical acts or b(r)ands (Zillmann and Gan, 1997) and the attractive prospect of long-term band–fan relationships to exploit. Within marketing, music-related research in the eighties looked at rather instrumental matters (in the non-musical sense), such as, for example, how to use music to get people to buy more products in supermarkets, to create mood in restaurants (Milliman, 1982, 1986) or the use of music in TV commercials (Gorn, 1982; Park and Young, 1986) – more about muzak than music.

Another strand of research has looked at the idea of hedonic consumption. Hedonic consumption, a term which makes it sound more like a pulmonary illness than having fun, focuses on the experiential and emotional aspects of consumer experiences. Popular music is very much part of the entertainment economy (Wolf, 2000), and the experience economy (Pine and Gilmore, 1999). Lacher (1989), linking to earlier work by Hirschman and Holbrook (1982), positioned the consumption of music as hedonic consumption, which is better explained by reference to fun, fantasy, emotive and experiential aspects of consumer behaviour rather than by the more traditional rational decision-making model. Hedonic consumption deals with consumer experiences of aesthetic and non-aesthetic products. Experience is seen as multi-sensory (Schmitt, 2000), evoking emotion such as joy, fear, rapture, ecstasy and so on. Hedonic consumption deals with issues such as perceived freedom, fantasy fulfilment, personal growth, experimentation with identity and escapism. It can involve altered states in mind and body. Justin Sullivan of New Model Army (Buckley et al., 1999: 683) describes it like this:

> I would challenge you ever to put on a New Model Army record and by the end of it not, if you're driving, not to be driving rather slightly faster than you intended to, or if you're sitting down listening to it, your heart will be going slightly faster than you intended to. It's designed to do that. The music is designed to do that. Basically we like things that are exciting. We're looking for some kind of a music that's exciting.
>
> (Interview with author)

Focusing more directly on the consumption of music in its own right and not just as a sales aid, Pucely and Mizerski (1988) showed that, for pre-recorded music, experientially-based measures were superior to more traditional gauges of consumer involvement, highlighting the importance of music as experience. According to Hirschman and Holbrook (op. cit.), hedonic consumption research should focus on performing arts, plastic arts, movies, rock concerts and fashion apparel. There has been very little research within marketing and consumer behaviour into rock music consumption specifically. Lacher and Mizerski (1994) found that the need to re-experience the music was the key factor in the decision to purchase recorded rock music.

As far as live performance – a key aspect of popular music – in general is concerned there has been some research into the ritual dimension (Gainer, 1995) and consumer sense-making processes (Caldwell, 2001). Gainer's conclusion from her interviews with consumers of live performing arts was that people use this kind of consumption to define themselves as part of a collective. Caldwell offers a general living systems theory (GLST) perspective to cover the theoretical gap in explaining and predicting the sense-making associated with live performance attendance. At the other end of the scale, focusing on the individual rather than the social, Holbrook (1986, 1987) and Shankar (2000) offer more personal accounts of individual music consumption experiences, including collecting.

Another interesting notion in marketing has been that of symbolic consumption. Symbolic consumption deals with consumption of products and services as sources of meaning – for example, Levy (1959), Hirschman (1980), McCracken (1988), Mick (1986), Brownlie et al. (1999), Elliott (1994) and Elliott and Wattanasuwan (1998). An important strand of thinking in symbolic consumption is that consumers no longer consume products simply for their functional value, but for their symbolic value, for what they mean to themselves and to others. Products have become commodity signs.

Experiences and their meanings are important for marketers attempting to understand popular music. According to Arnould et al. (2002), consumption meanings are relative to the communications and the communities which receive them. The relevant product offering contains certain meanings more or less shared and more or less agreed on by community members. They identify different types of meaning: utilitarian or functional, sacred and hedonic which can be transferred from producer to consumer. Hogg and Banister (1999) applied McCracken's (1988) model of meaning transfer to images of pop stars.

Furthermore, on the basis that one's identity is determined, at least partly, by what one buys, the kinds of music a consumer listens to, will symbolise something about them. Where their musical preferences are discussed socially, consumers can use this to strategically position themselves as belonging to a group with a desirable social identity. Music consumption can be used to enhance one's sense of own identity as well as social identity. Thus consumption can be turned into a statement about the consumer's self-perceived self-identity and desired social identity. Lived and mediated experiences serve as symbolic resources for self-construction (Elliott and Wattanasuwan, 1998). Consumers internally construct their self-concept and externally their social world. Lived experience has stronger value for the consumer than mediated experience. To sum up, there has been a little work done on the hedonic and symbolic consumption aspects of popular music consumption, and very little indeed on the marketing-managerial side.

Popular music studies

Shuker (2001: 3) states that popular music studies as a discipline:

> Embraces the economic base and associated social relations within which the music is produced and consumed, textual analysis, auteur study and the nature of the audience.

Key themes amongst popular music scholars include: musical practices and identities (Hargreaves and North, 1997), subcultures (Gelder and Thornton, 1997; Hebdige, 1979), individual and social identity (Antaki and Widdicombe, 1998; Bennett, 2001; Widdicombe and Wooffitt, 1995), the link between music and youth (Bennett, 2000) or society generally (Longhurst, 1995), fandom (Harris and Alexander, 1998), cultural intermediation by the record industry (Negus, 1999) and the analysis and characterisation of different popular musical genres.

Within popular music studies, Middleton (1990) identifies three different approaches to the study of popular music. The first of these is the structuralist approach, which examines how meaning is generated in musical texts, how the structure of the text produces meanings, how the audience member is constructed and positioned, and also covers musicological and semiotic perspectives on the subject. The second approach, the culturalist one, is about constructing consumption of popular music as an active rather than a passive process, oppositional politics in popular music, tensions and contradictions in popular music, music and youth subcultures, the individual as determiner of cultural meaning, creative consumption and consumer autonomy; see http://www.marillion.com/ or Collins (2002) for examples of fan power. And the final approach, the political-economic one, engages with issues such as the corporate power of the capitalistic music industry and its role in determining the tastes of a passive audience.

On the business side of popular music studies, Negus has said (1999) that corporate strategy is central to any consideration of musical mediation as it entails an explicit attempt to manage the production–consumption relationship. His research explores the relationship between corporate cultures and music genres, focusing in particular on cultural intermediation and organisational cultures. This is moving close to, but does not engage with, more purely marketing constructs.

On the consumption side, popular music fandom has a lot in common with football fandom, and sports brands in general. Fans are characterised (Harris and Alexander, 1998: 4) as:

> specialised audiences with very intensified relationships to content – those who do not have to be pursued because they are already captive in their 'fanatic' devotion to a star, text, or icon.

Fan–brand relationships are potentially intense, high-involvement ones, offering the opportunity for meaningful, experiential and hedonic consumption. Material written from a fan perspective (Smith, 2000), fan ethnographies (e.g. Cavicchi, 1999) and books on fan culture (e.g. Lewis, 1992; Hills, 2002) offer further insight into fan thinking in relation to the popular music product. As Larson comments (1995: 548):

> Music provides the security of identification with other like-minded peers. The teenager who identifies with Guns-N-Roses gains the solidarity of being soul mates with millions of other youth. Identification with M.C. Hammer connects you to a different group of peers.

As far as a more collective than individual dimension of consumption is concerned, there has been an extensive literature on subcultures (usually traced back to Hebdige, 1979), but for some time the value of subculture as an analytical construct has been challenged, and the notion of social identity is coming more to the fore (Bennett, 2001). However, what to call a group of consumers of a particular popular music brand remains problematic. Do they constitute a subculture? (too unwieldy a construct); a fan-base? (too commercial); a tribe? (a bit passé); a family? (too many criminal associations); a cult (prone to misunderstandings nowadays); a club? (too exclusive); a segment? (too commercial).

Marketing and popular music studies

The Rodman/Coates web-based bibliography offers almost 1500 academic articles on popular music. It can be seen that the subject coverage is very wide – from music videos to areas such as race issues, music genres, identity categorisation, song analysis, the counter-culture, and analyses of a wide range of popular artistes and performances. There are, however, very few references to business, the word marketing scarcely appears, and consumers, as such, are practically invisible. On the other side, as we have seen above, marketing and consumer behaviour studies have not engaged in depth with popular music.

There does not appear to be any systematic engagement with the strategic marketing or consumer behaviour literature or discourse by popular music researchers. Given the huge issue of, for example, commerciality versus creativity within the music business and amongst music fans, it is surprising that popular music scholars have not engaged more systematically with marketing-related issues or discourse.

No doubt each discipline's concerns are different, yet they share so many common bases. Both subjects have had to fight the charge of not being sufficiently scientific. Popular music has had to fight hard to establish itself as worthy of respect, both in its own right and as part of cultural studies. Both marketing and popular music studies draw on insights from psychology, sociology and anthropology. Popular music studies make greater use of insights from languages and literature (e.g. the notion of 'text' discussed below), and from cultural studies. But the linguistic turn has taken hold in marketing too, not just the hermeneutic–semiotic (O'Shaughnessy and Holbrook, 1988) but also discourse analytical perspectives (e.g. Hackley, 1998 as an early example).

A key issue which the two areas have in common is identity. Identity was the big issue in cultural studies in the 1990s (Barker, 2000). While cultural studies in the 1990s, and popular music studies within it, explored issues of agency, performativity and the subject, as well as identity in terms of place and musical scene, and more politically sensitive issues such as race and gender, on the whole, marketing's gaze was turned to brand and corporate identity. Consumer identity discussion made heavy use of the self-concept, a psychological construct which many cultural studies people would query. For some cultural studies scholars, the notion of the agentic subject is problematic, a contested site; for marketers, agency is taken for granted. Marketing's concern about identity is simply how to define, control and project either a brand identity or a corporate identity, or to link consumer constructions of their own identities with product or service attributes in a way which makes the purchase seem congruent with the individual.

Another issue which the two disciplines have in common is pleasure. Marketers call it hedonic consumption. Popular music scholars, too, know the meaning of pleasure. Here is Shuker (2001: 15) on the pleasures of the text:

> include the sheer tactile pleasure of handling record albums, with the accompanying rituals of setting the scene for listening … and studying anew the sleeve notes; and the physical pleasures of … active participation, most notably

dance ... the emotional pleasures to be derived from both the anticipation and consumption of familiar pleasures ... catharsis ...

There is space here for only a short review. The main point is that, given their common roots and their common concerns, the popular music business is a site in which marketing and popular music scholars could usefully conduct interdisciplinary empirical research.

The popular music industry and environment

The popular music business is part of the entertainment economy (Wolf, 2000), and the experience economy (Pine and Gilmore, 1999). In this section, we look at the key types of player in the popular music industry and their inter-relationships in the context of the business-environmental factors currently impacting on them. The mass marketing of music is similar to the mass marketing of other popular culture products, such as comic books, novels, films, video games and videos. Ownership of rights in these products is commonly assigned by their creators to large corporations with the financial strength, media connections and distribution networks to deliver the products and promote and publicise them through the mass media. Major labels have smaller labels, rather like publishers have differentiated imprints, that help them to handle different categories or genres of music and thereby better align the artistes with the targeted segments.

Figure 2.1 is a necessarily simplified diagram of the key categories of players in the music business together with, in some cases, an indication of their roles. This diagram does not do justice to the complexity of the business, but will serve for the purposes of this discussion to highlight the key areas.

The global industry is dominated by the major record labels BMG, Sony, EMI, Universal and Warner. It is to the major labels that classical marketing strategy terminology can most easily be seen to apply. At any one time, they will be scouting for new talent, sounds and looks, maximising the take from their rights, managing the back catalogue, timing new releases and culling unprofitable acts – pure product portfolio management, in fact. Each of them runs a wide portfolio of labels and artistes, with resource allocation decisions to make, trends to spot and competitors to beat. The corporate labels are like venture capitalists for creative artists ... and, like true venture capitalists, they come with strings attached (Harrison, 2000). The term corporate is of course highly charged in pop music parlance, being associated with the idea of suits (soulless business executives who do not understand music and are only interested in the bottomline).

A popular music act can be a solo musician, a group of musicians, a singer–songwriter or a solo singing star. It can be, for example, a heavy metal rock band, a boy band, girl band, a rapper or rap act. A common

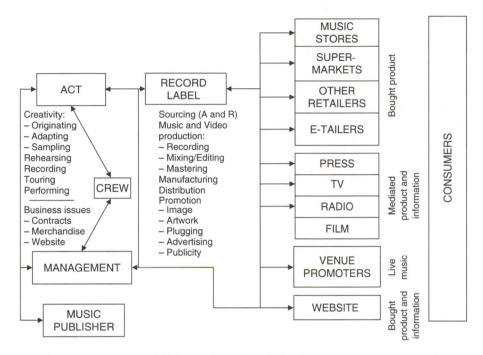

Figure 2.1 Key categories of players in the music business.

arrangement is for the act to have a manager, or management operation, which takes care of the business side of things, allowing the musicians and singers to focus on songwriting, composing, rehearsing and performing. The management typically negotiates a contract with a record label (unless the act sets up its own label). The record labels recruit artists, arrange and fund production, distribution, market research and promotional activity. The funding usually involves an advance on royalty earnings, out of which production costs can be clawed back. Relationships between band, management and record label can be extremely complex (Lendt, 1997). The act's material is recorded onto the appropriate audio and/or video formats, promoted to and through radio, TV and film and distributed through a variety of retail outlets. Many acts now have their own websites through which products and merchandise can be ordered direct. If the act originates its own material it will do a deal with a music publisher. Through its management side, the act will also need to consider issues such as brand identity, sponsorship, e-commerce, touring management, copyright protection, moral rights, piracy and royalty collection agencies (Harrison, 2000). Business arrangements between bands or acts and their management and record labels are an interesting read, for example Lendt's (1997) account of his time helping to look after the business affairs of Kiss is an engrossing read, particularly for the complexity of the business arrangements and description of touring planning meetings.

Like any other industry, the popular music business is currently faced with a wide range of issues creating opportunities and threats. Here are a few current examples. Firstly, there are considerable opportunities offered by the mass media and technology. For example, The Pop Idol TV programme is an example of an attempt to create a pop act live on TV with audience involvement, in fact giving the audience a say in the creation of the idol, whether this be an individual or a group. There have been some successes and some failures, but this programme has changed the way the industry and the media will do business, going far beyond the Top of the Pops or Saturday morning kids' TV programme formats. Another music performer brand who is taking advantage of media opportunities is Ozzy Osbourne, the self-styled Prince of Darkness, whose family documentary show has been a stunning success. Finally, David Bowie performed tracks from his new album 'Reality' in September 2003 before an invited audience in London, and technology made it possible to screen this performance in cinemas in places such as Tokyo, Rio and Sydney, with screenings in Europe being simultaneous with the actual performance.

One of the biggest threats to the music business is piracy, greatly aided by, but not solely dependent on, the Internet. Peer-to-peer file sharing via Napster and the resultant loss of revenue led to Metallica taking action against Napster. Currently, the Recording Industry Association in the USA is even suing individual consumers over the same issue. Meanwhile, in China, despite the presence of the major labels selling original product, billions are being made and lost through piracy.

Another environmental issue is the change in musical preferences and tastes, witness the explosion of interest in rap music over the past few years and the transformation of music store sales categories from being rock and pop dominated to rap and hiphop. In the UK, as an example of political and legal influences in the business environment, legislation on music venue licensing threatens to restrict or at least bureaucratically complicate the performance of live music.

Popular music and branding

The music business has plenty of examples of prominent brands. The stars are the brands (Wolf, 2000). What does not yet appear to have been dealt with in marketing or popular music literatures is the question of music brand identity. Clearly some of the major artists are leading international brands, with images and personalities and reputations that many buttoned-down corporate executives would love to be able to integrate in their own commercial brands – without of course rocking the corporate boat. Mainstream corporate brands such as Coca-Cola or Tommy Hilfiger seek to enrich their own brand identities by tie-ins with music brands, through sponsorship, product placement, celebrity endorsement, licensing or other deals. Naomi Klein, in her critical review of branding (2000), discusses the branding of music. She comments that brand managers see themselves as 'sensitive culture makers'. Artists and their managers and labels are alert to the value of tie-ins with major brands like Gap and Nike. Rolling Stones' tours have been sponsored by Tommy Hilfiger (clothes) and Jovan (perfume). She comments that:

> when Hilfiger launched the ad campaign for the Stones' No Security Tour [1982] full brand-culture integration was achieved. … The tagline was 'Tommy Hilfiger Presents the Rolling Stones no Security Tour' … The act is a background set, powerfully showcasing the true rock-and-roll essence of the Tommy brand.

A brand identity is the intended meaning projected by the brand's managers; brand image is what is received and/or interpreted by the audience. Popular music b(r)and identities/images are constructed along four dimensions. Firstly, the band 'internally' develops a working culture and organisational identity. Through the working processes of creating, rehearsing, recording, touring and performing, the band becomes 'tight'. It develops a strong musical identity. Secondly, this is then communicated as an external brand identity to the fans by means of the marketing communications process. Thirdly, in a process of 'discursive elaboration' (Elliott and Wattanasuwan, 1998) the fans then use the received and interpreted brand image to help with the construction of part of their own identities, individual and collective. Also, rituals of exchange, possession, grooming and divestment are important in the act–fan relationship for fans (McCracken, 1988). Finally, there is then a feedback process whereby the fans feed back, critically or approvingly, to the band, particularly at performances, but also through the website, fan letters, fan websites and fanzines. Unless these four dimensions are fully understood, the richness of the brand's meanings cannot be appreciated, or indeed managed.

Several different types of brands can be identified in the popular music business. Table 2.1 outlines these different types.

For popular music acts, external brand identity has a number of key dimensions. A popular music act's identity is above all a musical one, usually characterised by a genre, or mix of genres. Another key aspect of brand identity is commercial identity. As Shuker says (2001: 34):

> Also central to left analyses emphasising the economic, is the conception of 'authenticity', which is imbued with considerable symbolic value. Authenticity is underpinned by a series of oppositions: mainstream versus independent; pop versus rock; and commercialism versus creativity. Inherent in this polarisation is a cyclical theory of musical innovation as a form of street creativity versus business and market domination and the co-option of rock.

Table 2.1 Different types of popular music brands

Type of brand	Example
Performer/artiste brands	Madonna, Metallica, Limp Bizkit, NWA in other words individuals or groups which have an outstanding talent for originating or interpreting something creative
Content provider/mediator brands	Record labels, radio and TV stations, including of course MTV
Cultural intermediary brands	Record producers, such as William Orbit, fairly recently celebrated for his work with Madonna
Event brands	Glastonbury or Lollapalooza music festivals
Venue brands	Brixton Academy
Character brands	Artists' personae, e.g. Bowie's "Aladdin Sane, Madonna's "Material Girl"

Issues of commercial identity are very important in fan and academic discourse. There are major cultural distinctions made by fans between authentic acts and sell-outs. This is often a distinction made between rock and pop. It is also tied into anti-capitalist sentiment and rhetoric, as well as the separation between musical talent and corporate control. Being 'tainted' by commerciality can be a bad thing.

Another important aspect of popular music brand identity is the subcultural aspect. In the past five decades, there has been a significant number of subcultural identities such as Goth (Hodkinson, 2002), punk (Colegrave and Sullivan, 2001), crustie and mod. Some bands become closely associated with a particular subculture. This can be a threat to band longevity if the subculture becomes unfashionable. Joolz Denby comments about New Model Army, a band which has been in existence since 1980 and is still producing albums and touring:

> NMA have always occupied a niche of their own. This is extremely important in regard to their success and longevity. They were never part of a "movement" thus pigeonholing them and creating an end-time scenario in regard to the eventual demise of that movement.

(interview with author)

Some bands become associated with these subcultures. However, such attachments risk the act going out of fashion when the subcultural fashion changes.

Geographic identity, another important aspect of popular music brand identity, is often associated with a particular sound, such as rap with the Bronx and Brooklyn, or the Beatles with Liverpool. Coming from a particular place or country can authenticate the sound. Increasingly, as part of their political identity, it is common for bands to get involved with cause-related marketing (e.g. U2 and Amnesty).

There is also the issue of the balance between an act's collective and individual identities. Take for example, Kiss, the seventies US rock band (Lendt, 1997), where each of the four members had his own Kabuki-style makeup and was a character with a name and identity of its own. The band members' removal of this makeup and revelation of band members' identities became a media event in itself. More recently, in the UK, the Spice Girls was a group of female artistes each with her own individual band identity. These identities have now been spun off into their own celebrity orbits, with varying degrees of success. Perhaps more common in the rock scene are acts with one or two band members who are more prominent.

There is also the question of the identity life cycle. Like human beings and products, popular music acts have life cycles. Some can be fads, some fashions, some slow burners, some with staying power. Some popular music brands have considerable talent at changing and thereby prolonging their brand identity. A key brand manager of her own brand in this sense is Madonna (Morton, 2001; Taraborrelli, 2002), or consider David Bowie (Sandford, 1997) or Kylie (Scatena, 1997). Other artists use shock to gain and maintain impact, such as Marilyn Manson (Baddeley, 2000) or Jim Morrison (Hopkins and Sugerman, 1980). Other brands maintain longevity through a combination of talent, honesty and the richness of their overall contribution (e.g. Bob Marley (White, 2000)).

Unfortunately, existing models of brand identity (e.g. Kapferer, 1997) lose the richness of the reality they seek to capture. This becomes all the clearer if one reads any of the above biographies.

The music brand web

The dominant heuristic trope in popular music studies is arguably the 'text' (e.g. Frith, 1996: 158ff; Gelder and Thornton, 1997: 254–60; Horner and Swiss, 1999; Johnson, 2002: 704–12; Lewis, 1992: 52–5; Longhurst, 1995: 195–202; Middleton, 2000: 1ff; Shuker, 1998: 301ff; Titon, 1995, 2003). This notion seems so embedded in the discipline that its metaphoric and metonymic character appears to be overlooked. Nevertheless, to say that a performance is a text is to use a metaphor. In so far as this construct focuses attention on communicative aspects of the phenomenon only, it is metonymic.

Hall (1997) defines text as:

all practices which signify. This includes the generation of meaning through images, sounds, objects (such as clothes) and activities (like dance and sport). Since images, sounds, objects and practices are sign systems, which signify with the same mechanism as a language, we may refer to them as cultural texts.

Shuker (2001: 14) places the notion of text into a social context:

The 'meaning' of any engagement between a text and its consumers cannot be assumed, or 'read off', from textual characteristics alone. The text's historical conditions of production and consumption are important as is the nature of its audience, and the various ways in which they mediate their encounter with the text.

Using the text trope, a brand's identity can be said to be a system of signifiers, a web of significant texts, a collection of commodified meanings, a character and a story for sale.

In order to use this notion of text to construe the relationship between a popular music brand and its fans, we need to take account of all of the texts which the brand might weave together for fans to consume, whether auditory, visual or behavioural. Their aggregate communicative power constructs the brand identity. Figure 2.2 illustrates this idea.

Examining each of these aids to positioning a music brand in turn, we begin with publicity. This element is the one which enables the act to set out its stall, its musical and commercial values and identity. The lyrics express what the songwriter has experienced or felt and communicate them

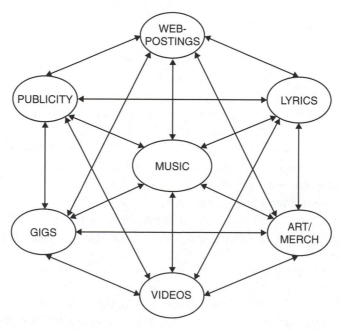

Figure 2.2 The music brand web.

inter-subjectively to the audiences. There is key to the fan's perception of the act's values, particularly when sung in performance, where the fan can see for himself or herself the authenticity or sincerity of the performer's sentiments. For fans it is important to be able to identify with the points of view expressed in the lyrics; not only that but to remember the words and be able to sing the songs. There is often a concern amongst fans to understand the intention behind the lyrics, but also a sense that the fan does not have to be constrained by the songwriter's intention.

> Maybe they have totally different emotions when they wrote the song than I have when I hear it, but that's all right with me. I don't need to know what their emotion was. I mean, it would be interesting, but I've got my own feelings with that song and if Justin's trying to get a message through in, well let's say, um, You Weren't There, which he kind of does, that's OK. That's his message. But if I get another message out, my own one – that's my message I get out of the music and in a way I can't be bothered with what they are trying to say with it.
>
> (New Model Army fan, interview with author)

The artwork communicates a visual culture with any number of referents, helping a band to create a look but also arguably to form a kind of visual micro-culture. When used in the merchandise or swag, these symbols are worn as signs of allegiance to the band or as, evidence of fanhood, and a signal to other potential fans. The T-shirts apart from being a lucrative source of revenue to the act, usually bypassing the label, can also carry lyrics, album covers, photos of the band. Videos, whether concert videos or arty music videos targeted at MTV, combine audio and visual elements with art direction and sometimes highly sophisticated production values to enhance the musical experience.

In terms of interactivity, it is the website and the live performance which are the key 'sites' in a band–fan relationship. A band's website is a vital communications tool enabling band to fan, fan to band and fan to fan communications. Fans use these websites to discuss the b(r)and, and what it means and stands for, as well as more practical issues such as planning to meet up before the next gig. In these discussions, fans solicit and offer accounts of how they first became fans, what the band means for them, the meaning of lyrics, personal collections of key life-moments in which the band's music has played an important part or with which it is associated, lending background thematic meaning or something to hold onto in difficult times.

Live performance is particularly important in the act–fan relationship, whether it be a rambling improvisation for the Grateful Dead or a tightly planned spectacular 'show' from U2. It is in live performance that the hedonic, experiential and symbolic aspects of the relationship become most intense, that fans and band experience a sense of flow and communitas. The performers can put a lot of thought into gigs. Here is Justin Sullivan, of New Model Army, a veteran of thousands of performances:

> I lose a lot of sleep over setlists … To me, it's not playing a series of songs, it's making something happen … It's a film. It's a story. It starts with something and it ends up with something else, and during that time you've gone somewhere and been somewhere through a number of different emotions … So, to that end you have to pick an order which first of all has a narrative kind of feel that works. I mean, most obviously, you start big, then go down in the middle and end big. Sometimes we start low and come up gradually. Those are the two most obvious ways to structure a set. There's more to it than that. There's more – mood swings – there's more to it. Then having discussed mood swings, then there's key changes. Key change is very important … Then there's the change of instrumentation. If I finish a song with an electric guitar, I've got to start the next one with an acoustic and I'm the last person to play and the first person … so there's basically all these different things go in to making a set list and then you have to pick the right one, and when you find a set that flows beautifully and reaches – all the right things happen in the right places, we tend to play that on a tour for like 2 weeks and every night the same, because it's right … but then what happens after 2 weeks, we'll get bored with it, we'll start to get stale with it and we'll change it.
>
> (Interview with author)

For example, fan behaviour at rock gigs can range from standing at the back just listening to getting into the middle of the moshpit and taking one's chances (Ambrose, 2001). Some fans find it hard to stand still:

> It's the speed, the intensity, the things going on. We're getting all this input and you have to do some sort of output or you're going to go totally into overload at a New Model Army gig. I can't understand that people stand still at New Model Army gigs. You have to channel some of the energy back out or you're going to be – well, I don't know, you're going to overload, you're going to go on tilt, you're gonna go bleep, blat. You have to channel that back out and without – unless you want to start shouting and screaming …
>
> (Interview with author)

Finally, an interesting use of 'text' is the practice of some fans of tattooing themselves with band emblems.

> Music fans – especially Rock or Alternative music fans – very often seek to publicly declare their allegiance to their chosen band by being tattooed with the band's logos, record/CD covers, lines from songs that have particular meaning to the tattooee, or names of band members, portraits, etc. This is done to

demonstrate solidarity not so much with the band themselves but with the other fans who are part of the tattooee's 'family' or clique. Fans of Rock/ Alternative bands also have a perception of themselves as 'individuals', 'outlaws', rather more discerning and daring than 'the average person'. Tattooing, which in the West has ambiguous status within the dominant culture and associations with punitive or stigmatised sub-cultures, and thus a 'daring' image, presents a relatively safe way of expressing Otherness.

(Joolz Denby, interview with author)

Popular music and the marketing mix

The marketing mix is a simple conceptual framework, more a checklist of elements, for the tactical management of brand–consumer relationships. In this section, the application of this tool to popular music brands is considered. Here, we are talking not just about the communicative aspects of a music brand, but its management as a 'product'.

Product

The 'product' is of course music, and more narrowly the particular sounds of the music made by the act. Arguably, the 'product' also includes the song lyrics and performance. In view of the possibility of recording music for replication and distribution for mass consumption, we need to take account of product format. Popular music is reproduced in various technical formats, the principal examples of which are vinyl disc, minidisk, digital audio tape (DAT), video, DVD, audio tape (cassette), MP3 and CD. Musical genre is another part of musical products – one only has to visit a retailer to see the changes in category on the shop floor as a consequence of the emergence of hip hop or R&B. Another product format, arguably the most important is live performance. In addition to the core product of music, there are ancillary products such as T-shirts and so on. Other product categories are release formats such as live albums, studio albums, singles, extended plays (EPs), and now video and audio are being mixed on EPs.

Place/distribution

Music is distributed over the Internet in either buy-from-shop or downloadable format, either by organisations like Amazon, different kinds of e-tailers or direct from the acts themselves. Much product is sold through high street music retailers, supermarkets and motorway service forecourts. From a popular music studies point of view, however, place signifies something to do with the places where music is originated and heard. Certain types of music, certain sounds, become associated with certain places, for example, Manchester (Haslam, 1999), Rio de Janeiro, Compton and Dakar. The places where live music is performed are almost highly significant for consumers.

Promotion

This includes interviews with acts, press releases, tour publicity, telephone interviews done by the band, radio and TV promotion and performance, features, photographs, video clips, album trailers/teasers, web-based promotion, especially through the act's and the label's website, merchandise, T-shirts, CD covers, artwork generally, music videos, live performance videos, publicity photos and so on.

Music is heavily mediated – via TV, radio and the Internet. The playing of a song on the radio, TV or web can be read as both a 'delivery' of the product experience as well as a promotion for the band or act. Links between the mainstream corporate brands and popular music include celebrity endorsement (Erdogan, 1999), product placement and sponsorship.

People

In mainstream marketing this element in the mix foregrounds those who deliver the service or salespeople who sell a product. In the music industry, this can include a wide range of people, from the band or act members, the crew and management, tour management, producers, freelance and label employees, session musicians and a whole host of cultural intermediaries involved in bringing the 'product' into being. Also, DJs in clubs and on the radio, or VJs.

Process

Most acts engage in five major or core processes: origination of material, rehearsal, recording, touring (e.g. Alan, 1992) and live performance. The first four of these work tasks are back office tasks with mostly no customer exposure or contact. It is in live performance that the band's process interacts with the consumers' process.

Physical evidence

The physicality, tangibility or materiality of the product is represented by the technological medium which carries it (e.g. CD, vinyl and DVD). But there is a much more important sense in which physicality is important, namely the servicescape. This relates to where live music is performed. These venues range from smoky bars, to a wide range of venue sizes, up to stadia which can take 100,000 people, as well as major open air festivals such as Glastonbury, and clubs (Garratt, 1998; Malbon, 1999).

Price

The price is basically the money charged for the recorded product or for entrance to see a live performance. Related to this is the question of perceived value for money, a factor which is not far from fans' minds.

A marketing mix for popular music brands

The flaws of the mix concept are well known. Its simplistic nature is often criticised (Jobber, 2001: 19–20). As indicated above, key issues in the popular music business do not always sit well with or fit comfortably within the list of seven elements. At the same time, there is little point in completely reinventing the wheel, particularly when moving into a new area of application. So, a slight re-casting of the mix to make it more suitable for the popular music business seems in order, and the following is suggested (Table 2.2).

This mix model is more suited for use at band level than by a record label managing a band's marketing efforts. The first three elements are seen as the more important ones to get right in the popular music business, and the first two are arguably the most important of all. This arrangement of the mix foregrounds the softer aspects of music brands.

Table 2.2 A marketing mix for popular music brands

Element	Description
People	The singer(s) and/or musician(s)
Product	Music genre, sound and lyrics
Performance	The live performance process, including the physical performance space
Promotion	All forms of promotional communication mentioned above
Place	Physical or electronic distribution of the product
Physical evidence	Technical format (e.g. CD, MP3), and release format (e.g. album, single)
Price	The money charged for the recorded product or for entrance to see a live performance

Future research directions

As suggested above, there could be considerable value in interdisciplinary work in the area of popular music for both marketing/consumer behaviour and popular music studies. There are five clear lines of exploration which suggest themselves:

- Research into the marketing-managerial side of major labels, with a focus on their innovation strategies, product portfolio management strategies, their relations with technology and the media, and on co-branding with mainstream commercial brands through product placement, celebrity endorsement, licensing and sponsorship.
- The development of a comprehensive theory of performer brand identity which takes account of the particular characteristics of the popular music business.
- Research into the contribution of popular music fan websites to the formation of brand identity and image. Apart from a direct focus on popular music band and fan sites, this could be linked with ongoing research into mainstream commercial online communities, and also with other areas of cultural marketing and consumption, such as sports, film and literature.
- The development of a theory of live popular music performance, with a specific focus on the relationship between the music act and the audience, taking account of critically important themes such as ritual, flow, communitas, trance, shamanism, coherence, symbolic aspects of interaction, identity work, catharsis and so on. This could lead to an integrative conceptual framework which marries key issues in marketing and consumer studies, such as meaning transfer and hedonic consumption, with insights from music, theatre, dance, performance art and so on.
- Finally, a challenging research objective would be the development of a comprehensive theory of popular music consumption which takes account of perspectives from relevant disciplines.

Conclusion

In this chapter, we first looked at the nature of music and marketing and consumer behaviour's engagement with popular music (or relative lack of it, with some honourable exceptions). Consideration was then given to popular music studies' concerns, and these were compared and contrasted with those of marketing. A gap between the literatures was identified. Given the salience of popular music in contemporary popular culture, its strong brands, the passion of its consumers' involvement and its links with the corporate world, it was felt that much could be learned from interdisciplinary research between marketing/consumer behaviour and popular music studies.

Then, the structure and environment of the popular music industry was outlined and examined. Following a discussion of music brands, and different dimensions of their identity, a music brand web model was offered, as well as an adapted marketing mix for popular music brands. Finally, four directions for future interdisciplinary research are suggested: music brand identity, online music fan communities, major label marketing practices, performer brand identity and live performance.

Acknowledgement

Daragh O'Reilly gratefully acknowledges the kind and constructive help of New Model Army, and their fans; Chas Critcher and Kathy Doherty of Sheffield Hallam School of Cultural Studies; Gretchen Larsen of Bradford University School of Management; and members of the International Association for the Study of Popular Music e-list (http://www.iaspm.net), whose inputs helped to shape his understanding of issues in this area. Any errors are entirely his own.

Chapter 3

Marketing in the film industry

Finola Kerrigan

Introduction

It is only possible to engage with marketing issues by understanding the wider environmental context in which marketing takes place. This chapter aims at setting film marketing within the wider context of the film industry. Although the importance that marketing plays in ensuring a film's box office success is recognised, understanding of the process is not and very little academic attention has been given to studying the marketing of films. Most recent academic attention has focused on predicting success for films according to various characteristics they possess. Other research has focused upon the role of critics in developing positive or negative word of mouth for a film. Another focus has been upon the industrial structure and its role in film marketing. The marketing of film differs from the marketing of the majority of art forms included in this book in that the majority of film does not receive public funding. Like rock music, those in the film industry can only afford to nurture new talent and take risks by achieving a level of commercial success with others. In saying this, there are some public funds available to support film making and distribution of films both at national and European levels.

The chapter starts by discussing the difference between the artistic and commercial views of the film industry. It examines the source of the American domination of the global film industry. The chapter then proceeds to discuss the nature of marketing within the film industry and the development of marketing research. Finally, the marketing tools used in the marketing of films are identified and unpacked.

The usual starting point for academics discussing any area of arts marketing is the debate regarding the commercial versus the artistic nature of the arts, in this case, film. Is the commercial only achievable by the sacrifice of the artistic? One of the foremost debates that prevail in the study of the film industry is concerned with whether it can in fact be viewed as an industry at all. There is a separation of the notions of industry and art form in a simplistic manner, differentiating between 'the film industry' and 'cinema'. The former, by virtue of its phrasing, implies that the film industry can be seen in purely industrial terms while the latter intimates that film is, in essence, an art form and therefore the rules of industry cannot be strictly applied to it. Common historical discourse on the matter divides film-makers into two camps. Americans, that is Hollywood, are seen as approaching film making from an industrial angle while Europeans believed film to be the preserve of artists where industrial models could not be applied without sacrificing the necessary artistic values of true film making. Puttnam (1997: 114) sums up this difference using the words of a cinema critic in 1926, 'Film is not merchandise ... Indeed, precisely because film is not merchandise we can compete with America ... In the cinema, Geist(spirit) can balance the monetary supremacy of the competition.'

Such a separation between art and industry is neither accurate nor productive in relation to film as both elements are evident, to greater and lesser degrees in each and every film that is produced. In order for a film to be realised, it is necessary to secure a budget, irrespective of size. This debases the proclamations of those who support the theory that film making is merely an art form, as commerce does enter the equation to some extent despite the regard or lack of regard which the film-maker attributes to it. The reverse is also true. In following the procedures necessitated by film production – creation of a storyline and script, shooting the scenes, the verbal and visual processes inherent in a films' genesis – there is an intrinsic artistic quality in all film making.

The failure to recognise this duality has resulted in the concentration of studies upon the artistic aspects of film to the detriment of an examination of the underlying industrial mechanisms, which produce such art.

These two – generally diametrically opposed – elements which constitute the film industry, culture and economics must be awarded equal importance in the drive to sustain the film industry into the future. The fact that the European film industry is not as commercially successful as its American counterpart is not surprising if one examines the structures which are in place in America in terms of production and distribution and the historical context in which this is founded. This is reinforced by an examination of the motivation behind film making in America as opposed to Europe. The former views the film industry as just that, an industry, while the latter has traditionally placed cultural consideration over commercial gain. This spirit of cultural protection is evidenced by the words of Jean-Luc Godard: 'Films are made for one or maybe two people' (Puttnam, 1997: 291).

American box office domination

Despite sporadic success of European films both within their home countries as well as overseas, the US still dominates the European box office. According to the European Audiovisual Observatory (EAO), cinema attendance remained stagnant in Europe while in America it continued to grow, surpassing all attendance figures since 1957 (EAO, 2003: 5). In addition, '... a number of European markets clearly lacked successful local films. The European market was, however, above all lacking in European films that were successful continent-wide' (EAO, 2003: 5). Although the average number of films produced in Europe exceeds that produced annually in the US, American films continue to have substantially higher average production budgets and also still dominate in terms of box office revenue earned.

The top 20 films in terms of box office revenue were all US productions or co-productions between the US and one other country (New Zealand, Australia and the UK). It is indicative of the poor performance of non-English language films that the co-productions which achieved top 20 status were all with English speaking countries (EAO, 2003: 9). European film-makers are still producing more films than their American counterparts, with 625 films produced across the European Union in 2002 and 628 in 2001, while in the US, 449 films were produced in 2002 with 462 produced in 2001 (EAO, 2003: 11–20).

These figures show the prevailing dominance of American films in the European market as well as the failure of European films to travel beyond their own market. Despite the number of films produced annually in Europe and the popularity (although stagnant) of going to the cinema, European films are not gaining the same success as American films outside their national borders. In order to understand the current situation, it is necessary to look at the structure of the European film industry and to explore the power relationships that exist between the different stages in the product life cycle of a film and between the various actors operating at each of these stages.

Why does America dominate?

The reasons behind the Hollywood domination of the global box office have long been a source of investigation and many explanations have been proposed. This is the same for other film making regions. Although recent years have seen success for South American and Indian films outside their own territories, such success is still not comparable to the financial success and notoriety achieved by Hollywood films. The problem faced by many film industries is a combination of a lack of business acumen, reluctance of many to watch non-Hollywood, non-national films and structural shortcomings (Kerrigan and Özbilgin, 2003).

Structural problems

The basic structures in place in the European industry are disjointed and fail to provide the level of support offered by the much more cohesive American structures. It is interesting to note that the vertical integration, which is now an integral part of the American film industry, was a European invention. Charles Pathé saw the immense potential of the American market and sought to exploit it. His visionary tactics form the basis of the film industry in America today. Pathé introduced vertical integration seeing that the real money to be made emanated from the distribution of films rather than from their manufacture.

It may be disputed whether film production was ever viewed as an industry in Europe. In the US the Movie Business was always viewed as just that, a business that had to make a profit in order to survive. After Edison's development of the Kinetoscope, those who took advantage of his advancements were able to conduct thriving businesses, initially in the 'nickelodeons' and subsequently in the movie theatres. In fact, Edison's influence in creating the structured industry that exists today cannot be underestimated. The early years of the film industry in the US were dominated by law suits between Edison and his fellow Trust members (an industry formation of the early innovators in the film industry) and those film entrepreneurs who were not Trust members (Balio, 1976). However, while Edison dominated the market for equipment and films in the US, his lack of international foresight resulted in his inventions being used in England and France free from the threat of litigation (Huettig, 1944).

One of the main aims of the Trust was to harmonise the activities within the industry. They wished to gain exclusive control over production and distribution channels to the industry. They did so by renting prints to the exchanges for a fixed fee each week and had taken control of the vast majority of exchanges by this time, forbidding them from sourcing product from the independents. The exchanges in turn rented these prints out to the nickelodeons. Such levels of standardisation were not adopted by the last link in the distribution channel, with the exchanges charging the nickelodeons varied fees in accordance with the quality of, or demand for the prints being hired.

This grouping can be identified as the first monopoly to exist in the film industry. During that period, such co-operation to protect patent rights and in effect, the creation of a monopoly was commonplace in all of the main utilities and in manufacturing. In parallel with many fledgling industries, there was a developed spy system in place by this stage (Dyer McCann, 1987). Robinson (1996) highlights the aggressive nature of the Trust members in enforcing its provisos and the penalising measures of license cancellation as a response to non-compliance with the dictates of the Trust.

The prohibition on new members led to the opposition forming a coalition of its own (Robinson, 1996). Dyer McCann (1987) credits John J. Murdock with the creation and strengthening of the independent sector during the

Trust. He saw the opportunity of sourcing films in Europe and exploited this. When it was obvious that these European films were not enough to satisfy the American audiences he encouraged Americans to commence the manufacture of films under his protection. The independent sector soon became organised and market leaders emerged. The General Film Company (GFC) was formed as an independent grouping to the Motion Picture Association of America (MPAA) but was restricted to MPAA members and proceeded to take over all of the licensed film exchanges with the exception of Fox's Greater New York Film Company. Fox had refused to agree with the GFC over pricing details, so the GFC retaliated by cancelling his license and refusing to deliver on contracted shipments. William Fox issued a lawsuit against this action, which was instrumental in the demise of the Trust.

In opposition to the Trust, the independents established the sales company, which centralised control over the independent film exchanges. When they were investigated for violation of the Sherman Antitrust Act, this caused internal difficulties, which resulted in the division of the members into three distinct groups. These groups released their films through Universal, Mutual and other disparate companies.

The development of the feature film

In recognising that the public wanted more sophisticated films than previously on offer, the independents created features of higher quality than had previously been in existence (Balio, 1976). Adolph Zukor (1954) was one of the first to believe in the American audiences' capacity for longer features. Zukor bought the distribution rights for the French production Elizabeth, but felt that in order to achieve success with features, it was necessary to produce them in the US. In order to do so he needed the permission of the Trust. He approached Jeremiah J. Kennedy, the head of the Trust, who dismissed his idea of feature production saying: 'The time is not ripe for feature pictures, if it ever will be' (quoted in Zukor, 1954: 49).

In January of 1916, the Motion Picture Patents Company was prohibited from retaining their present organisation by decree. Their subsequent appeal was dismissed in 1918 and this ended the matter. Nevertheless, as Robinson (1996) points out, this lawsuit was not the single influencing factor in the fate of the Trust. Robinson cites five factors that contributed to the demise of the Trust; the strength of the independents' in their organised opposition; the financial drain ensued by constant litigation; the failure of the Trust to look to Wall Street for finance; the inflexible nature of the organisation and finally, the loss of the European markets which resulted from WWI. Despite the relatively short-term impact of the Trust on the US industry, in the long run, it can be argued that they were instrumental in the creation of a cohesive, structured and competitive international industry which remains today (Anderson, quoted in

Robinson, 1996: 110). This is in part due to their success in implementing Hamiltonian strategies coupled with the creation of a united opposition who would go on to form the studio system, which dominates the worldwide film industry today. The above sections have shown how the Hollywood studio system began and the reasons for the subsequent domination of the global film industry by the majors. The following section will examine the current situations with regard to marketing practice in the film industry and outline the key marketing tools that are used in the marketing of film.

Marketing of films ... you mean posters and trailers?

Many, even those within the film industry, understand marketing activities as the creation of posters and trailers, advertising and promotional activities in advance of a film's release. This chapter will show how marketing is much more than this, and must be considered right from the point of conception of a film, in other words the beginning of the product development stage. The main stages of activity in the film industry are development, production, postproduction, distribution and exhibition and there is a need to focus on marketing in all of these stages.

Many film industry professionals do not regard what they do as marketing, although on a daily basis they are packaging each film and marketing it to a number of people from technical crew to financiers to the cast. Only once these stages have been completed does attention turn to marketing the film to the general public. Although the marketing stages involved in bringing a film from conception to the market can be laid out in a linear fashion, many of these stages occur simultaneously. Durie et al. (2000: 5) define film marketing as '... any activity that assists a film in reaching its target audience at any time throughout its life'. This is developed to identify the goal of marketing as '... to maximise a film's audience and, by extension, its earning potential' (Durie et al. 2000: 4). This view of the role of marketing in the film industry is shared by Weise (1989: 13). The identification of the target audience is key to the success of the film, according to Lukk (1997: xxi), 'most marketing executives will concede that the most that they can accomplish is to get moviegoers to taste the movie in the first week of its release. After that, word of mouth takes over.' This is because marketing – as defined by Durie et al. (2000) above – does not take place in the marketing department alone. Weise (1989) urges film-makers to think about what they are trying to achieve and what their capabilities are in meeting the needs of a project right from the development stage.

Early market research

Although marketing in the film industry is now presented as a finely honed activity, with the major Hollywood companies investing heavily in marketing intelligence and advanced market research techniques, this view is overly simplistic and was certainly not always the case. It is important to examine the development of the use of market research within the film industry as this identified many of the key marketing characteristics of the industry from quite early on. Although the methods used were crude, they did aid early film-makers in gaining a fuller understanding of their audience.

Certain European film-makers are scathing of the practice of audience research as carried out by the majors in the US, but lack of direction or knowledge of the appeal of a project from the early stages is likely to restrict the effectiveness of the marketing campaign. All too often, such research is left until the latter stages of production when it is ineffectual. Puttnam articulates the European situation by stating that: 'Many film-makers in Europe still regard research with distaste' (Puttnam, in Ilott, 1996).

An essential aspect of Kotler's (2002) Marketing Concept is market research. While market research is widely used in the US film industry, its introduction into the European industries has met with some resistance, particularly on the Continent. Recruited Audience Screenings (RAS) are events where a film is shown to an audience consisting of members of the target audience with the purpose of testing various aspects of the film to see if it does in fact appeal to the target audience. The Danish Film Institute has introduced a system of RAS to the industry but is hampered by the fact that there are no specialist film research companies in the country. The situation is different in the UK, where a number of companies specialise in RAS. Unsurprisingly, with US films accounting for 86 per cent of box office revenue in the UK (EAO, 1999), their client lists are mainly composed of US companies operating within the UK.

The origins of market research in the film industry

Initial audience research was socially motivated with psychologists and sociologists recognising that film could be used as an effective research tool. The films themselves were not being investigated; they were merely used to draw in members of the public in order to collect data. Early forms of market research were evident in the American film industry by the 1920s when Albert Sindlinger began to plant ushers in the cinema toilets where they would discuss a film with audience members who had just exited a performance (Jowett, 1985). Attempts to ascertain consumer demand only really came about with the recognition that using film as an efficient method of social research necessitated the identification of the interests and preferences of the audience. Small-scale studies of audience preferences began with simple observations of content in the early cinema forms. This proved sufficiently popular to support the foundation of the industry that flourishes today (Jowett, 1985).

In the 1930s, industry professionals began to be more scientific in the collection and analysis of the customer base. This was in response to the depression combined with the restrictions of the self-censorship, known as 'the Code' instigated by the industry in the face of criticism on the grounds of the negative moral impact of films on the population. Immediately after World War II, Chambers (1947) identified the need for Hollywood to introduce sustained research into film production and audience composition in order to retain its lead in the world markets. He stressed the adoption of a global strategy to establish a sufficient understanding of the overseas markets in order to compete successfully (Chambers, 1947).

The 1930s also heralded the introduction of the 'sneak preview' as a means of determining success and failure factors of a newly produced film. These early RAS did not have the advantage of todays more sophisticated testing systems. Their biggest impediment to accuracy was the lack of discrimination employed in audience selection. Those running RAS's are careful to attract clearly defined audience segments in order to determine accurately the film's potential impact on the target group. They also endeavour to ensure that each participant returns a fully completed questionnaire; there was a tendency towards self-selection in the early years, whereby only those who enjoyed the film completed the questionnaire.

Frameworks to identify the marketing tools involved in the film industry

Litman (1983) identifies three decision-making areas that he believes are important in ensuring a film is successful in the marketplace; the creative sphere, scheduling and release pattern and finally the marketing endeavour. The problem with such a framework, is the separation of 'the marketing endeavour' as a final and separate consideration. This chapter proposes a more holistic approach to marketing activities. As marketing is concerned with developing, packaging and communicating, marketing activities range from the very early development processes through the budgeting processes to the exhibition and distribution strategy.

The role of the star – actor, director, producer

To date there has been a lot of attention paid to the role played by the lead actors (stars) cast in films. The literature discussed below does not provide a definite answer as to the marketability of films in relation to 'the star', but it is recognised that the star can often be a point of reference in consumers choosing particular films. In addition to this, many of the other creative roles can prompt a decision to select particular films from the available offerings; this will be discussed later in this section. Jacobs (1968) divided the factors influencing film choice into five loosely defined areas, with the principle stars seen as the most important factor in attracting an audience. The importance of a star's earning capacity is recognised by the Hollywood Reporter with their 'Star Power' service. It has a database of over 500 actors and actresses around the world, with an indication of their box office potential.

The importance of genre, script development, target audience and budget will be discussed below, but these factors must be considered in choosing appropriate creative personnel. The impact that these individuals may have on the ability of the film to crossover from one audience segment to a wider audience should be evaluated. The aim of the marketing campaign for many small films is to precipitate a film in crossing over from a niche market to a mainstream audience.

The appeal of 'star quality' has not diminished. On occasion, this appeal is over estimated, as some films do not support big names. This can be problematic for film-makers when trying to secure production finance from the majors. Certain stars have been associated with playing particular character types and appearing in certain types of film. If such stars switch genre, this can be confusing for the potential audience. Latterly, research has shown conflicting results regarding the role of the star in the ultimate success of individual films. De Silva (1998), Sochay (1994), Neelamegham and Chintagunta (1999) and Sawhney and Eliashberg (1996) found that star involvement in a film had a positive result on the box office performance. Ravid (1999), Austin (1989), and Litman and Ahn (1998) concluded that the inclusion of a well-known star in the cast of a film played no significant role in increasing earnings. Litman and Kohl (1989) identified that the star had a small role in increasing revenue but was not the most significant factor. De Vany and Walls (1999) found that those films that featured a star were more likely to have a longer run on more screens than those without. However, as they point out, this may be linked to the fact that such films are likely to have a greater budget than films without stars, which may account for this. Evaluating the impact of stars on the box office performance of films is problematic as often it is dependent on the star in question, the image that this star has and how they are received by the intended audience for the film.

The star is not always the main attraction. For many cinemagoers, the director or cinematographer of the film may be a major draw. For example, the films of Quentin Tarrantino have a certain style and following. This is true for many directors, Pedro Almodovar, Stephen Spielberg, Gus Van Sant, Lars Von Triers and so on. In each case, the attachment of such a director indicates a certain style, genre or quality which appeals to the intended audience. A problem arises when this style is deviated from, as the previous audience can be alienated without the new audience fully accepting the work of such a director. For example, *A Life Less Ordinary*, starring Ewan McGregor and Cameron Diaz was not as commercially successful as anticipated. Many believe this was due to the mixed messages communicated due to the distinctive track record of the film-makers in previous partnerships with Ewan McGregor. This was the third film written by John Hodge and directed by Danny Boyle. The earlier films, *Shallow Grave* and *Trainspotting* had achieved cult success and this, their third collaboration, again starring Ewan McGregor, was eagerly anticipated by their fans. Despite the attempts of the marketing team from their distribution company, Universal Pictures International, to communicate that this was a very different film stylistically to the earlier films, there were still expectations that the film would be another cult classic. Boyle and Hodge's earlier success had awarded them the opportunity to work on a bigger budget, more mainstream film, but this early success also dogged them with a 'cult' label.

The creative sphere

As the end product of the film industry is in itself a creative product, within this it is difficult to distinguish the 'creative sphere' from that which is not creative, but this thesis is not concerned with debating and defining the role of creativity in organisations. Litman (1983: 159) defines the creative sphere as 'the total creative effort expended in making the film', and within this he stresses the importance of the story. This elevation of the story is echoed by experienced film-makers such as Neil Jordan (1997) who stressed repeatedly that the quality of the story was one of the most difficult, yet important, tasks to achieve. Jacobs also includes the story as a key feature in his (1968) framework. Linked to the appeal of the story is the genre. It is impossible to consider the role of the story without discussing the genre of the film.

Genre

The identification of a film's genre is essential as the tastes of cinema audiences move with fashion, with one hit in a particular genre inspiring a revival, as was the case with Les Craven's *Scream* films, which heralded a revival of the teenage horror film. There is an element of chance involved in identifying what will attract audiences when the film is completed. Ellis (1995: 102) and Bowser (1990) examined the trademark genres that existed in American Film in the 1920s and remain today. The Western typified America and the American film of the time. The Comedy became very popular in the 1920s when the first comedy features were made. This was the era of Chaplin, Harold Lloyd, Harry Langdon, Buster Keaton and the infamous duo of Laurel and Hardy. 'Though the introduction of sound required extreme modifications of style and introduced a new group of comics, the comedy, along with the western, the gangster film, and the musical, remains among the most distinctive, indigenous, and important American contributions to film forms' (Ellis, 1995: 104–5).

Another popular genre of the time was the love story. These were originally referred to as 'women's pictures'. Although the love story had been around since the beginning of the film industry, it reached its popular plinth in the 1920s as by this time, women constituted the largest cinema going social group. This is in contrast with the situation today where the main target audience for films are young males as they are now the most frequent cinemagoers. This type of light entertainment appealed to the populace as it enabled them to escape from the humdrum of everyday life. This has remained part of the quintessential appeal of the Hollywood blockbuster to date. Genre continues to be a key determinant for financial success (De Silva, 1998; Litman, 1983; Litman and Kohl, 1989). However, it can be difficult to predict the genres which will appeal at the time of a film's release, as the lead-time between development and theatrical release is nearly 2 years, the result can be producing in a genre that has run its course or suffered from overkill (Litman, 1983: 160).

Ellis (1995) highlights the popularity of adaptations of successful novels and plays of the time. This enthusiasm for adaptations has not faded, the recent success of films such as *Bridget Jones Diary*, *Charlotte Gray*, *High Fidelity* and *The End of the Affair* are testament that the trend towards popular adaptations has not ceased. However, the success of the original novel alone does not ensure success as was seen by the relative commercial failure of *Captain Corelli's Mandolin*.

Target audience

Durie et al. (2000) stress the need to identify the target audience for a particular film in order to focus the marketing campaign. The target audience and any potential crossover audience may be determined by studying the success or failure of similar films at the box office. This can highlight the successful and unsuccessful strategies employed in the production and marketing of such films in order to determine potential audience size.

Durie et al. (2000), share the belief held by Tim Bevan from Working Title Films that it is essential to know a films' target audience from an early stage in its development. Bevan admits that it has taken him a long time to recognise this necessity but urges the writers whom he produces to imagine the trailers and the target audience before writing at all. The identification of the target audience is closely related to the genre of a film as discussed above. The necessity for film-makers to identify potential audiences for their chosen genres was recognised by the European Commission who commissioned a study on the success rates of particular film genres in an attempt to focus European film-makers (Routh, 1996: 8–11).

Word of mouth

Many commentators believe that it is impossible to control 'word of mouth'. However, identifying the most likely audience for a film and focusing on bringing it to their attention can go some way to ensuring that word of mouth is positive. Durie et al. (2000) also look at the impact of 'word of mouth' and reviews on a film's success or failure. He differentiates between 'want-to-see' and audience enjoyment. Film marketers can create 'want-to-see' through the marketing campaign. However, the ultimate aim is to achieve audience enjoyment and therefore 'good word of mouth' in order to sustain the film in the market. Accurate targeting of the film can assist in positive word of mouth.

The experience of Neil Jordan in relation to his film *The Company of Wolves*, provides an example of where a film was failed by its marketing campaign due to incorrect targeting (Jordan, 1997). This adult allegorical fairy tale was distributed in the US by Miramax, who marketed the film as a horror movie and targeted this audience. Audience expectations of a horror movie were unfulfilled resulting in the film being slated by audiences, which ultimately created negative word of mouth and commercial failure; the film was failed by its marketing campaign. Negative word of mouth can undermine the most sophisticated marketing campaign (Katz and Lazarsfeld, 1955).

Critics and avids

An essential role in creating and sustaining good 'want-to-see' and word of mouth is played by the critics and what the film industry calls 'avids' – the mavens or opinion leaders from among the consumers. Much research has been carried out regarding the role of critics and awards in predicting box office success (Austin, 1983, 1989; Cameron, 1995; D'Astous and Colbert, 2002; D'Astous and Touil, 1999; Eliashberg and Shugan, 1997, Holbrook, 1999). Findings here are inconclusive but there would seem to be an overall acknowledgement that good critical reviews can help a film to achieve box office success. The question of the role of awards ceremonies seems more complicated, films with Oscar (Academy Award) nominations, more likely of achieving box office success than nominees and winners of festival prizes such as Cannes, Venice and Sundance. There has been evidence from Austin (1981) to show how the influence of critics and reviewers only impacted on the more 'esoteric films' and therefore did not heavily impact on box office receipts in the main.

Production values

In the early film industry, production values, such as impressive sets and crowd scenes involving large numbers of extras were identified by Jacobs (1968) as influencing the level of audience appeal. In today's terms, this would translate into the appeal of elaborate special effects and the use of digital mastering in order to impress the audience. However, De Vany and Walls (1999: 308) stress that, 'heavy spending on special effects or "production value" is the most risky strategy for making a movie a hit'.

Development

The above factors are all important considerations when packaging a film, but often considerations pertaining to the marketing of a film occur too late. In the development stage of a films life cycle, it is important to identify the genre, target audience and so on in order to select the correct creative talent and to make appropriate budgeting decisions. The approach to film making in the US is still based on the principle of market success, despite the rise of the independent production sector. In Hollywood, films which are not easily classified by target audience and genre, have little chance of surviving the development process. In Europe, the percentage of projects proceeding from development into production is extremely high in comparison to the US. 'Hollywood spends around 7 per cent of each film's overall budget on development compared to Europe's more characteristic 1–2,' (Finney, 1996: 17).

This disparity is mainly attributed to the pay structures existing in Europe with production companies reluctant to invest money in projects that need further development. In a panel discussion as part of the 1998 London Film Festival, Andrea Calderwood, Head of Production at Pathé Entertainment, confirmed that production companies are unwilling to become involved in the script development stage preferring to wait and see the fully developed project before committing to it. Therefore, the scriptwriter is likely to hurry along the process of development of a script due to financial necessity. Due to the budgetary constraints which this imposes, independent film-makers in Europe rarely carry out cohesive audience research at this stage. This failure in the European film industry has been recognised and programmes like the European Commission's MEDIA Programme as well as national level programmes have been established to address this problem.

Distribution – scheduling and release

A wealth of debate surrounds the issue of whether the majors or the independents can secure the most successful distribution deal. While it cannot be denied that the majors are ideally suited to distributing big budget, high profile films, independents and specialist distributors are often more suited to the distribution of smaller films. As they invariably have lower prints and advertising (P&A) budgets, they are required to execute a more exact and focused distribution campaign than the majors and this is often more successful for these films. Goldberg (1991) summed this question up as whether to aim with a rifle or a shotgun. PACT (1994: 55) found that, in relation to UK productions, those which were independently distributed, recouped a significantly higher proportion of their budgets than those distributed by the majors. The average proportion of budgets recouped, from all media, by independent distributors in the UK and US were 17.75 and 35 per cent, respectively. In contrast, the figures for studio-distributed British films in the UK and US were 6.75 and 20.6 per cent, respectively.

In fact, August 1989 heralded a new era in film marketing in the US when Miramax released sex, lies and videotape. According to Perren (2001: 30), 'sex, lies and videotape helped to set the standard for low-budget, niche-based distribution in the 1990s and to lay the groundwork for a bifurcation within the entertainment industry'. This led to each of the major Hollywood studios purchasing a specialist distribution company to handle quirky small films.

The power of the majors to secure preferred playdates, length of run and maximum levels of prints emerged in the PACT submission to the Mergers and Monopolies Commission in 1994. This was especially true for films that were distributed by the majors in the US, a phenomenon can easily be explained. The majors control the distribution of the overwhelming majority of films in the international market and for this reason it is imperative that the exhibition sector co-operates with them in order to secure a constant flow of product.

Latterly academic attention has shifted to look at the release strategy as well as the characteristics of the film itself. Jones and Ritz (1991), De Vany and Walls (1996, 1997, 1999), Neelamegham and Chintagunta (1999), Zufryden (1996), Jedidi, Krider and Weinberg (1998), and Litman and Ahn (1998) all look at the impact which the number of screens on which a film opens, runs and closes has upon success. In general, the greater the number of screens a film is released on, the more likely the film is to achieve financial success. But, this explanation is overly simplistic. The number of screens that a film opens on as well the length of the run which films achieve is dependent on the budget which the distributors have for P&A. The cost of each print is in excess of £1000 and one print is needed for each screen showing the film, in this way, smaller films with lower P&A budgets will be restricted in terms of the number of screens the film can be shown on at any one time. In addition the major film studios, due to the integrated supply chain at their disposal, can negotiate longer guaranteed runs in cinemas than independent distributors.

Ratings

Litman also emphasised the impact that a film's rating can have upon the success of a film. Austin (1981), in agreeing with Litman draws upon Brehm's concept of psychological reactance 'which focuses on the specific motivational and behavioural response of individuals for whom a given freedom has been threatened or eliminated' (Austin, 1981: 384). When a film is rated R or X in the US (18 or X in Europe) the film has the aura of something forbidden. The publicity gained by such films as *The Last Temptation of Christ*, *Crash* and *Natural Born Killers*, when the censors wanted to outlaw them, was invaluable. This controversy created 'must see' – the feeling that one is missing out on an important cultural reference by not seeing a particular film – which is what every film marketer strives for.

Brehm's (1966: 9) theory predicts that the individual 'will be motivated to attempt to regain the lost or threatened freedoms by whatever methods are available and appropriate', the more a freedom is threatened, the more it is sought. Therefore, when applied to the ratings systems of films, the more forbidden it is to see a film, the greater 'want-to-see' – the industry term for very strong word of mouth, which creates great anticipation for a particular film – is created. To support this belief empirically, Austin draws upon Herman and Leyens (1977) work (Austin, 1981). In a study of films transmitted by Belgian-based French language TV station, RTB, they concluded that, 'qualifications make the movies more desirable for the television viewers … movies with advisories are watched more than the movies without them' (quoted in Austin, 1981: 390).

It is undisputed that the American industry has more star appeal with more internationally recognisable stars. In addition, as outlined above, they control the major worldwide distribution networks and have a major foothold in the exhibition sector. In this way, they dominate the worldwide film industry. The distribution sector is undoubtedly the most instrumental element in a film reaching its audience. Irrespective of the talent of the writer, director, technical staff and stars involved, if a film fails to secure a distribution deal with one of the majors or a respected independent distributor, it will not be widely exhibited and will certainly not recoup its production budget. A good marketing campaign, which is coherently planned with the production team and distributor from the earliest possible stage, is essential in order to secure good box office receipts. Durie et al. (1993: 13) stress, 'the goal of film marketing is to maximise the audience for a film and, by extension, its earning potential.'

European film-makers are at last acknowledging that they must make money to survive in all sectors and that while there is a place for artistic and sensitive films which do not achieve major box office success, these must be subsidised by blockbusters. The recent success of non-Hollywood films like *Billy Elliot*, *Monsoon Wedding*, and *City of God* around the world is testament to the fact that a film-maker can retain his/her creative integrity while achieving commercial success, one, therefore, does not exclude the other.

Yet again, we are witness to the fact of the major players from the American film world dominating – and in so doing, restricting entry by independents – largely European, into the market. Although investigations by the MMC in the UK, the Antitrust authorities in the US and the European Commission's Directorate General for Competition (DG IV), to date there has been no proof that this domination is taking place unfairly. It will be interesting to note how this develops with the continued growth of the multiplex sector and their specific arrangements with their parent companies. It is, however, unlikely that we will again enter into a situation resembling that which existed during the reign of the Motion Picture Patents Company. It is difficult to know how Europe should tackle the historical domination which the US has over its markets, but progress cannot be made until European filmmakers acknowledge that, in film, there is no natural separation between commerce and art.

Conclusion

This chapter has sought to examine the major drivers behind the dominant position the American Film Industry holds over global box office. Historically, the structural problems which are seen to dog the European industry emanate from the organisation of the industry itself combined with a reluctance on the part of the Europeans to adopt industrial and marketing tactics readily embraced by Hollywood. While acceptable growth could be achieved in its domestic market, the US majors felt little need to dilute their effort and develop a foothold in Europe. However, as the home market became saturated and demand for its product in Europe rose, the majors found it relatively easy to mobilise its marketing machine and take a significant share of the European distribution and exhibition market.

Europe's policy makers are belatedly employing some of these techniques in order to develop the European industry. The American major's domination of the distribution sector continues to cause problems for the European – and indeed American – independents. The additional problems, which Europe has in relation to language and culture, are merely asides to the question of industrial organisation and market awareness. It is upon these areas that the national policy makers are concentrating their effort to increase the commercial success of the global film industry and loosen the stronghold that America currently has over this market.

Acknowledgements

I would like to thank the University of Hertfordshire for funding the research that went into this chapter. In addition I would like to thank the various film industry professionals whom I have interviewed during my research.

Chapter 4

The marketing of theatre

Iain Fraser

Introduction

Suitable definitions of theatre are as elusive as for anything else – but dramatic art may serve. The Concise Oxford Dictionary has drama as a 'set of events having the unity and progress of a play and leading to catastrophe or consummation'. Many think of it as being building based, but often it is not. It is thought to have its roots in prehistory and religious or spiritual ritual. Through the ages and across the world, theatre has been performed at the poles, in hospitals, in prisons, in concentration camps and the gulag. Specialist forms of drama have been developed for therapeutic purposes (Røine, 1997). Insights into the human condition, art, therapy and entertainment – all are there. Drama takes many forms including state – subsidised theatre, professional for profit theatre, political theatre and theatre in the open air, touring and repertory companies, amateur, school and youth theatre.

What is theatre marketing? Is it a function, identifying an appropriate marketing mix and implementing tactical programmes to serve the artistic director? Or is it more, a philosophy putting the customer at the heart of things and around whose wants the product and marketing mix is designed? Of course artistic directors or producers can be seen to use their instincts to devise a blend that can be sold. For them, marketing is about tactics. It is therefore about promotion through advertising, telephone selling and publicity in part, but principally by use of the seasonal brochure and mail shots. Pallin, outlining the responsibilities of staff in a theatre, describes the role of a marketing/publicity manager as selling the show (Pallin, 2003). This takes place through a range of activities including raising the public profile of the theatre, and attracting sponsorship. Theatre marketing also produces posters, leaflets and advertising and organises their distribution and arranges press and photo calls. The role as described can be very much seen as a tactical one with no evident development since the 1980s. Few professional marketers nowadays would be content with such a role.

Theatre is a people business, needing teamwork backstage and front of house. In essence, we reach out to the audience to pull them into an intimate experience. Soft skills and judgement borne of experience are needed. Whether in the subsidised or non-subsidised theatre, artistic directors are required to bring in audiences. In the for-profit sector, the day of the theatrical producer is said by many producers to be ending (Iverne, 2000). Certainly the promoter's business seems to have become even more risky. But theatre is a risk business. Arguably few other fields of endeavour depend so much on the market-based judgements of the producer and impresario.

The work is done, the doors open – will an audience turn up?

Policy frameworks are dealt elsewhere in this volume. Pick (1986) covers the ground comprehensively. Many of the issues are relevant not just in the UK but worldwide. Heilbrun and Gray (2001) give comprehensive consideration to the economics of the arts in general. As far as theatre is concerned, a wide spectrum is evident in relation to a number of national policies, yet the same theme emerges. How does one ensure a vibrant sector when entrepreneurs regularly find they cannot make a profit through offering the most demanding fare, art on the artists' terms, as it has been described?

In the US, theatre is unashamedly commercial or reliant on community effort. It is argued that such a system is more democratic, in that companies are forced to solicit support on a wide scale from individuals – and that the tax deductibility of donations is a suitable recognition of the sector's importance. Despite the difficulties this might be said to bring (e.g. it has been variously reported that between two-thirds and three-quarters of the staff in arts organisations in the US are fund-raisers) the community sector has grown consistently. In the UK, with the advent of gift aid, we now have such a system but tax deductibility works at the basic rate. It is thought this will in the long term continue to reduce the percentage of total income that theatres obtain from the box office. Such pressures exist elsewhere. Caust (1999) outlines some of the policy issues that have arisen due to the imposition of economic rationalist policies in the Australian cultural sector, with reference to concurrent changes in policy in the UK and the US. She argues for the predominance of artistic objectives.

At the other extreme, there are governments that fund theatre companies to such an extent that 80 per cent of their income comes from the state. They therefore are substantially less reliant on box office income. Such companies are able to rehearse for long periods, bringing astonishing depth to their productions. Examples can be found in the Baltic States, for example, where marketing in any sense is not practised or well understood, though there is still far greater emphasis on the visit of school pupils, for example.

Some knowledge of both the history of the arts and the comparative study of arts management and management science is desirable for the theatrical entrepreneur. There is clearly some chance of misunderstanding different cultures and societies, yet it seems that there are instructive examples to be found and some insight into cultural policy.

As is well known, theatre had roots in religious and quasi-religious backgrounds. The Greek Thespis in 500 BC managed an artistic festival in conjunction with an independent jury. 'Additionally, there was of course an independent sponsor, the choragus, who financed the festival. During the festival, a project organisation was established to manage events and supervise the performances, which were attended by more than 10,000 visitors' (Hagoort, 2000: ix).

The golden age of theatre in Elizabethan and Jacobean England (which produced Shakespeare, Marlowe, Jonson and Webster among others) was formed through the entrepreneurship of Henslowe and others. The situation is too complex for a detailed description here, but London at one point contained a creative cluster of half a dozen competing theatrical companies, from which companies toured nationally in the summer months or when plague had shut their London premises. Entrepreneurs set out to make a profit through expanding the audience for theatre, building a theatre custom designed for the purpose rather than the inn yards and barns previously used (Cook, 1995). In Jacobean times, indoor premises were used during the winter months, markedly affecting the nature of the dramas written. Different companies developed different house styles, some being notorious for their blood-and-thunder melodramas, others presenting more sophisticated fare. Growing demand was reflected in the capacity of the new theatres. Up to 4000 people were thought to have attended a single performance – there is a reference to there being no casualties when the Globe fire occurred, a bystander remarking on the fact that such a crowd escaped through only two exits. Methods of promotion included the extensive use of playbills. These were intensively distributed and displayed, and used by the literate as what we would now call programmes.

Over a 100 years later, David Garrick notoriously gave up his partnership in a wine merchant's as he felt he could make more money by acting – and became a rich man in doing so (Benedetti, 2001). Examples of the actor-manager continued in the UK for many years, although their large-scale touring companies (operating for profit) led an often-precarious existence. They were known to use mailshots for promotion: for example in London in the mid-19th century, one promoter posted out several thousand to boost sales.

The role of the actor-manager managed to survive well into the 20th century, but faced with increasing difficulty. Some interesting examples of promotion and showmanship – that indispensable component of the producer's toolkit – can be found. For example, in 1926, 'Henry Baynton's Shakespearean Company' was scheduled to visit Dundee in Scotland. Four weeks beforehand, the local paper noted that ballot papers were available for collection from the venue, the King's Theatre. Patrons could vote for any seven plays from 25 listed. The seven most popular would be performed, and a prize of dress seats would be given to the voter whose choice matched that of the public as a whole. The ballot closed 1 week before the company arrived in town. The plays finally given were Hamlet, Twelfth Night, Romeo and Juliet, Julius Caesar, Merchant of Venice, As You Like It and Macbeth. Offerings such as Cymbeline apparently did not make an impact. The newspaper is silent as to the names of the individual winning and indeed as to how many votes were cast.

Post war, it was clear in the UK that the preservation of a traditional body of classic and large-scale theatre required subsidy, in the form of intervention from either local or central government. High art and entertainment were steadily diverging. Private sector entrepreneurs found it increasingly difficult to make a living through large-scale productions. Awareness of the importance of cultural education and the larger needs of society led eventually to the foundation of the Arts Council to dispense subsidy at arms' length. But some differences in philosophy were soon highlighted. Its wartime predecessor, the Council for Encouragement of Music and the Arts (CEMA) had maintained as one of its policies the encouragement of music-making and play-acting by the people themselves (Pick, 1986). It therefore assumed that government support for amateur activity would be required. However, Lord Keynes, first chair of the Arts Council, ensured subsequently that the role of the new body was restricted to support for the professional arts, a policy that has continued to the present day.

By comparison with these days of New Labour, it seems extraordinary that after the war the incoming Labour government gave such great support to the Arts. What underlaid this post war philosophy? The then Minister of Education, Ellen Wilkinson argued, 'Only the best is good enough for the working man' (quoted in Drummond, 2000). It was then accepted that art forms were different, offering a spectrum of challenges – nowadays it is politically correct to argue that all art forms are somehow equal or equally valid.

This bureaucratic framework was established to facilitate the management of the arts. The same ethos was also evident in the attitudes and values espoused by the BBC, something expressed well by Sir William Haley, Director General of the BBC. In 1946 at the time of the incoming Labour Government, Haley saw every civilised nation as a cultural pyramid with a lamentable broad base and a lamentable narrow tip.

Haley's conception was of a BBC through the years which would slowly move listeners from one stratum of this pyramid to the next. Outlining the purpose of the Third Programme (now branded BBC Radio Three) he set out what would now be called a mission statement stating that the Third Programme was designed to be of artistic and cultural importance. The audience envisaged was one already aware of artistic experience and will include persons of taste, of intelligence and of education. It was therefore, he concluded, 'selective and not casual, and both attentive and critical'.

Such conviction was quickly apparent in the development of the system of theatre subsidy too. Thus the public subsidy of non-profit theatre companies was systematised. In the UK, what remains of the philosophy that informed that immediate post-war period? Despite the experience of the 1980s – said to be the most hostile atmosphere for the public subsidy of theatre there has been – this structure of arms' length distribution of government funds – seems likely to continue. The system has its virtues but some weaknesses and paradoxes. Driven by the need to demonstrate high occupancy figures, subsidised companies sometimes put on programmes containing highly commercial elements. For example, the Royal National Theatre in London recently presented *My Fair Lady*, claiming it attracted people who would not otherwise enter the building complex. The hope was that they would be encouraged to move from one level and genre to another that is seen as more demanding, part of the justification for subsidy. A similar dilemma confronts the BBC when it finds itself competing with more and more commercial offerings rather than developing the sort of programming that would be beyond the private sector.

John Drummond, drawing on his wide-ranging experience as a festival director and arts manager, restated one of the key arguments for publicly funded subsidy. It is his belief that the arts need public subsidy to retain some freshness through innovation. The truth is, he argued, that if you let the public decide what you do you will become both repetitive and lacking in imagination. 'What the public want is always more of what they have already experienced and liked. The real challenge is to find ways in which they can be persuaded to listen to something they do not immediately find attractive, so that essentially that experience extends their knowledge and their taste' (Drummond, 2000: 148). He argues that the task of the marketing manager was essentially to promote the programme chosen by the artistic director.

Amateur drama

We have already seen that Arts Council policy from its very beginning omitted much consideration of the amateur theatre movement. In the UK, very little government funding is directed to amateur or community theatre, this role being taken up by local authorities. In Sweden, by comparison, around a quarter of government funding goes to support amateurs. And other Scandinavian countries, France and the Netherlands also devote relatively more to amateur work than in the UK (Feist, 1997). In the UK, the very word amateur has come to have a pejorative meaning. Many disparage amateur theatre, yet historically many noted actors first appeared with amateur companies (Giesekam, 2000). A high proportion of professional arts organisations have grown out of amateur roots. Frequently amateur companies hire in professional actors or singers for lead roles, and in past times professional companies often involved amateur actors. Many professional actors have prolonged periods of unemployment and while resting – the term applied to actors while not professionally engaged as actors – seek and obtain other ways of earning a living. So the boundaries are by no means clear. Amateurs aspire to professional standards.

It is difficult to maintain that this transformation is a seamless one. The barriers put in place by the institutional snobbery of administrators and reviewers are too great. I recall the hurt with which one amateur performer recounted being told by a director of the Scottish Arts Council (SAC), 'what you do is not art,' something he had remembered for over 20 years. Of course amateurs in any walk of life cannot be expected to achieve professional standards and certainly not consistently. Perhaps however amateurs come close more often than professionals would like to credit. In particular, I have been a member of audiences at amateur theatrical performances, and at times one could sense the absorption of the audience in stage proceedings quite as much as in professional performances.

In Scotland, in common with many other countries, many amateur societies sprang up at a time when there was little professional activity to offer an alternative. For some, especially in isolated areas, the motivation was social and with the aim of providing entertainment. Other groups tried to develop a distinctly Scottish dramatic condition. Still others were concerned with the political potential of theatre (Hutchison, 1977: 14). A recent study (Giesekam, 2000: 2) demonstrated that amateur theatrical activity in Scotland remains strong. The nation, with a population of 5 million, has an active voluntary sector. 'The total audience for amateur, youth and community theatre, at well over a million people, easily exceeded the audience for professional theatre – and they can't all have been shanghaied into going by the 40,000 or so people who are regularly involved in such activity.'

Commonly a further distinction is then made between mainstream and community theatre. Those involved in community theatre see themselves as more radical, involving excluded sectors of society in representing their lives on stage. This emerges in the face of what is seen as the dominance of bourgeois life in mainstream political theatre. Themes in such dramatic work tends to focus on racism, gender and sexuality. The underlying philosophy can also extend to the formation of the groups themselves. Theatre groups can involve, for example, those with learning difficulties (such as Chickenshed Theatre in London); or there are examples of theatre companies involving the elderly and other socially excluded groups.

Regardless of motives, all these groups are reaching out to different sectors and different audiences, not just the stereotypical middle-aged and middle class. Joan Littlewood's Theatre Workshop, for instance, had a clear political agenda and did much to change the direction of British theatre after the war. Kenneth Tynan once remarked 'Others write plays, direct in them and act in them: she alone "makes theatre"'. Nowadays, people find it hard to understand why her work was seen as so revolutionary. Much UK theatre was then more comfortable – 'a mirror held up to cosiness' as Peter Brook called it (Littlewood, 2003). One must be careful not to patronise. There is a story of Joan Littlewood negotiating to bring ballet to London's Stratford East, traditionally a deprived area. The company manager asked whether her audiences would be able to enjoy it, to be told 'they will if you are good enough'.

For these attenders and participants, motivations range from seeking entertainment to personal development to exploiting the political potential of theatre. It is arguable that the audience and the actors are involved together in the process. Kelly (1984) talks of cultural democracy – an idea that revolves around the notion of plurality and equality of access to the means of cultural production and distribution. Bouder-Pailer reviews the literature concerning theatre audiences. She hypothesises four dimensions (social hedonism, intellectual enrichment, arousal of emotion and entertainment), concluding that more research is needed (Bouder-Pailer, 1999; Giesekam, 2000). A number of attempts have been made to segment audiences.

Policy for subsidised theatre in the UK is moving more towards the situation where market-based plans are required, focused on increasing audiences and widening access. There is an increasing awareness of the need to make the results of market research reports more widely available – after all, public money has been spent on them.

A recent publication *The UK Cultural Sector: Profile and Policy Issues* (Selwood, 2001) claimed to be the most comprehensive piece of research ever to be undertaken into the subsidised cultural sector (press release, 2001). Any researcher is struck by the dearth of reliable information. There is perhaps no gap harder to assess than that between the impact and value of cultural activity.

Selwood (2001) concluded there was an absence of reliable and consistent data among official bodies as to how money is spent. Feist (1997) points out some of the problems in detail. For example, when respondents in national surveys have been asked questions regarding visit frequency, there is no attempt to discern whether thinking about amateur or professional performances. The well-known halo effect is also a concern.

The fact that there is no one agency responsible for gathering data on the cultural sector in the UK, and no single source of information about funding, is problematised by Selwood (2001). Official data is described as broad brush, and of little value in establishing a picture of specific areas of cultural activity. National policies and objectives are set out on the website of the Department for Culture, Media and Sport (DCMS). It seems hardly too much to say that one could not imagine a mission statement for an arts organisation that would not fall within the ambit of the declared policies. To anyone who has worked in a commercial organisation, the lack of sharpness seems tangible. Even when sound data has been obtained, its distribution is often restricted. Researchers in the arts field are often refused data, collection of which has been funded by public money.

Selwood (2001) also questions the extent to which DCMS objectives are delivered. The research findings question many assumptions maintained by the cultural community. Examples include the belief that subsidised theatre is more innovative than commercial theatre and that there is an economic impact from cultural venues and events. And it is unclear, says Selwood, what is the nature of the relationship between the subsidised cultural sector and the creative industries. What we need therefore is evidence to substantiate these assumptions so that policies can have an impact.

Clancy argues there are a number of policy initiatives in the developed world – the concept of access for all (both horizontal and vertical), the impact of technology and the instrumental use of cultural policy – for example attracting tourism or aiding urban renewal (Clancy, 1997). To provide the evidence linking cause and effect is problematic. So many well-meaning folk find it hard to have their effectiveness questioned; yet no need is self-evident. The very term itself – 'the Arts' has developed a pejorative meaning. At least when one comes across the term creative, there seems to have been a distinctive attempt to avoid the use of the word arts. It seems often to be used in its place. The case for the arts must be made.

Theory and practice

Management theory requires the consideration of organisational objectives, strategy and tactics. These relate to audiences. Strategic marketing management is nothing if not about segmentation and positioning. Segmentation has been carried out using box office data. This has often been on some form of recency, frequency and monetary value (RFM) analysis. Such an analysis identifies intenders, rejectors, lapsed attenders, heavy attenders (four or more visits per year), and so on (Kahan, 1998). Discussion of Customer Value Matrix also takes place (Marcus, 1998).

Bennett (2002), investigating competitor analysis of grant-aiding provincial UK theatre companies, concluded that competition in what was essentially a mature and static market had greatly intensified in recent years. Theatre managers seemed to be echoing the commercial sector in increasing competitor analysis, predicated on the assumption that their competition comprised other theatres and other arts venues rather than leisure, sports and general entertainment. However, few resources had been invested in competitor analysis and activity tended to be ad hoc and informal. Bennett concluded that in the absence of professionally commissioned market research, this work had not been used effectively and a more structured approach would be helpful.

Other key marketing issues concern audience development and product design. The evolution of the role of theatre marketing in recent years seems to be giving marketers a greater role in these areas. Too often, theatre managers have accepted only the need for publicity from their marketing staff. Marketers have always felt their skills deserved some input into decision-making on strategic issues. Tactical issues naturally occupy more of a marketer's time, such as the consideration of the relative effectiveness of advertising, selling, direct mail, sponsorship, publicity and merchandising. Analytical work on the marketing mix and dispassionate calculations as to the effectiveness of various forms of promotion has its place. For staff of subsidised theatres, it seems that a disproportionate amount of effort goes into the preparation of a season's brochure. Touring promoters tend to rely on newspaper advertising and listings. Reports of Internet marketing confirm its potential. Electronic-flyers (e-flyers) and text messaging too have shown promise. With the expansion of published media, the number of listing opportunities has increased. There are magazines – both in hard copy and on-line, and of course newspapers.

Yet marketing tradition indicates that our primary audience will be most easily drawn from existing and lapsed users, from their families and friends. We therefore need to capture this data at the box office and use it. How simple! Suppliers of box office software claim to make this more straightforward every year. However, difficulties remain. For example, how should the theatre classify the customer who comes to four performances of one show in a year? Is this customer intrinsically better than one who attends four different shows in a year? How effective is cross selling? Theatre going is still a social activity and perhaps, if it is not that, it is nothing. Perhaps more can be done to make theatres more comfortable for the lone attenders? Existing systems and databases may tell us little or nothing about these issues. As one marketing manager said, we have a list of names and addresses but we know very little about them. We also know less than we would like about the others who come with the ticket purchasers.

Study of the literature of arts marketing, and particularly theatre marketing leaves one wondering why so few writers explicitly include reference to the role of the theatrical impresario, producer or festival director. It is given to few to take so many decisions relating to the outcome. The impresario must know his audience. The best have a deep and instinctive understanding of what will sell, of what their audiences will buy, for any theatre has many audiences and many segments. 'The critical element in theatre management is an understanding of the nature of the community of which the theatre is a part. From this we hope to develop an accurate judgement of the public taste' (Paul Iles, quoted in Crispin, 1999: 72).

What is an impresario? According to the Oxford English Dictionary, 'one who organises public entertainment'. The term refers to the person who hires a show or act that is already in existence, hires a performing space and presents them there. A producer has an even wider scope, creating his own show from the ground up – finding and paying for the play, the director, the cast, the publicity, the marketing and anything else that crops up (Inverne, 2000). To what extent are these lines blurred? Famous figures in UK theatre range from the Grades to Bill Kenwright, Thelma Holt to Cameron Mackintosh and Peter Hall to Joan Littlewood. Peter Hall, quoted by Inverne (2000) provides many insights useful to our discussion. It is seen as a very personal business, one where the ability of a commercial producer to survive is increasingly questioned. 'Commercial theatre could not work now – it is specialist, hand-made and very expensive' says Hall.

An alternative view (Bennett and Kottasz, 2001) suggests that the 'artistic director' or 'general manager' is the figure most commonly responsible for new product development. They tested the hypothesis that a new product ought to be designed in consideration with their views. The research concluded, among other things, that theatres had become more marketing oriented, yet this had not crowded out the sector's commitment to education and challenging as well as entertaining audiences. The paper's concluding remark suggested that the key factors causing lead users to identify the elements of a successful new production were not yet known. In the genre of blockbuster musicals, one example of a successful producer/impresario is Cameron Mackintosh, a man who immerses himself in the details of a show, working extremely hard to shape it. Yet he has had his failures. In his memoirs, Alan Jay Lerner, lyricist of *My Fair Lady* among other musicals, tells the story of how he and his partner the composer Frederick Loewe, insisted that in other countries they used identical stage sets in the belief 'it might have been the chandelier that did it'. Such superstition, such alchemy!

Practice

Much theatre is venue based. Not so long ago, theatres could be categorised as producing or receiving (now more commonly called presenting). The one had a permanent company putting on a season of shows, rehearsing one while performing another. The other would have a far smaller establishment, putting on touring shows for one or more nights. The two were seen as requiring very different management and in fact marketing skills. When receiving managers tried to produce shows, they were known to become a cropper – and producing managers were not always sufficiently adept at knowing what their customers might buy from a touring promoter, nor indeed might they be skilled at negotiation with promoters.

Commercially run theatres still rely on long runs, producers designing and developing a product which will be popular enough for them to spread fixed costs over a large number of performances. Even the best, however, find themselves with a turkey from time to time. Aficionados of small scale, intimate theatre argue that large-scale productions in large auditoriums – even when produced night after night to the highest standards – are not theatre. As one critic said, having viewed a production of *Phantom of the Opera* in a 3000-seat theatre, it was more akin to cinema.

Modern direct marketing relies in large part on the capture of individual customer details at the first sale, so that the marketer can begin a relationship with that customer, subsequently treating them differently over time in order to generate repeat business. There is an overlap between database and direct marketing. Database marketing is used to hold and analyse customer data, helping to create marketing strategies. Direct marketing focuses on using a database to communicate directly to customers so as to attract a direct response. 'A marketing database is a list of customers' and prospects' records that enables strategic analysis, and individual selections for communication and customer services support. The data is organised around the customer' (Tapp, 1998: 45). Direct marketing is a way of acquiring and keeping customers by providing a framework for three activities: analysis of individual customer information, strategy formation, and implementation such that customers respond directly. Data relate to customers, to transactions and to communications. Basic software functions require name and address processing, being able to make selections, analyse the effect of campaigns and make reports. Many companies are awash with unusable data; always one must ask 'what do I need the database for?'

Relationship marketing was first defined by Berry (1983), and does not mention direct marketing. The terms sometimes are used interchangeably. Segmentation can be carried out using behavioural data or profile data. The customer's lifetime value can be calculated and used to calculate the allowable marketing spend per customer. Cluster analysis can be used to sort customers (and non-customers) into segments according to lifestyle needs. Responses can be modelled on a campaign-by-campaign basis. Statistical methods lie at the heart of the superior control and targeting that direct marketing can offer.

When Roger Tomlinson wrote his guide to box office management 'Boxing Clever', he was able to point out the changes that had taken place with the introduction of credit card booking and telephone management (Tomlinson, 1993). He correctly foresaw continuous change – but who could have foreseen the full extent of the potential brought by the Internet and by e-commerce? Good box office practice is at the heart of most marketing work in the theatre. The marketing guides produced by Tomlinson for the Arts Council of England advocate this in a clear and logical fashion, providing 'a step by step approach to capturing information from customers, to managing and extracting the data recorded in computerised Box Office systems, and to the key calculations and analyses necessary to understand and interpret it for marketing purposes'(Tomlinson, 1998).

Yet it seems unlikely that some of the analyses recommended by Tomlinson are carried out rigorously by the majority of theatres. Of course, staff can rightly claim that they have a good and detailed understanding or feel for their local market. There are many examples, though, of research that shows that there is no substitute for an independent analysis in greater depth. Anecdotal evidence alone suggests the time of staff is still too constricted by day-to-day pressures. Investment in the necessary software, and more expensive still, in training the staff in the necessary skills, seems unavailable in all but the largest public sector organisations. Some detailed research is required. It is arguable in fact that the necessary software is still not cheap enough.

Data capture is the name given to capturing details for a buyer of tickets in such a way that one can start to build a relationship. To the purchaser, it should seem an incidental part of the evening, and one that takes no longer than necessary. There have been many examples of models constructed, some involving regression and some involving cluster analysis. Only those who have worked through such exercises can fully appreciate the range of assumptions made, sometimes on evidence that is largely untested. In any case, however sophisticated the methods used, the marketing analyst must always try to understand the need to devise methods that can be used.

There is clearly a great skill involved in putting together an attractive package. Touring promoters and impresarios often mix well-known stars in a package. There is a great art in this. In old Athenian drama, satirical comedies or other forms of fooling followed tragedies. Sir Thomas Beecham always used to follow orchestral programmes with what he called a 'lollipop' to serve the same purpose. This 'lollipop' was a piece of music which was in contrast to what had gone previously, and which was of a soporific or soothing nature. The objective was to lower the emotional temperature of the audience to the normal so that everyone walked out happy and comfortable.

How else can theatres draw in audiences? Commonly a body called a theatre club, a friends' society or some other such name is attached to a theatre. These bodies may be formal or informal. For example, they may be able to nominate directors, or may at the other extreme have no influence. A new artistic director might well disapprove and feel that the club members will not like what the director may want to put on. There is said to be such a society where there is great competition to become chair – because the society contributes so much by way of subsidy that the chair is able to lay down the law concerning the production of a particular play in the following year – and even to cast a key actor. An artistic director recounted this tale to me with horror. Americans have developed mechanisms to handle this better, asking patrons to nominate separately desired playwrights, plays and actors in such a way that the linkage is not overt, and allows the artistic director to combine flexibility with a sharp sense of the wishes of those on the mailing list.

Friends' societies have the potential of an important point of contact with regular customers, that known as a membership scheme or friends' society, and were well examined by Raymond (1992). Such societies can have varying aims and titles, ranging from a playgoers' club only loosely attached to a particular theatre, to a membership scheme operated and driven by the theatre and offering a wide range of options with different levels of benefits. Fraser (1998) reported on a study, part of the aim of which was to identify exemplars that were of major benefit to any particular theatre. The study showed very few UK theatres – perhaps 10 per cent – possess a truly effective membership scheme. These schemes are clearly able to generate large numbers of core attenders. Subscription income, net of costs, may amount to a significant contribution to the theatre's annual running costs. Investment of resources is required to produce good results. Membership schemes require the allocation of full-time staff to maximise benefits.

The craft of marketing in theatre administration and management is a vital one, akin to entrepreneurship and needs a combination of skills of a high order. Invariably today there is more competition than ever before, and more need for effective promotion and marketing, whether tickets are being sold by word of mouth to youngsters' parents or advertised by some impresario on a large scale.

The poster designer can do much of this. Cameron Mackintosh attributes much of his success in promotion to the design of posters. He tries to develop identifiable vivid images that burn themselves into the memory. There were the green eyes for the *Cats* poster, the starving child backed by a tattered French tricolour for *Les Miserables*, the mask for *Phantom* and so on. 'A good poster says everything and nothing. It allows the imagination to take flight. Posters that explicitly say "this is what you are going to get" usually mean you are not going to get it. But after you have seen the show, it should become clear that the good poster has everything in it; because it has caught the spirit of the show with something very simple. However, it is a very complicated process to make it simple' (Mackintosh, quoted in Inverne, 2000: 27). The copywriter, too has a key role. But how can a copywriter manage to convey the unique experience of being there? The copywriter must bring this unique experience alive to prospective customers. He may be said to be writing a review before the event.

As for amateur and community theatre, marketing principles hold good here too. It is true that the choice of repertoire is driven by the need to maintain an income stream. Society members are embedded in networks and communities and families and extended families to whom they sell tickets. Income is largely from the box office (Giesekam, 2000). Often this has to be bolstered by fund-raising events and by sponsorship. Membership fees can be a significant cost. People join societies to act or help behind the scenes.

This writer was struck when presenting a seminar to societies from all over Scotland, just how few claimed to train the younger members in selling techniques – yet they mostly complained about the difficulty of filling theatres.

Rhetoric

In strategic terms, language used relates to bringing in young audiences and audience development. This term is variously defined. Maitland (1997) calls it 'a planned process which enhances and broadens specific individuals' experiences of the arts'. Kolb (2000) refers to audience development as an expression of the need to extend the range of the audience. Indeed, she accepts that audiences are skewed. Few cultural organisations have an audience which consists of the broadly based spectrum of society although this is the espoused goal of many mission statements.

Does the term actually relate to pulling the audience through a set of experiences so that their appetites would be developed, and they would move up to the next stage on the ladder? Are we trying to develop a larger audience for Beckett? Or is audience development about focusing on introducing a higher and higher proportion of the population to attend shows of any kind?

The debate has been around for years. Mokwa (1980) quotes an unpublished speech by Paul Fromm in 1978 arguing for policies which deepen audience experiences, arguing that the education of a minority of arts patrons will serve as a nucleus from which a healthy arts culture could grow. Opera America (1999) makes another attempt in saying 'the goals of audience development are increasing awareness of, and participation in, the activities of an opera company, which include, but are not limited to attendances at performances. This involvement can and should manifest itself in ways that extend beyond ticket sales, to participation in the company's leadership, volunteer core and donor groups, or voicing support for the company and its value in the community'. The term means so many things to so many people.

Young audiences are another issue. Gazing round at the sea of grey-haired members of the audience, I heard a marketing manager tell me more older people were coming along every year – and they were 'empty nesters', hungry to resume their old habit of theatre-going. Why should he try so hard to bring in the young? It would cost them a lot of money to put correct damage done earlier. Surely it was a job that must be done inside schools? Certainly he would expect special funding for such a project. Clearly we must aim to widen access. Definitions change as they relate to political climate. With the advent of the Thatcher government in the UK and the tendency to adopt a business-based approach, saw the formation of ABSA, The Association for Business Sponsorship and the Arts. Not long after the coming to power of the Labour government, ABSA became Business and the Arts.

Future trends

In the age of the web, the Internet and the mobile phone, it has never been easier to exchange marketing information, nor in fact to make it available. There are many reports of experiments (see, e.g. *Limelight* or the *Journal of Arts Marketing*). Around 50 per cent of UK households now have access at home to the Internet. The comparable figure for market penetration of mobile phones is over 80 per cent, making short message service (SMS or texting) more attractive, not least since the relative penetration is even higher among the young. When theatre is promoted through e-flyers, these of course require the previously obtained consent of the recipient. Generally speaking, these flyers seem to be designed for simplicity, due to the need to allow for variable standards of capacity in receiving PCs. Often these are quite basic text-focused appeals, making special offers, often relying on respondents logging on to an e-mail site. Their great advantage is that once the e-mailing list is in existence they can be deployed swiftly. In practice though, proof reading is a problem. As with brochures, it is necessary to take the very greatest care to ensure details are correct – particularly phone numbers.

There have been attempts to stimulate interaction with a website. For example, that for the Official Rocky Horror Show Website invites visitors to print out a full-colour (or black and white according to choice) poster to be pinned up on your company's notice board. This sign-up sheet is to help you 'get a group of like-minded fun folk together to have a great night out!' The website goes on to show how you can forward the e-flyer to your friends. Other examples of this technique can be found, some even stating 'It is not the intention to encourage spam or chain letters. Please send this only to friends who would be genuinely interested'. Perhaps the most dramatic flyers this writer has seen are those for dance companies – those for Northern Ballet Theatre are notable. Multimedia trailers have also been produced for *Wuthering Heights* and for Rambert Ballet at Sadler's Wells.

Advertising performances on SMS text messages poses a number of problems. For example, one is limited to 160 characters to deliver a message so it has to be part of an integrated campaign. A number of theatres report good results from using SMS on their database, and say it is both cheaper and more effective than direct mail. The speed of the technique suggests it is suited to stimulating last minute ticket sales. For example, Sadler's Wells had 26,000 mobile phone numbers on their database. In one experiment, from among those who had opted in to receive marketing information, around 4000 were sent an offer. This resulted in 100 ticket sales, 8 per cent responded stop to unsubscribe and in addition there were two e-mail complaints. This was considered successful. Other examples are given by de Krester (2002).

More and more fully searchable sites relating to arts marketing and theatre marketing too have become available. For the amateur sector, see www.amdram.co.uk; www.noda.org.uk and amateur theatre webring, www.btinternet/~scda/. For professional links see www.artdes.salford. ac.uk/visavis/ and www.arts-research-digest.com. In the US, www. operamerica.org/parc is of interest. Others have high aspirations too, see that of Knowledge Services for Arts Management (KSAM) and its website www.ksam.org.uk. It specifically aims to incorporate details of work carried out at the public expense. I remember my irritation when I was one of a group of activists who wished to save a theatre building. It had been released for sale by the owners, who had promoted it as a bingo outlet. We had charitable status and a letterhead demonstrating we could attract figures of substance as patrons. Unfortunately, data on the market locally which had been obtained by the Arts Council – using public money – was not available to the action group as 'they were not currently in receipt of Arts Council revenue funding'. When this writer approached the particular market research company directly to see if they would sanction release of the date, he got a dusty answer. 'If the Arts Council could not care, why should we?' The Arts Council's website is useful; others such as the Arts Marketing Association's are open to members only.

There are many signs of a growing realisation that there has to be more co-ordination and networking between venues. In Edinburgh, The Audience Business has been able to develop understanding of audience behaviour in the region – but efforts are hampered by lack of funding. There is still very little known and made publicly available concerning the effectiveness of cross selling in the arts. A number of studies have of course been carried out, but methodologies have not been made available publicly. Before conclusions are drawn, there follow some case studies that illustrate some of the points discussed in this chapter.

Discussion

Theatre – presenting or producing?

A presenting (or receiving) theatre is one that earns income from hosting shows, normally touring shows originated elsewhere. Financial arrangements vary. Companies may either pay rental charges or the theatre takes a share of the box office proceeds, commonly 25 per cent. Some other permutation of these may be agreed. Sometimes a minimum guarantee is required by the promoter, or a 'first call' (all the ticket proceeds until a specified number of seats is sold). The contract terms and conditions for a particular show would also stipulate the costs for setting up the show (get-in) – and striking (get-out). Leaflets and posters would generally be supplied by the touring company for overprinting by the theatre. Local advertising would be handled by the theatre and agreement as to payment of costs made.

A manager of a presenting theatre may find that every agreement is different in some respect. Managers require good judgement as to what will sell to their local audience, and considerable negotiating ability. In a theatre concerned with the minimisation of risk only rental terms will be offered, but the theatre thereby foregoes the opportunity to earn larger sums from the proceeds of ticket sales. Very often local authority owned arts centres would insist on rental agreements, ignoring a possible 'topside' in favour of covering the 'downside'. The management of a presenting theatre is often concerned by the range and quality of touring shows – is there enough good 'product' in a particular category? At the time of writing, for example, there is said to be a shortage of good shows aimed at children (and of course their accompanying parents).

The producer takes the bulk of the risk in theatre. For touring shows, this risk is spread through performances in numerous venues. Through constantly demonstrating they can provide good houses, some theatre managers can build up good reputations for their venue and hence find it easier to win better terms. Managers of producing and presenting theatres require very different skills and temperaments. The manager or artistic director of a producing theatre requires to choose and produce a number of plays during a season. This involves high cost and therefore risk.

In Britain, most provincial theatres are subsidised, usually by both the local authority and the regional Arts Council. In recent years, reduction in subsidy in real terms has led to many theatres closing. Among the survivors there is greater emphasis on commercial considerations, theatres requiring to maximise the income from bar and catering, and a sense of greater competition (Bennett, 2002). The pressures to increase revenue have also resulted in a blurring of the differences between presenting and producing theatres. Traditional producing theatres often now host touring shows, for example late night comedy. In addition, some share the costs of a production with another theatre or send a production out to other theatres on tour in an effort to generate a surplus.

Further consideration can be given to the problems involved in combining the roles of a presenting and a producing house.

Case one: Whitehall Theatre

The 740 seat Whitehall Theatre in Dundee is an unusual organisation. First there is its legal structure, of a sort common at the time of the purchase of the theatre. For 20 years, the theatre building has been owned by the Whitehall Theatre Trust and managed by the Whitehall Theatre Company on behalf of the amateur musical and dramatic societies of Dundee. Around a dozen of these societies were shareholders in this not-for-profit organisation. Throughout this 20-year period, the theatre has had no revenue subsidy, but nevertheless has managed to keep going. Indeed the fabric, though old-fashioned (the building dates from 1928), has been kept in relatively good repair. The necessary money to do this has been obtained in a number of ways including donations from local charitable trusts. The attached theatre club or friends, gave donations generated by the efforts of volunteers (who among other things work front of house for performances). The amateur societies had often staged benefit evenings, and most years there were seven or eight performances of a show called *Sounds Spectacular*, profits going to the theatre for capital works. Additionally, sometimes the theatre generated a modest revenue surplus. Costs were kept down too; it was often possible to find volunteers to carry out maintenance without charge if the theatre paid for the materials.

This Dundee theatre lies about 60 miles north of Edinburgh, the capital of Scotland, where the nearest larger theatres are. Dundee currently has a population of 150,000, there being around 500,000 people within an hour's driving time. Within 3 miles, there is Dundee Repertory Theatre (Rep) with 420 seats, a producing house but increasingly inclined to present touring shows as well. However, in relation to the Whitehall, the Rep is seen by promoters as expensive and anyway is often fully booked. The Whitehall's main local competitor as a venue is the local-authority-owned Caird Hall (holding over 2000, it has wings but no fly tower). The Whitehall also faces competition from the Gardyne Theatre in nearby Broughty Ferry (seating 320, the Gardyne is part of an outlying college campus owned at the time of writing by Dundee University).

The Whitehall Theatre building is generally described as being of no great architectural importance, the architect being constrained by both the brief and the site. One theatre expert describes it as a 'former cine-variety venue of quite paralysing dullness'. The building was originally supposed to serve as a cinema and a theatre combined, the auditorium being 'boxy'.

Reviewing the last 20 years, it seemed that whenever money was required for some urgent work to the fabric, it had been found. But in recent years, it had become apparent that a change of emphasis was needed. The report of a consultant (RGA consultants, 2000) reinforced that view. If the theatre directors and trustees – all volunteers – were to raise the finance needed to bring the fabric up to the standards required in the 21st century, it would need not be just a fund-raising campaign but capital grants from the City Council and from the SAC. This in itself would require a professional approach and a professional manager. No longer would it be possible to open for just 60 or 80 performances a year. Previously it had never even been necessary to calculate the number of customers each year – why was it necessary when so much of its business was related to the income from hires only, and attendances for these were the responsibility of the hirer and had little direct effect on the Whitehall's income?

By 2003, much progress had been made. The full-time general manager had been in post for a few years and had developed a good touch in picking out touring shows that would 'sell' to the Whitehall's audiences. He was in part guided by the influence of promoters of touring shows whose judgement he had come to trust. It turned out that when attendance figures were calculated, the Whitehall was found to be selling around 52,000 tickets a year, a very creditable performance when comparisons were made with professional theatres locally. The theatre was scheduled to put on 126 performances that year – over 50 of them professional, most of the professional shows being for one night only.

The Whitehall had become home to Dundee Schools Music Theatre (DSMT) as a result of a joint bid for lottery funding with the local education department. DSMT was one of only five such groupings nationally to be chosen to perform a schools' version of 'Les Miserables'. About 30 of their rehearsal sessions a year were held in the theatre. The association was prestigious for the theatre, though bringing goodwill rather than cash. It was hoped, too, that eventually DSMT would provide a transfusion of new blood to the amateur societies.

From the point of view of the theatre board, promotion of shows had always presented difficulties. The amateurs invariably sold their own tickets. They had their own mailing lists and in fact rented the theatre, removing the risk from the Whitehall itself. In considering sales development, there was therefore a temptation for the Whitehall management to concentrate on promoting professional shows. It was not easy to promote a single evening of a professional show, yet the theatre had to do this 30 times a year.

The chairman of the operating board reviewed matters. From the time he first became involved, he was convinced that the theatre devoted insufficient resources to promoting shows although equally he could see they had little cash available. Mostly they paid for posters to be put up, and leaflets sent out periodically to their mailing list of 7000. Back in the year 2000, the consultant had thought it possible to increase the number of performances to around 180 a year. Currently, over 40 were attributable to three long established amateur musical societies. The other shareholding societies held their shows in the Gardyne or in community halls. He had heard them say they did not think they could fill the Whitehall – but he also knew few societies trained their members in techniques for selling tickets; most of them saw it as a chore. Perhaps 30 performances related to school or youth groups, including the *Gang Show* and the balance were professional shows.

The professional shows were a mixed bag, some taking the theatre on a rental basis, but most had negotiated a split of ticket money. They ranged from comedians to tribute bands, musical groups or singing acts to *The Singing Kettle*, a Scottish phenomenon of a show that pulled in the children – and grannies. In fact it had been known to perform at the Whitehall 10 times in a year, often selling out. Most years a hypnotist would rent the theatre for one night, sometimes two. The theatre also hosted the occasional performance of ballet or opera. The professional acts in general, though, were mass market and entertainment rather than art.

The chairman and general manager often discussed programming. The chairman wondered about cross selling and whether it was possible. He well understood the need to brand the venue, but had heard a member of an amateur society talk disparagingly of the standard of one of the other amateur shows he had heard. 'They'll get us all a bad name.' He knew of course that many regular attenders at professional shows looked down on amateur performances. How could you attract customers to them? Of course, the theatre got the rental incomes of the amateur societies anyway and the theatre earned money from the bar, from the sale of coffee and ice creams. And what about the Memorandum and Articles of Agreement? This made clear that the objective of the trust and company was to nourish amateur companies.

Yet the theatre had to build audiences and build performances. Surely there were ways in which the venue could be made to promote shows, and successful shows would promote the venue. He had wondered whether some of the strands of programming could be expanded, to include for example jazz or comedy. Could management try to put more effort into this so that more buffs were tempted back to another performer in the genre? Could the Whitehall encourage a group of existing attenders to suggest to the general manager which artists should be targeted?

At this point, the chairman met an old contact, the maverick publisher John Calder who was involved in a professional touring production of a play by Samuel Beckett. Would the theatre like to host this production of *Waiting for Godot*? Good terms were available – the actors had formed a co-operative, and the Whitehall would get 50 per cent of the box office.

Case two: Scottish National Theatre

With the advent of a Scottish Parliament in 1999, hopes rose again that funds would be made available for a national theatre. Over the decades, there had been a number of attempts to win a pledge of funding for such a body, but hitherto without success. This was not just a Scottish issue. Successive British governments had refused to subsidise the arts on the scale that was normal in many European countries. Many of the idealists who had sought a Scottish government with powers devolved from Westminster did so because they felt a movement towards European practice would improve matters, and people in the arts were no exception.

Scotland has a number of theatres subsidised by the SAC, a body set up to distribute government funding in the form of an annual block grant. Unfortunately for artistic communities the value of this SAC grant had not been maintained in real terms. The subsidised theatres were locally based in their respective communities and for many years had claimed they were under funded. Too much of their income was needed simply to maintain buildings and staff, rather than on productions. Actors were in any case underpaid.

So there was general concern that the establishment of a national theatre would reduce the funding available to existing theatres.

In other countries the model seemed to be that the national theatre had been housed in a brand new and expensive building in the capital city. But did Scotland need to build a new theatre as the home of a new company? Surely subsidy should go to the performance of drama itself and not on buying bricks and mortar. Then there was the issue of its location. There was already a growing feeling that Scotland's capital, Edinburgh, was home to too many national institutions, and a suggestion that it be housed in Edinburgh's Royal Lyceum theatre proved unpopular.

How then could a plausible case be made that additional money should be set aside for a national theatre? Hamish Glen, the then artistic director of Dundee Rep, and chair of the Federation of Scottish Theatres, advocated the development of a new model – a national theatre as a commissioning body. The funding would be additional, and revenue support to existing theatres through the SAC would be maintained.

The ensuing productions would then tour a range of medium-sized venues. This new company would complement the existing infrastructure and would attract the best of Scottish theatrical talent back to Scotland. Successful Scottish actors such as Brian Cox pronounced the concept exciting enough to interest them.

A plan was produced and money set aside for the initial costs. In September 2003, the Scottish Executive announced the provision of funding for the national theatre – £7.5 million is to be spent on commissioning, producing and touring work round existing theatres throughout Scotland. It remains to be seen how the scheme will work. The suspicion remains that the old dream that the Arts in Scotland would be given government funding at European levels – or even English levels – will not be fulfilled for some time to come.

Case three: Promoting the Lemon Tree

The marketing manager of the Lemon Tree was reviewing his promotional policy. The Lemon Tree is an arts centre, owned by a charitable trust of Aberdeen Council. There is a limited company which operates the catering and which feeds back the profits to the trust. This varies from £50,000 to £100,000 per year. The building houses two arts spaces: the studio, with one bank of raked seats capable of holding 180, and the café, which can actually hold 575 on evenings it is run as a nightclub. In practice, the café offers flexibility in its seating capacity, depending on how many tables and chairs are set out and of course how many tickets are sold. It is run as a presenting venue. Over a 12-month period over 500 events are put on. Around 80,000 people buy tickets for the venue each year. Recently, for *WYSIWYG*,

19 events were put on in 7 days. When thought is given to increasing the number of shows, however, attention has to be paid to some practical issues. For example, there are difficulties in putting on events in the café and studio simultaneously, because of the amplification needed for acts in the café.

As far as promotion is concerned, Lemon Tree management puts their main effort into brochures, the copy for which is provided by the marketing manager. The brochure, of 48 pages in full colour, is sent out every 2 months after being put to print in a hectic 5-day period. They print 30,000 copies, around 17,000 of them being distributed through Grampian Region Arts, an offshoot of the distribution business Edinburgh Arts and Entertainment Ltd. (EAE) and subsidised locally. The remaining 13,000 are sent out to those on the mailing list. The Lemon Tree controls the list themselves; they had painful experiences when the council managed it on their behalf. Their list management policy is active and they prune it on people who have not bought a ticket for 18 months. Naturally this can lead to complaints when people who consider themselves loyal are omitted. They reckon that they capture 70 per cent of addresses at the box office.

Together with the printing and mailing costs, the brochure accounts for over half their promotional budget. In addition to this, Lemon Tree used to advertise significantly but have cut this right back.

Six years' experience suggests to the marketing manager that the Lemon Tree attracts several different and distinct audience segments, and that cross selling does not work. The local audiences are considered conservative in their artistic tastes.

The Lemon Tree management find it very hard to get reviews in the local media. When shows are on for one night, of course, reviews are useful public relations (PR) but cannot be effective in generating additional direct business. The local daily newspaper is not seen as being helpful, but the evening paper runs a column on Thursdays every week on events at the Lemon Tree. The marketing manager is convinced press releases do little good; and worse, they take a long time to write which could more profitably be used doing other things. However, he keeps in touch with five or six journalists. He sends likely material off to them by e-mail and waits for any reaction. Most journalists, he says, feed off bad news.

Case four: Theatrical impresarios

An impresario is a commonly used term – the dictionary definition of which is – *'organiser of public entertainments, esp. manager of operatic or concert party'* (*Concise Oxford Dictionary*). Impresarios can be showmen or women, occasionally hucksters. Yet without their activity, social life would be the poorer.

Most of human history is unrecorded. One of the first in performing arts management of whom we know much is Philip Henslowe, who operated in London in Elizabethan times, being responsible for the building and operation of the first purpose-built theatre of early modern times. Henslowe kept a diary recording theatre receipts, payments to playwrights, cost of costumes and other day-to-day details. Shakespeare was latterly one of his partners.

Demand among the population for this rapidly developing form of entertainment grew quickly. Before long, there were four theatres in fierce competition. Scholars believe a performance attracting a full house would have an audience amounting to as many as 4000 customers, this drawn from a London population that may not have exceeded 200,000. Performances took place in the afternoon during daylight, and were promoted through the distribution of playbills. Flags were flown before a performance, and trumpets sounded. Clergy complained that for every hundred called to church on the Sabbath by a church bell, trumpets heralding a theatrical performance attracted a thousand, taking people away from church – demonstrating how popular Sundays were for theatre-going.

Closer to modern times, the American Florenz Ziegfeld put on a strong-man show at the 1893 Chicago World Fair. It was failing till he added sex appeal in the form of swooning ladies. He became known for the 'Ziegfeld Follies' that combined well-known personalities with beautiful, glamorous chorus girls. The shows were seen as daring and on the edge of what was respectable. He was far from being the first to sell products on the basis of sex appeal, but he learned to make large sums of money.

Case five: Stratford East

The Theatre Royal, Stratford East in London, has for many years been a famous venue in UK theatrical history. Not least, from 1953 it was home to Joan Littlewood's Theatre Workshop. Joan Littlewood left in 1975 following the death of her collaborator Gerry Raffles. Since 1979, Philip Hedley has been artistic director.

In 2003, Stratford East was still trying to attract new audiences to the arts. How do you attract urban youth to the theatre? How can you develop new contemporary musicals to represent the eclecticism of multicultural London? What do you put on stage to attract the target audience?

The product must have the potential to draw an audience for whom theatre seems to have nothing to offer. One of the main objectives was to re-establish the reputation of 'Theatre Royal' as 'a unique theatre producing important and innovative work attracting new audiences'.

The 'product' in this case is a hip-hop version of 'The Boys from Syracuse' renamed 'Da Boyz'. The music from the original 1938 Rodgers and Hart Broadway show was sampled, re-mixed and re-invented by DJ Excalibah and MC Skolla. The original plot stems from Shakespeare's 'A Comedy of Errors'.

In the new show, modern urban music sounds – hip-hop, garage, R&B and bashment – were included.

The entire purpose of Da Boyz was to involve local youth in the arts. The marketing plan involved several levels:

- *Participation* – the cast was largely drawn from local talent, either past or present members of their Youth Theatre or from open auditions conducted during December and January.
- *Education* – 'Da Boyz' was used as the basis for schools workshops in music, drama and dance, over 4 months before the opening of the production. Outreach workers even went into schools' assemblies to give talks (or more accurately, raps) and reached and involved literally thousands of local kids.
- *Involvement* – members of the Youth Theatre were involved in the marketing of the show by distributing stickers, flyers and posters and even selling tickets to friends and family.
- *Entertainment* – Da Boyz was not to be staged like a traditional theatre production but rather more like a hip-hop concert. The plan was to go to great lengths – even taking the seats out of the stalls and extending the stage – to ensure the best possible experience for the target audience and challenge any negative perceptions of arts they may harbour. Excalibah himself is on the decks on stage, adding a final live mix.

An appropriate promotional package was clearly also required. A show targeted at teenagers should be promoted in ways they will respond to, using media they access, rather than relying on traditional methods. As penetration of mobile telephony is higher among this group than any other, and texting is their preferred method of distant personal communication, the inclusion of text messaging into the promotional mix seemed appropriate.

So it was decided to mount a text campaign using SMS to create awareness of and involvement in the show. The campaign involved:

- an outward push to 10,000 (20,000) accurately targeted local mobile phone numbers;
- the facility to get a free Da Boyz logo and ringtone;
- the use of the above logo as a money-off voucher for show tickets;
- a viral element which allows respondents to have the outward push message sent to friends on their phone list.

As far as can be known, this is the first time an SMS campaign has been used for a theatre production in such a highly targeted and relevant way.

These were not the only promotional tactics. Mailshots and flyers were added to website activity. Promoting the show to the press was given great importance, too.

In a review conducted after the end of the run, the importance of the education programme and the pricing policy as supporting elements in the theatre's marketing mix were stressed.

In the final analysis, the show was held to have met financial targets over a run of 43 performances. The extent to which the marketing targets were met was more difficult to evaluate. To this analyst, there was so much effort put in to such a different marketing mix that any attempt to isolate cause and effect could be only partially successful.

Examples of the messages include the following:

1. DaBoyz: The ultimate HipHop experience @ the Theatre Royal, Stratford frm April 24th!C them 1st! RPLY YES 2 get MONEY-OFF tkts PLUS a Daboyz logo 4 UR phone!
2. **Header: DA_BOYZ**
   Sorry, but U have already received UR DaBoyz text voucher. C **www.da-boyz.net** 2 get Daboyz logos & tones!
3. DaBoyz@Theatre Royal Stratfd!£1 off tkts!Show this txt @box-office! Logos&tones on Da-boyz.net.Invite a m8, TXT us UR name&UR m8's mob. no., e.g. Tom 07984064157
4. We did not understand UR text. Please reply with UR name & UR m8's mob. no., e.g. TOM 07984064157 & we'll send a DaBoyz text voucher 2 UR m8's phone.
5. FRM UR m8 xxxxxxxxx: DaBoyz @ the Theatre Royal, Stratford frm April 24th!C them 1st! RPLY YES 2 get MONEY-OFF tkts. 4 DaBoyz logos & tones C Da-boyz.net
6. Sorry this person has already been invited to C DaBoyz @ the Theatre Royal, Stratfrd. Try another m8. Rply with UR name & UR m8's mob. no., for example, TOM 07984064157

Conclusion

Recent years have seen many changes. Subsidised theatres are increasingly forced by standstill or shrinking funding to generate more of their own income. PR and publicity, once considered sufficient to promote a show, are no longer enough on their own. The marketing of theatres is increasingly seen as requiring professionally trained specialists, who are knowledgeable in the design of the marketing mix and the deployment of the whole armoury of the promotional toolbox. They must be able and willing to analyse box office data, increasingly being made available in some detail. They are consulted by the theatre director and explain audience behaviour and changes.

The death of theatre has been proclaimed many times. But the unique attraction of theatre is of a live and often intimate experience and the work done by marketers to keep the craft alive is largely intangible as much of it is done from behind the scenes. The author has only to walk up the High Street in Edinburgh during its annual festival to be tackled by countless young actors promoting a huge range of productions. It is evident that young people are still committed to pursuing self-fulfilment in the performing arts in general and theatre in particular. Contemporary theatre managers require skill in balancing the needs of funders, audiences and artists in producing and maintaining a vibrant theatre sector.

Acknowledgements

Many people helped me in the preparation of this chapter. However special thanks are due to Barry Burke, Andy Catlin, Jonathan Lewis and Kathy McArdle. Any mistakes remaining are of course my own.

Chapter 5

The marketing of opera

Peter Fraser

Introduction

I cannot remember which opera it was, but I was undoubtedly well into my teens when my father ventured to take me along with my brothers to my first performance. We had been frequently exposed to a range of experiences in the arts including theatrical events ranging from the first pantomimes to Shakespearean drama. But opera seemed to be regarded as of a different nature, something special. Previously only my youngest brother, the most musical of us three and the only one who was musical in a practical sense, had been taken to visit a touring production that visited the Scottish city where we lived. Later when we were still at school our father took us down to London for a long weekend, where on our itinerary were outings to the Royal Opera House (ROH), Covent Garden, to see *Aida* and *Tosca*. I remember the operas, not least because of the spectacle and the music – some of which was familiar to me from recordings – but also because our father took a box. It was probably the first time I had been so close to the operatic stage. I remember being interested to find firstly that the view from a box was extremely restricted and not nearly as attractive as it seemed from other seats. To this day I remember aspects of the productions of course but more than anything the fascination of some of the theatrical effects. In particular I recall the 'torches' mounted at the side of the stage. The 'flames' around each rim were cut out of a material such as tissue paper or cloth. Illuminated from within, they rippled in a jet of air that hissed up through the torch. I remember being fascinated by this example of theatrical illusion and wondering whether they looked more realistic from other seats in the opera house.

So early on in my experience of opera I became exposed to the varied offerings of regional, touring and national companies, including international companies visiting the Edinburgh Festival. In this chapter I will try to highlight some of the particular issues and themes in the promotion, presentation and marketing of opera and the ways in which the marketing of opera has developed in the UK and elsewhere at such apparently different levels. From my position as a consumer and now as a researcher in the field, I will draw out some threads from marketing theory and touch on themes in relation to perspectives from complexity and complex responsive processes (Stacey, 2001). The significance of the social or group experience in particular will be highlighted.

But for the marketing of opera the product experience is the key. I have since wondered what drew me and still draws me to opera, or music theatre as it might better be described. It is perhaps something of a puzzle, not subject to rational analysis. It will be seen from this perhaps that the music was not necessarily what made the most impact on me. I learned no musical instrument and at school I was the kind of singer who was told to stop singing. The fact that I listened a lot to recordings of opera, as well as many other forms of music, rather escaped me. Perhaps it is not surprising that it took me some time to get hooked on opera. Later on, I remember being taken to a performance of *Così Fan Tutte* at Perth Theatre, a relatively intimate venue of the sort now rarely used by touring opera companies. I felt enchanted by the production, again attracted mainly by sets, costumes and lighting. But I was not familiar with much of the music. I recall vividly, though, a moment when the strings began introducing an aria. The hairs on the back of my neck rose and my spine tingled. A physical action was giving rise to a strong and tangible physical reaction. Soon afterwards I found that this aria was regarded as a classic. More recently a conversation with my brothers revealed that decades later, all three of us recalled with warmth different details from this same memorable performance. Perhaps, I thought, I did have some sense of music and I could trust a little more my reactions and instincts. I was lucky in that Scottish Opera, founded in 1962, were by the late 1960s increasing both the number of performing seasons and locations. They did not have their permanent base at the Theatre Royal in Glasgow until 1975 and their growing national activity helped disguise the decline in the number of touring productions from elsewhere. But by the time I was an undergraduate I was enthusiastically buying some of my own opera tickets.

The case of Scottish Opera raises the issue of how far opera is regional, national or international. Based in Glasgow, it has performed abroad as well as showcasing its work at many Edinburgh Festivals. Perhaps seen as regional elsewhere, within Scotland it carries the burden of national expectations, funded though the Scottish Arts Council by the Scottish Executive. It is not just seen as being of national significance but consumes a relatively high proportion of the nation's annual arts funding, more than any other single organisation. ROH is in a similar dilemma though a national company in a UK context. The recent complications of resulting political interference in ROH have been well analysed elsewhere (Towse, 2001). On both grounds such organisations make a tempting target when things do not go according to plan. Recently a letter published in a Scottish newspaper argued that opera should not receive government support on the grounds that it was not part of Scottish culture. However, for me and for those of my generation, who can scarcely remember a time without live opera and indeed Scottish Opera, it is now very much a part of the cultural environment and has helped form and make me what I am. I cannot explain why, but after experiencing a performance, particularly a good performance, I feel better and healthier for it.

As with most great experiences in the arts, the power of a good opera performance is indeed beyond words. John Adams, whose 1987 work, *Nixon in China*, has been considered one of the most successful of contemporary operas, has reflected in an interview on its ridiculous state of affairs. Adams went on to add 'the complex mix of ingredients, and the unreality of the experience, means that it's always occurred to me that opera functions on the archetypal level, that is seems to go beneath the level of consciousness to make its effect... What opera wants is a theme that has the power to go deep, deep down and stir up those dark, muddy waters' (Goodall, 2001: 82). Similarly, Beecham suggested more generally that 'the function of music is to release us from the tyranny of conscious thought' (Atkins and Newman, 1978: 80).

Lord Harewood, a noted opera enthusiast, has described this process as 'the law of operatic exposure which converted so many servicemen in wartime Naples to the most visceral of all reputedly intellectual pursuits – if you once get them into the Opera House for a half-decent performance of a good opera, they'll return; the problem is to get them there in the first place' (Harewood, 1972). Indeed, my father may have been an example of this very phenomenon. He always claimed that as a wartime soldier in Italy he once helped to catch a Tosca as she threw herself off the back of a stage in Trieste.

Opera: the product and its nature

What is opera and what human needs does it meet? At one extreme it is simply a representative of consumer pleasure and sensation seeking. Perhaps it seems odd to devote significant space to a discussion of the nature of the product but this issue often lies at the core of many services and arts goods. Conventionally the argument would focus on the circumstances of the service delivery. In the case of the performing arts, the products are 'experience goods' of the most extreme kind. With some exceptions we will come to later, they cannot be experienced or tested before purchase and they have high intangibility factors. As the issue of intangibility may also include its difficulty, it is often doubly intangible. Furthermore, in developing experiential models to explore buying behaviour, the inaccessibility of imaginative and emotional effects presents a challenge to researchers (Bourgeon-Renault, 2000).

Historically, opera performances have always been rare and special occasions. Part of the process was traditionally claimed to include some preparation by audience members as well as performers. Opera is particularly challenging in its complexity and the power of its experience. The issue of opera is further muddied by its multi-faceted nature, engaging most of the senses much of the time. Nevertheless, people tend to talk of going to the opera or going to see an opera, not necessarily of listening to it. Hearing an opera may nowadays suggest an audio broadcast or a recorded performance. This alternative mode of engagement leads some to be critical of the theatrical experience, pointing out that if a singer is moving about energetically on steps or a steeply raked stage, their singing is not likely to produce what are technically the best sounds. Indeed, the physicality of the performing arts tends to be downplayed in TV relays and recordings. In the theatre I remember being shocked at the sheer physical effort displayed by singers. Theatre lighting may reveal not just the sweat glistening on their faces, or soaking their costumes, but more dramatically a spray of saliva as they almost literally spit out their words. This can to an extent undermine the experience or at least to highlight how far it can fall short of the ideal. 'The dramatic side of opera is not very attractive' reflected Tyrone Guthrie of a previous generation. Singers, he suggested, 'have to live a vagrant life, and their career, a comparatively short one, is devoted to the presentation of a limited number of roles in circumstances which rarely permit the dramatic side of the performance to be anything but a stereotype surrounded by a shambles' (Guthrie, 1961: 221). Forty years later and from the perspective of the 21st century, perhaps events have improved somewhat. However, Guthrie concluded by saying that if 'operatic composers had intended their interpreters to concentrate their full energy on the music, they would not have planned their work for the stage' (Guthrie, 1961: 231). But he also goes on to suggest that he has experienced few really fulfilling nights in the opera house, something that appears to be a reflection on the difficulty of realising this complex art form.

Opera then may be a combination that offers you the worst of everything. Acting is one of many separate elements that taken individually might be perceived as of poor quality but in context can work well enough. The whole can be greater than the sum of its parts. For example, performances that seem weak, heard as a broadcast or audio recording can nevertheless make a significant impact in the flesh. It is a paradoxical situation. Furthermore, as with other performing arts experiences and as indicated in the introduction, there is a strong social element in the theatrical experience including the relationship with an audience and the way in which the presence of spectators transforms the nature of the event. The role of the audience in responding with clapping, laughter and other responses makes its own contribution. We know from the letters of Mozart and Verdi, for example, how often arias and stage action were interrupted by applause and encores, a way before the age of audio recording for audiences to get to know the music. A spectacular scene change might draw prolonged applause, for example, something that in those days seemed to be recognised with pride rather than something taken to be unsophisticated (Weaver, 1977: 14).

But what about the available product range? In the centuries since the first operas were created in early 17th century Italy, the number of works produced must run into several thousand internationally though many are now lost. This of course is a very different question from how many are still performed and recorded. 'You could say for sure', comments James Fenton (2003), 'that in 1999 there was a plausible and available recorded repertoire of at least 300 operas, even if some of those included were rarities, and others, perhaps, stinkers'. The size of this pool would have astonished the critics of a few generations ago, he says, but points out that this remarkable growth is due to its expansion backwards to incorporate performances neglected for many years such as those of the baroque. 'Strange then that the part of the repertoire least certainly alive is the modern, the new, the freshly commissioned.' Others have made similar comments on the ageing of the core product. Recalling 1959 performance statistics from Zurich Opera on their 125th anniversary, Roth (1969: 237), observed that:

> The average age of operas performed in the first season, 1834–5, was twenty-four years. In 1891–2 it was fifty-six years and in the jubilee season 1958–9 it had already risen to ninety-one years. Now, ten years later, it must exceed the century.

An obvious business development solution to this ageing might be for the opera companies to commission new work and offer new experiences. An interesting phenomenon in this respect was the sudden emergence in the middle decades of the 20th century of successful English operas written by Britten, Tippett and others. Before then it had been generally held that English opera had failed to produce any work to rival the early and isolated promise of Purcell. After initial collaboration with Glyndebourne, Britten went on in 1948 to found with his partner and creative collaborator, Peter Pears, the Aldeburgh Festival. Based at the remote Suffolk seaside town, it too has confounded sceptics by thriving after the death of the founding partners. Its artistic activity covers not just small-scale opera but orchestral work, recitals and literature. This rural community also hosts the

Britten–Pears Young Artist Programme (formerly the Britten–Pears School for Advanced Musical Studies) designed to combine training and performance activities at the Festival and on tour (Aldeburgh Productions, 2003).

Some operas on contemporary themes have achieved both critical and popular success, *Nixon in China* being one of the more obvious examples. Some directors of opera are keen to create more contemporary work, though how much public demand exists for this is not clear. New work normally means difficult work. However, new product development (NPD) at least as much as in any other sector, is fraught with financial and other problems. The gestation period required by a contemporary composer can be several years and the consequent costs make this a highly risky process. This can be contrasted with the likes of Rossini, who was able to take early retirement on the basis of his opera proceeds. Such composers worked in an environment in which they had to produce work at very high speed, Verdi notoriously describing his situation as that of a galley slave. But at least in past times such composers had the practice to develop their opera-writing skills.

Relating marketing frameworks to opera, the core offering would normally be taken as the single performance. Each performance is a different event sold separately. The nature of the experience is inevitably complex and the augmented product will include all the normal features of a visit to a theatre, encompassing fleeting encounters with a wide range of staff (box office, front of house, bar and so on) as well as the opportunity to purchase a programme that not only offers the potential of a keepsake but may help audience members prepare, understand and interpret. Most opera companies make some attempt to sell books and recordings related to the specific work or season being performed. Some companies offer additional attractions. Performances are sometimes preceded or followed by a free talk on the opera or its composer by a member of company staff or a performer, using story or personal experience to highlight some of the challenges or attractions of the work and its origin. These talks tend to be occasional offerings, perhaps one per run or venue. They enrich the experience for existing ticket holders and while they can be very enjoyable, are broadly educational in nature. Technology offers other opportunities for promotion and education. English National Opera (ENO), presenting the UK premiere of *The Handmaid's Tale* by Poul Ruders, produced a CD giveaway featuring the voice of Margaret Atwood, author of the source novel, as well as extracts from the recording of the Royal Danish Opera premiere. Scottish Opera is currently producing promotional material about the company on CD which it is hoped will highlight their strengths and achievements as well as enticing some recipients to attend performances.

If the repertoire has aged, then arts audiences are also ageing in line with wider demographic patterns. The growth in the 'grey market', broadly taken to mean the over-50s, is at its most obvious when a glance round the auditorium demonstrates clearly a relative scarcity of young people. Reinforcing this impression of maturity, Sue Broomhead, Head of Development and Marketing at English Touring Opera (ETO), chimed in with research findings when she described their typical opera goer as over-50, well educated, with the ticket purchaser mainly female. This was later qualified somewhat by descriptions of the diversity among audience membership and behaviour at different ETO UK venues (Broomhead, 2003).

There has been a rash of interest by arts organisations and arts researchers in how to attract young attenders (Harland et al., 1995; Harland and Kinder, 1999). The issue here is not just the need for all products and services to cultivate the next generation but clearly the awareness of lifetime value. The danger here is that the grey market itself offers more possibilities than it used to. With increasing numbers of people retiring early, and living more actively for longer and with more time and disposable income to explore the arts, the grey market itself offers opportunities for segmentation (Lancaster and Williams, 2000) and development. I once commented on this to a young arts marketing manager whose response was 'oh no, we have enough of them'. Yet at least in the UK, some research funding bodies are keen to see more applications for grants to research the needs of individual members of these grey segments and their consumption of the arts.

Some literature on opera marketing

Starting perhaps with Michael Kelly (1826), who sang in the first *Figaro* for Mozart, acclaimed performers, producers and directors have written autobiographies and other accounts of the creative process and performance of opera. Yet despite its importance, how the audience comes to be present for a performance is rarely touched upon. Similarly, academic literature on opera and its marketing, at least in the marketing and related journals, seems extremely limited. Most of the writing has addressed the genre from a musicological and historical point of view. There are a few exceptions. Currie and Hobart (1994) address the question of whether opera can be brought to the masses (defined as socio-economic groups other than A and B). This particular phrase, to the masses, seems to concern them. Their research was based round questionnaire activity and attendance at an arena opera production of *Carmen* held at the National Indoor Arena, Birmingham. They point out that ticket prices were a third of the equivalent at ROH. One of the issues here concerns the objectives. If the aim is indeed to move people on to a more traditional offering of opera in a theatre, how far are the experiences comparable given the clear differences? With reference to questionnaire feedback suggesting that cost is a barrier, Currie and Hobart (1994) recommended that prices be reduced. This however is not normally a realistic assumption given the expenses involved. Public understanding of the economics of opera is limited. Some assume, for example, that if a performance is sold out then the company should put on more performances to make money, not appreciating that in many cases, the more performances the more subsidy required (Greig, 2003). What can be done is to use larger auditoria, outdoor arenas and the like, all of which require larger forces and technical support in the form of amplification. In this sense it changes the nature of the experience. Only the most popular and spectacular operas are likely to be considered for this mode of presentation.

Moving on to address the art itself, which comes first – the words, the music – or the drama? Some composers such as Salieri or Richard Strauss have even made this debate the subject of an opera. Opinions have differed. Martin (1970: Preface), for example, believed that 'for most casual opera goers a performance is primarily a theatrical rather than a musical experience, a reason, possibly, why Puccini with his superb sense of theatre is more popular than Wagner'. Some influential opera producers such as Ebert came from extensive experience in theatre and believed that the distinction was misleading (Ebert, 1999). Peter Hall is a contemporary parallel. This view would also be supported by some marketing managers who find evidence of greater crossover between audiences for opera and drama than between opera and other performing arts such as dance or orchestral concerts (Greig, 2003). Its power varies from venue to venue, however (Broomhead, 2003). Researching among adult Canadians, Fisher and Preece (2002) focused on the phenomenon of culture vultures in relation to five art forms – theatre, symphony, opera, choral music and dance. Education, income level and age were found to be clearly significant but weak as predictors of attendance compared with attendance at other arts events, including movies. Finding that the more people attend one art form, the more likely they are to attend another, they called for more co-operation among arts organisations in promotion and advertising among other activities (Fisher and Preece, 2002). Clearly, given that attendance at any performing arts event is a minority activity, this makes a lot of sense. Among the cross relationships they identified, they confirmed that opera attenders were also likely to attend theatre. However, this was not reciprocal, opera goers being promiscuous arts attenders and theatre goers relatively monogamous. Perhaps surprisingly, relationships between attenders at choral concerts and those at opera were weak, as unsurprisingly they were between pop music and opera. Attenders at opera performances represented the smallest category, and attendance frequency was also relatively low. How far this was related to cost or access – it seems likely that performances of opera would be less widely available – was not explored.

Opera can also create benefits for the wider performing arts. ENO, London-based, fostered in 1978 the spin out of ENO North, later to become Opera North. As there was no existing orchestra in the Leeds area, one had to be created to serve the opera company. This orchestra now has a life of its own performing apart from the opera company and making recordings.

Explorations of opera have traditionally addressed musicological issues of the genre itself, its origins and development. But there are other less obvious perspectives. To cite just a handful of examples, some have addressed the politics of opera (Bokina, 1979); the sociology of opera such as status (Ahlquist, 1997) or its relationship to death and disease (Hutcheon and Hutcheon, 1999). The theme of opera on film, video and TV (including live broadcasts) has been addressed at length by a number of authors (Citron, 2000; Fawkes, 2000). Literary theorists have questioned why so much emphasis has been placed on musical meaning yet relatively little attention paid to the inherent drama and poetry in the form of the book or libretti and the contribution of the words. Instead this part of the experience is ignored or denigrated (Levin, 1994: 6). There is a continuing debate about the advantages and disadvantages of performing in the language of the audience rather than that of the original opera, a debate that does not seem to have lessened with the increasing use of surtitles.

Marketing of opera

How do individuals make their first acquaintance with opera? Perhaps through hearing music in TV advertisements, perhaps through radio or the recorded repertoire. In my own case, I would say I was lucky. My parents had an interest in it. They did not discuss opera much. Our conversation on opera was rudimentary, tending to address whether we liked a performance or not. But they took us along and persisted in their efforts to expose us to other art forms including the performing arts. Outside my family, there were some school visits to theatre as well as to schools concerts by the Scottish National Orchestra, but not to opera. When, in my school music classes, schoolteachers tried to expose us to classical music, it was to recordings of orchestral pieces, not opera. Nowadays, by comparison there are no special schools' performances of live orchestral music in my native city. Touring costs have risen and the local authority concerned is no longer prepared to meet the expense. This is not however a universal experience and some are willing to provide support. It adds however to the impression of regional and national diversity.

Sometimes people make its acquaintance through work. A friend of my brother's once reflected that he did not like opera. He was asked if he had ever tried it. 'Yes, I once went to ROH with some clients. It was gey drear' (very dreary). What did you see? '*Götterdämmerung*'. It has to be said that this is probably not the ideal first opera to which to take someone. Not only does its first act alone last for 2 hours, longer than some entire operas, but the whole performance lasts 5½ hours or more. Furthermore, it is the final night of a cycle of four and while the operas were composed to be seen individually, to experience the final one in isolation from the others undoubtedly undermines its dramatic and emotional impact. I have taken people to their first opera, sometimes to see something relatively modern or superficially unappealing. One of the keys I think is to take them to something that has a pretty good chance of being a good performance, but otherwise there are no rules.

What implications might there be for marketing of opera? And how do companies attract and develop their audiences? What does the academic literature have to say about opera marketing? Texts on the marketing of the arts and the performing arts, including chapters within more general texts include (Colbert, 2001; Hill et al., 1995; Kolb, 2000; Kotler and Scheff, 1997; Mokwa et al., 1980; Sargeant, 1999). Lowe (1995) has presented what is in effect a case study of entrepreneurial behaviour by a Swedish opera company; while Ikavälko (2003) has focused on issues around sponsorship of a Finnish opera organisation. There are analyses of individual venues. The opera house experience can be heavily product oriented. Lynch (2002) describes the efforts in Sydney to orient activity around the customer and implement a more holistic approach.

In a recent article exploring the future of opera, Graeme Kay (2002) acts as devil's advocate and summarises some of the reasons for being pessimistic. He argues that in the UK at least, public perceptions of opera are in general believed to be more negative than those for other art forms. There is prejudice about opera, suggesting that it is suited only for people who are both snobbish and elitist. This might be called the 'Glyndebourne effect' fostered by scarce and expensive tickets as well as images of formally dressed toffs eating from picnic baskets and drinking champagne. 'Dressing up' carries its own costs in terms of time and money, and so creates additional barriers. Summarising some recent research, Kay takes this theme further and points to a claim that young people were being put off attending concerts because of the 'rigid formality' of concert settings; and that a majority of 6–14-year olds could not name a single classical composer. He acknowledges that the population in general is ageing, and worse, that education in the arts at school and university level does few favours for performing arts in general and opera in particular. Nevertheless not all is gloom and doom. An Arts Council of England (ACE) survey claimed that in 1999–2000, 6.4 per cent of the UK public had attended an opera performance and furthermore a later investigation confirmed that the number of attendances (as opposed to individual people attending opera) seemed to be on the increase. This could at least partly be accounted for by an increase in the number of available performances.

Creation of the product

One of the key issues in assembling the ingredients for the product is the casting, the selection and employment of the artists. This raises all kinds of issues, not just the technical suitability for a particular role, but the social and other skills to fit into a team and contribute in a production or indeed to a range of productions in a well-balanced season. Some operas are rarely performed for the very good reason that specific parts are very difficult to cast. The world of opera is a small world in which 'everyone knows everyone else' (Broomhead, 2003).

One of the other strong themes therefore would be the relationship with other opera companies. While there is strong competition and local rivalry between public and private sector, between one organisation and another there is also a great deal of collaboration. Co-productions are increasingly important. No doubt collaboration is at least partly driven by the relationship with public funding but there are in the UK two or three discussion forums, such as the Opera Music Theatre Forum (OMTF) where opera companies put their 'bids on the table' for the next few years, one of the aims obviously being to ensure that not everyone decides to mount the same opera at the same time. All are after all driven at least partly by the same wish to increase public attendance at opera performances.

In-groups imply out-groups. If a house employs one singer frequently in prime roles, building on the professional relationships involved and developing the company brand, then by definition they exclude or reduce the opportunities to hear others. So the employment by ROH of Callas in the 1950s and 1960s tended to rule out the engagement of Tebaldi (Lebrecht, 2001). Gossip about particular artists may suggest that some are wayward or difficult to manage in some way. The task then lies with issues akin to internal marketing, managing the personal relationships to build what some have called a family atmosphere. A whole range of minor actions can make a significant difference to the warmth of the backstage atmosphere, including increasing the appropriate use of backstage parties (Padmore, 2002).

In charge but not in control? The role of the marketing department

The tension between theory and practice can always be illuminating. When opera marketing managers are asked how they learned, the response may well be, I learned by doing it. Many are young, and female. Few seem to hold say, degrees in marketing or to have any kind of formal or professional training. In that sense the activity seems informal. Of course, jobs in the arts are not generally well paid and marketing skills in industry tend to be well rewarded. One opera marketing manager commented critically on her peers in the arts and how they dressed and presented themselves. It was important, she argued, to behave in a way that encouraged others, particularly those on company boards, to take marketing seriously.

Of course, many of the smaller companies have no marketing department. Much of the responsibility for achieving sales might be left to the receiving theatres or in effect contracted out. But even in the larger and integrated organisations, where is marketing? Do opera companies fit the dreams of every enthusiastic marketer, offering a full service department with marketing somehow being represented on the board? The answer appears to be no. The processes normally considered as marketing seem to be subdivided. To judge from the behaviour of the major national organisations such as ROH and ENO, there is a split between marketing and public relations (PR). Fund-raising, in the sense of raising private sponsorship in various forms, is also considered a distinct skill that may even be contracted out. In terms of addressing different public then marketing is not just a matter of addressing customers. Relationships with government ministers will need to be cultivated, a task that definitely tends to lie with the Chair and CEO rather than with staff in any marketing department (Colvin, 2003). What about relationships with private trusts, philanthropists and public sector funding bodies? Lobbying and survival is after all a highly political issue. If an opera company is to be successful in increasing its support from national or local government then it almost certainly means that there will be losers, perhaps those operating in areas such as Poetry, or Jazz. If opera is perceived as expensive, which it is, it is all the more important to ensure high levels of attendance by members of the public. Arts organisations therefore have to invest substantial resources in researching and quantifying their own performance in order to feed this back to their various stakeholders.

One of the more interesting marketing developments in recent years was partly supported by ACE under their New Audiences Programme and was available nationwide. *Operatunity*, a kind of Fame Academy for opera singers, was a TV project commissioned by Channel 4 and broadcast as a four-part series in February and March 2003. Produced by Diverse Ltd in partnership with Channel 4 and ENO, two winners were rewarded with the chance to sing on stage in an ENO production (Waldman, 2003). Two of its objectives were to introduce opera to a wider public as well as increase awareness of ENO; and to amateur and professional musicians. The series was held to have had some considerable success, obtaining extensive national media coverage, but how far this translated into increased attendance nationwide is not yet clear.

Promotion

Traditionally, approaches to advertising and promotion emphasise mailing lists as the main tool with the use of brochures, newsletters, leaflets and flyers, and newspaper advertising. More recently e-mailing and texting have been added to the use of websites. Compared with their industrial counterparts, the opera marketing process is complex, with promotion potentially required for each individual opera and venue. Some opera marketers lament the limited budgets when compared with their commercial competitors. Yet given that some budgets are limited, great care must be taken in the design of leaflets. It is almost certain that the same audience may contain both experienced opera goers and those attending for the first time. One singer said that in preparing himself psychologically for the coming performance, he thought of those in the audience who were seeing the opera or an opera for the first time and those who were seeing it for the last (Waldman, 2003). While the leaflets have to be both informative and enticing, care has to be taken to avoid making the leaflet patronising to opera regulars who may already know the plot and music well (Broomhead, 2003).

Some companies such as Scottish Opera have their own in-house graphic design department, arguing that this saves significant sums of money. The nature of the single performance product may lead companies to produce for the same opera production, different leaflets or flyers to suit the target markets at different venues. Such leaflets may have been produced in a wide variety of formats, including for outreach and educational work some material in comic strip form (Greig, 2003). In a similar effort to reach new public among 'non-users', in 2001 Opera North promoted *Paradise Moscow*, 'a block-busting musical comedy by Shostakovich' by distributing beer mats to down market pubs and other outlets. Relatively cheap to produce, the upper face contained basic details and a teasing description of the story, while on the reverse side, the design gave the performance details for the tour. How successful this was is not known, but one competing marketing manager thought this was in danger of creating the wrong image for a relatively highly priced product.

Complimentary tickets represent a key tool in the marketing armoury, if very expensive for arts managers to provide. However, they are essential for a variety of purposes. Firstly, for professionals, for critics from the media who have to be attracted to performances in the hope of reviews and other media coverage. Good national reviews at an opening night can provide superb material for subsequent brochures, regional touring and subsequent revivals. Lebrecht, however, describes how the use of complimentary tickets at ROH was set in a context in which 'critics and journalists were tolerated as long as we sang from an approved score'. Their availability is a privilege that offers latent power. On at least one occasion a hint was given by ROH senior management that unless a hostile story was withdrawn, the newspaper might find itself without free tickets (Lebrecht, 2001: 4, 5).

Secondly their careful distribution can be significant in building goodwill and differing levels of political support. In the early days of the ROH after the war, Kenneth Clark 'was forever badgering {the general manager, David Webster} for free tickets to give to contacts who might be "valuable allies" from many points of view'… sometimes senior politicians. 'In return for free seats, the Royal Opera House amassed a list of powerful people who could be called upon in time of need to press its case with government' (Lebrecht, 2001: 75). Attracting national and international celebrities is also helpful to the image of such a product.

Finally, in the case of performances not selling well, tickets can be heavily discounted or even given away, a practice sometimes known as papering the house but which can be effective in meeting differing social aims, for example, enticing celebrities or those of high status, or to those considered deserving in other ways, such as nursing staff at a local hospital. More unusual or extreme approaches include BOGOF, or Buy One Get One Free. One opera house offered any seat in the house for £10, though this was for a notoriously obscure and unsuccessful production – what might be called a fire sale.

Using complimentary tickets to obtain influence over critics is credible when the house has status. What options are open to the new or small-scale festival? In the 1960s and 1970s, the publisher John Calder ran a small-scale arts festival at his Scottish country house, Ledlanet, with opera featuring prominently in the programmes. To appeal to Scottish interests, entertainment presenting Scottish themes and artists were incorporated and Calder would often be prominent in his kilt when addressing and mixing with his festival audiences. Creating a mailing list was of critical importance. However, to build his audience, Calder obviously needed to have coverage in the local and national press and today still remembers his struggle to attract music critics (Calder, 2003; Fraser, 2003). At high opportunity cost to his festival finances, pairs of complimentary tickets were sent to the reviewers at a range of appropriate publications. However, a lack of response persisted. In those days, road links and communications in general were somewhat less good than today and to many the location must have seemed obscure and unattractive. Calder eventually asked the editors whether they would consider publishing unsolicited reviews. So it came about that the first anonymous accounts, written by the impresario himself, were printed. Later, as his Ledlanet Nights Festival developed, it obtained national coverage on its own merits.

It is in the nature of an experience product that networking and 'word of mouth' (WOM) can be invaluable. The use of WOM, both positive and negative, has tended to be neglected in the marketing literature and it is only in recent years that it is being addressed, mainly in the context of entrepreneurial and other small-scale marketing (Silverman, 2001; Stokes and Lomax, 2002). Yet it is characteristic of opera that it is harder to establish conditions where WOM can work. Companies seem to be energetic in creating opportunities for supporting publicity whether in outreach work generally (Greig, 2003) or in the performers singing informally in a variety of unexpected venues such as restaurants or town market places. One company set up a series of events in the lead up to opening, including a recital/talk at the local community college, recitals and leafleting at a local major hotel and an English heritage property. All these took place in the final week when booking at the venue rose by nearly 20 per cent. In terms again of the local and the small scale, such activity also creates a taste of the experience, a real buzz, unpredictable and unmeasurable in its outcomes, that may or may not feed in to increased attendance at the theatre (Broomhead, 2003). At some of Scottish Opera's outreach work, perhaps a performance of songs and arias in a school is priced cheaply and the task then is seen as moving the newcomers on to experience work in a theatre and subsequently a full opera performance (Greig, 2003). For the productions themselves, positive WOM would best feed off a long run of performances. But all the work of opera companies has to be put on in strictly limited runs. It can therefore mean that by the time WOM operates, large numbers of customers are disappointed. In opera, even if a production is sold out for its entire run, there is rarely an immediate opportunity to extend it. Opera musicians and conductors are increasingly booked up well in advance, sometimes for years. The only response available to success is to plan to revive it at the earliest opportunity, when with cast changes it may or may not meet with a similarly enthusiastic reception. But this approach can work. For this reason, some productions become historic and are still regularly revived after a period of many years. Jonathan Miller's 1982 production of *Rigoletto* for ENO was considered to fall into this category, as was the 1958 Visconti/Giulini *Don Carlo* at the ROH. Acclaimed productions can also be borrowed or bought in by companies in other countries. More formally, some companies have embarked on programmes of co-productions in order to share costs and risks. Co-productions can save significant proportions of such costs, the difficulty being that most companies have very high fixed costs. Such savings, while very worthwhile, can therefore form only a small proportion of the total. A different challenge awaits the marketer when a production has been mauled by the critics and may have a large number of contracted performances still to run. Subsequent revivals offer a period of months or years in which it can be substantially rethought and presented differently, though there may be relatively little that can be done without significant expenditure to modify sets and costumes.

An issue related to WOM and the emergence of enthusiastic communities of advocates or missionaries lies in the creation and support of friends, volunteers or other formal support networks. The importance of volunteers varies, some of the organisations as at Aldeburgh or Scottish Opera being professionally run. Some arts organisations claim they are critical to survival or alternatively that they are an underused resource. Here, loyal patrons are encouraged to participate in a range of activities; to subscribe, or perhaps taking part in additional social events that overlap with fund-raising or sponsorship campaigns. Arts managers can however seem ambivalent to them. On the positive side, they can improve attendance figures, contribute significant sums of money and enhance the life of the organisation. However, they can be somewhat ineffectual and to management, time consuming, like all voluntary activity being dependent for success on a few livewires. By definition they are representative of existing users rather than non-users. Their contribution varies from group to group. Some prioritise the social aspects of their activity, not seeing their aim as expanding their membership. Others are dynamic and highly effective, contributing a significant proportion, for example, of audiences (Fraser, 1998; Hayes and Slater, 2003). Friends can be of greater significance for touring companies where some local champions can be important in keeping interest and attendances alive. However, it seems difficult to categorise these enthusiasts, who might formally belong to the friends or be involved with unrelated local membership organisations such as rotarians (Broomhead, 2003). It is impossible, Broomhead commented, keeping in contact with them all but it is important to try as only the people who operate in a particular location know how it ticks.

Credence qualities are very important to the box office in making the intangible tangible and reducing the potential risk. A star singer, a creative producer whose last effort was acclaimed by critics and public alike; or an experienced team – all these may be powerful elements for success. Managing limited capacity is a critical issue in services marketing. If buying tickets is expensive, those who have limited funds or who are risk averse may be inclined to await reviews of a production before committing to purchase. The theatre is also subject to the same patterns of social behaviour or other recreations, whereby Mondays are normally less sought after than Friday and Saturday nights. So it may be hard to sell all of the seats for the first performances, and later ones can quickly be oversubscribed.

Detailed national and international statistics for opera performances are not maintained. From conversation I have gained a sense that there is more opera available in the UK than is commonly known and that the number of concert performances of opera in the UK has increased. Music colleges and amateur companies contribute to this. Some opera companies have offered performances with discounted ticket prices, or presented in cheaper format as concert or promenade performances. In particular, companies are increasingly anxious about the ageing nature of their audiences and devote some time and effort to attracting younger non-users. One recent example of this was seen at the Edinburgh Festival where several companies collaborated to open their doors free of charge, hoping to draw new audiences across the arts. One of the contributors to this scheme was Scottish Opera, who were justifiably proud of presenting their first *Ring* cycle for over 30 years. It must have seemed a wonderful opportunity to expose novice opera goers to music theatre at its grandest and most spectacular. However a performance of *Götterdämmerung*, free for those aged 26 and under, attracted an audience of just 237 to the Edinburgh Festival Theatre. No doubt it did not help that this took place on one of the hottest afternoons of the year.

We have already highlighted the potentially negative attitudes of much of the UK public towards opera, and this, combined with the strongly political nature of dependence on government support, tends to give ready fuel to critics in the media. Furthermore, there is a feeling among some arts managers that the press, particularly the tabloid press, can be quite malevolent in its coverage of the 'elite' arts. Much of the activity of marketing and PR staff is therefore devoted to trying not just to feed out to the media positive stories but trying to counter negative ones. One opera company commissioned some atmospheric paintings from a well-known local artist which it used to decorate the exterior of the theatre. Quite soon there was a critical press report about the extravagance this represented but the reality was that the marketing manager had negotiated a special rate with the artist well below the typical gallery prices his work was fetching. In a similar way, following the well-intentioned 'free' Edinburgh Festival performance, Scottish Opera came in for much criticism for the low attendance. Hostile press reaction to the low attendance included a piece by Bowditch in which she argued that this 'free' policy was misconceived and that 'there are things – Wagner is one – which are only truly appreciated by people of a certain age'. Furthermore, there are other reasons why trying to attract the young may be inappropriate, not least as they seem to be burdened by more and more debt.

> The idea that a customer in their twenties is so much more beneficial than one in their fifties, a notion we all tacitly give credence to, is as dangerous as it is discriminatory. It gives us an excuse to value people less the older they grow.
> (Bowditch, 2003)

Indeed, research and the experience of others suggests that there is truth underlying this argument. At what point do you pitch the appeal to younger people? 'Significant numbers of people' says Peter Bellingham of Welsh National Opera, 'start to go to the opera after the age of 30 – people seem to mature into it, and so the idea should be to focus on young professionals. But it's a hard nut to crack – you're fighting against so many other attractions' (Kay, 2002: 1452). It is also argued that young people tend to be more impulsive, to avoid booking in advance and to have shorter spans of attention than the 5½ hours needed to experience *Götterdämmerung*.

Pricing

Whether from opera house to opera house or from production to production, the variation in prices is considerable. Conventionally seats in different parts of a theatre are priced differently and further variation may obtain from production to production or night of the week. In the UK this can range from over £200 at the top to £10 or so at the lower end. Many opera houses pride themselves in offering a range of discounted opportunities, not just in existing houses but in outreach work. Standing space is limited but can also be sold off. Some opera houses have experimented with promenade performances, removing the seats from the stalls area. Some of the cheaper seats at ROH are the slips with restricted view bought by those who do not mind not being able to see, especially music students. Similarly, but depending on the wishes of the music director, a final dress rehearsal may be opened to students or other attenders, either free or at a nominal price. One marketing manager reported that she experiments with pricing regularly and monitors sales in some detail on a daily basis. Perhaps paradoxically, while there is concern that pricing at the top end may exclude a high proportion of potential customers, in opera as in sales of other status goods and services, premium pricing sends out other signals. She reports the well-known phenomenon that it is always the higher priced tickets that sell first. But she cannot raise prices at the top end as for her company this would be considered, both internally and externally, politically unacceptable.

Special policies may be applied for different circumstances. For example, contemporary opera is potentially difficult in terms of the box office. People neither know the music nor the drama and pricing may be adjusted to ensure good seat occupancy, as with the recent production of *Sophie's Choice* at the ROH. Pricing is well known to be particularly difficult to research.

Education and outreach

To address this, opera companies, in parallel with other performing arts organisations, have established outreach activities in both communities and schools (Tambling, 1990, 1999). Broomhead (2003) talking enthusiastically about ETO's experience of creative work that involved a mix of both school-children and children with special needs, commented that this activity is provided from their basic budget and they get no separate funding. It was, she said, incredibly rewarding to see how the 'mainstream' children would learn in opera making from those with, say, learning difficulties. More conventional work with schools was also good in breaking down preconceptions. Children would, in effect, persuade their parents to take them to the opera. The amount of education an opera company can carry out must be relatively limited but many efforts are now made to support understanding, from pre- or post-performance talks to surtitles to more informative programme notes. All these small-scale initiatives can help to address the concern that nowadays audiences are less and less prepared for opera performances, not least in the attention span that is demanded of them.

Touring: the issue of place

The key task of opera marketers is to remove barriers to attendance, perceived or real. Obvious and immediate barriers to opera attendance – in no particular order – include image, cost, venue and access. These are related. The economics of touring presents a real problem as the labour intensive performing arts become increasingly expensive in real terms. National companies such as in the UK, The Royal Opera or in the US, the Metropolitan Opera, used to tour frequently whether in the 1930s or the 1950s. Scottish Opera, as I have implied, started off by presenting a series of seasons around the country and only more than a decade later gained its permanent home at the Theatre Royal, Glasgow in 1970s. Since then, touring by Scottish Opera has increasingly been scaled back to small- and medium-scale productions. If, living in Dundee, a modest sized Scottish city of 150,000 and with a catchment area in North East Fife and Perthshire potentially attractive to performing arts companies, I want to see opera, I have restricted choice. I can stay in the city and see the occasional annual amateur production. I can catch the infrequent simply staged production of a popular opera such as those by Ellen Kent using companies such as the Ukrainian National Opera of Odessa from the former Soviet states. Sometimes Scottish Opera visits with Opera-go-Round, scaled down productions again mainly of popular operas and performed with piano accompaniment. All these have their merits. However they are only a partial substitute for real opera, a fully staged opera supported by a full orchestra. Furthermore, if frequent attendance at performing arts events is taken as five or more performances per year, as referred to in Fisher and Preece's Canadian study, then many arts actives or devoteds are being deprived (Fisher and Preece, 2002). The opportunity to build opera-going as a habit is lost. This may also partly explain the promiscuous buying behaviour suggested elsewhere, or alternatively this may be related to the eclectic nature of opera as an art form.

ETO offers another strand. Unlike, say, Glyndebourne Touring Opera or Scottish Opera, they have no theatrical building they can call their own. They have developed an increasingly ambitious programme of touring within the UK, mainly in England, with the support of ACE. ETO currently visit in the range of 25–30 theatre venues per year, offering capacities ranging from 400 seats upwards, with other miscellaneous performances in restaurants, schools, stately homes and elsewhere. Next year in London they will add the larger 1000 seat Hackney Empire when it reopens after a major restoration. Their artistic policy, encouraged by ACE, involves visiting a list of the sort of venues which do not often host opera, and offering those works that are suited to these smaller venues. Their repertoire is consciously different from that of the more popular works toured on a large scale by commercial companies, and they have recently adopted a policy of two new productions per season rather than one new and one revival.

As their range of receiving theatres increases, they are also moving away from their 'one size fits all' policy and creating productions in two sizes, as it were. One of their more recent pairings, Handel's *Ariodante* and Britten's *Turn of the Screw* exemplifies their aim of dealing in operas from among those that are less well known. Venues range from Richmond in London to Ulverston in the Lake District, where over the years they have established a loyal and enthusiastic clientele. Visits to such places can therefore generate a real sense of occasion. These vary enormously, with Cambridge or Bath being 'opera-savvy', to Preston or other communities where the arrival of opera is less welcomed. There are many other challenges in touring, not least that sales are made not from your organisation and its website but from the receiving theatre. Website links make a sale more likely, however. But the challenge for touring opera companies is that they do not know much about their customers when customer data is held by the receiving theatres.

The role and branding of the venue and the contribution of the structure is worth some mention. For the student of theatre architecture and history, the venue can itself be worthy of special study and appreciation. Some customers, faced with a choice between different locations for the same offering, have been known to travel the greater distance to experience the ambience they prefer. In some theatre buildings it is possible for members of the public to pay for backstage tours, gaining insights into the ways in which the dramatic illusion is mounted.

The brand is often the building, particularly at a provincial venue where the sector is represented typically by receiving theatres in which opera might represent only one strand of a season's entertainment offering. In Glasgow, for example, an increasingly wide range of activities is being mounted. The marketing manager is in fact responsible not just for Scottish Opera performances whether at their home base or when touring, but also the marketing of their Theatre Royal base. Programming of touring productions is increasingly important in its role as receiving theatre. Activity includes a series of lunchtime talks by celebrity speakers, held in the auditorium itself. Forthcoming speakers include a noted sports commentator as well as writers, the aim being to attract the sort of people who might not normally be attracted to opera and might never have entered the theatre before. The hope would be not just to gain income and build awareness but perhaps even to cross-sell (Greig, 2003). Similarly, on the other side of the globe at Sydney a new commission called Testimony and based on the work of Charlie Parker was the catalyst for widening partnerships and brought Jazz into the classical arena (Lynch, 2002).

Management of the building is often separated from the artistic management of the programme, the artistic production. Lynch (2002) describes the introduction at Sydney of an holistic approach to management integrating administration, building operations, programming and theatre functions (Lynch, 2002). A building itself can have a major impact on perceptions and the core experience. If the venue is hot, dirty and overcrowded this is problematic.

As with other service offerings, the role of the customer in affecting the experience for good or ill is also worth exploring. One regular at ROH says he only attends performances on Fridays or Saturdays as he hates the atmosphere created in the bar and circulation areas by the corporate customers, often referred to as suits. Extraneous noise can be particularly destructive for the opera goer. Many have complained that the etiquette of theatre attendance is in decline and this can detract from the experience, bringing on attacks of feelings close to misanthropy. By definition, audience development programmes will if successful attract those unused to theatre in general and opera in particular. Some first attenders have arrived at the opera carrying popcorn or other potentially noisy snacks. The significance of etiquette in history has been addressed by Elias (1994). The control required of opera audiences is significant and must be similar to that for a concert where Elias points out that the audience has to keep its movements under very strict control and he argues that over time, 'the tendency to restrict the movements of the audience has markedly increased'. The emotions of people are stirred, yet 'as far as possible no muscle must stir. They should be moved without moving' (Elias, 1986). 'Only at the end may an audience indicate through the strength and length of its movements, of its applause, how strongly it has been moved in silence before' (Elias and Dunning, 1986).

Opera etiquette, a perennial problem, features strongly in several opera websites. Respect for the boundaries of the performance is stressed with a wide range of examples ranging from timekeeping to wearing strong perfume. Cooper (1997) addresses a wide range of problems caused by audience members, ranging from the more obvious such as 'please don't applaud until the music has stopped' and 'please don't sing along with the music', to the less obvious such as 'please don't climb over other people's seats when arriving or leaving' or even 'please, if you must spit out lozenges, do so quietly'. In a lifetime of opera and theatre-going, my concentration has been distracted also by doors opening and closing, glasses and bottles clashing in the bar areas, lift machinery, and even, during a performance of *Siegfried*, an ambulance siren in the street outside sounding at virtually the same time that the singer was putting a horn to his mouth. The audience reactions can be imagined. The obvious management response is to focus on those elements that can be readily improved or are most obtrusive. Before a performance, announcements about mobile phones are now commonplace. Otherwise the audience members are partly responsible. As one correspondent said, 'The enforcement of such etiquette is simple if no one in the audience tolerates aberrant behaviour; the more it is allowed by the organisers or individual members of the audience, the more it will occur. So it's up to us, really' (Etiquette, 2003). In an effort to manage expectations, dispel the

Glyndebourne effect and ease non-users into what might be unfamiliar settings and behaviour, some opera house websites such as those of ENO give guidance about what to wear.

In recent years there has been an emphasis on upgrading performing venues. Helped by lottery and private fund-raising, long overdue programmes of reconstruction have been carried out in London both at ROH and ENO's home the Coliseum. Milan's renowned opera company, La Scala, 'has found itself at the centre of a court battle as preservationists fight to stop work to pull out the stage and backstage area. The building plans are part of an ambitious restoration programme on the 18th century venue, begun 6 months ago. Italian environmental group Legambiente has begun legal proceedings, arguing the space is as historically important as the theatre's delicate boxes and galleries' (BBC, 2002).

This may raise also the issue of changes to the supporting environment. Though opera has been performed in venues ranging from Roman amphitheatres to tents to factory premises, the failure and conversion of traditional theatrical venues to other uses cannot be very helpful in enabling access. Turning again to my native city in Scotland, the theatre building that used, right up to the 1960s, to receive touring productions is no longer available for theatrical performance as it has been converted to a nightclub. In relation to the performing arts in general, large numbers of venues have disappeared (Bennett, 2002). The theatrical equivalent of multiplex cinema, which revolutionised and regenerated film-going does not seem to be feasible. Opera with few exceptions has to find a home in performing arts venues that tend to be mixed in the repertoire they mount. So if a person living in that particular part of the country wants to see opera, then they have to be prepared to travel to Edinburgh, Glasgow, Aberdeen, London or elsewhere, adding to the time and expense. It has to be said also that in the UK the development of touring has been inhibited by bureaucracy. When companies are dependent on subsidy it cannot be a free market and the issue of boundaries has been a serious constraint in the eyes of many patrons. It would seem common sense for the best use of public funds that opera companies in different parts of a country should be encouraged to tour with their productions. Yet for many years in the UK the issue of who pays has created a barrier to this sort of activity. Only recently has a settlement been reached between the government funding bodies within the UK. ETO has been able to cross the border into Scotland and perform at Perth Theatre and conversely Scottish Opera has been able to increase the number of its performances in the north of England.

Finance

Today, opera companies are not-for-profit organisations. Historically, this was not always the case and in the past some impresarios such as Oscar

Hammerstein made fortunes from mounting opera (Stockdale, 1998). Nowadays the financial objectives may mean little more than avoiding loss, with any surpluses from popular operas offsetting losses on the more adventurous. From the customer's point of view, however, this is sometimes hard to reconcile with what seem like high ticket prices. More than any other of the performing arts, opera has a socially exclusive image, which is believed to discourage attendances. Undoubtedly this is partly related to price. Opera-going can be expensive, not simply in regard to the ticket prices but the associated costs. Travelling costs may well be one of these. But the financial climate has changed. The economic issues concerning opera present an increasing challenge. John Culshaw, writing 30 years ago, reflected on his first experience of Wagner operas after the war at the ROH. Neither I, he says, nor any of the colleagues who came with him could possibly be described as rich.

> Indeed, we were all on salaries which it would be generous to call modest; some were men with very young families; yet in those days we could afford to go to Covent Garden, and, what is more sit in very good if not the very best seats. Our precise equivalents in London today could not afford to go at all, except possibly in the cheapest seats.
>
> (Culshaw, 1976: 84)

Unarguably, almost 30 years after Culshaw wrote, the situation for young people is even worse. Top ticket prices at ROH are significant. This has a number of consequences, not least that as people pay more for tickets they may expect a higher standard of service and not just the performance itself. Price can perhaps only be lower, and access wider, with the support of government subsidy. As Lebrecht (2001) points out, this problem is unlikely to ease. While companies in New York and Paris face the economic challenge by investing in new purpose built opera houses with 4000 seat capacities, the more conservative tradition in Italy and the UK is to refurbish existing theatres which keeps costs per seat comparatively high.

Some champions of the market would argue that there should be no government or public subsidy for opera. Any such support, they argue, encourages waste and significant effort has to be invested in bureaucracy and other indirect costs. In recent years, UK entrepreneurs such as Harvey Goldsmith and Raymond Gubbay have mounted productions of more popular and spectacular opera in large public arenas such as Earls Court or the Royal Albert Hall. Such productions have often met with critical and commercial success. Nevertheless, to the purist there are many compromises. Not only is the repertoire again limited to the most popular and spectacular of operas, but due to the size and constraints of the venue, amplification of voices is necessary.

Recently Gubbay has announced his new venture, a new company and season to be launched at London's 1130 seat Savoy Theatre and which will mount operas sung in English, at a top ticket price of £50. Public subsidy or funding will be avoided. To achieve this, costs have been significantly reduced by an approach which involves no star names, young singers, orchestra and chorus hired on a project-by-project basis; as well as simple sets. The offering, which is aimed at a middle brow rather than high brow segment will consist of a season of nine operas in the first year, two of which are yet to be decided. The listed operas include *Barber of Seville, Marriage of Figaro, Carmen, L'Elisir d'Amore, La Traviata, La Belle Hélène* and *The Magic Flute* (Higgins, 2003). A parallel for this type of model can be seen in the construction industry, where many companies used to employ skills directly but the more common model now is one in which all activities are subcontracted, keeping overheads to a minimum.

Education

We have already commented in the introduction to the book how arts education is receiving less and less attention in the UK school curriculum. Publicly funded secondary schools used to consider music a critical part of education, something all youngsters needed to be exposed to. Before the days of TV and radio, the performance of music used to be considered part of the home and social life of many families. Large employing organisations often ran works musical clubs, choirs or brass bands. In this secular age, church choirs as well as amateur orchestras face considerable difficulty in recruiting members.

Yet there are encouraging signs to support the belief that opera is a long way from being dead. The UK regional companies such as Opera North, Scottish Opera, and Welsh National Opera have managed to maintain high artistic standards despite periodic financial vicissitudes. There are a large number of small-scale opera companies, often working with limited subsidy and the support of friends' societies and networks. Some such as Pavilion Opera or Garsington are resolutely private sector in their philosophy, following what might be called the Glyndebourne model, with high seat prices, little or no public funding and always engaged in a search for generous patrons and philanthropists. Others range from amateur to semi-professional to professional ventures offering young singers attractive and demanding roles in new or rarely seen operas. A feature of the last few years in the UK has been the welcome appearance of touring companies such as Chisinau National Opera from Moldova and suchlike countries in the former Soviet Union. To an extent they have addressed the gap left by the touring companies of previous generations. Yet they offer special occasion events, stopping in a location for only one or two nights and their repertoire is narrowly focused. Performances are spectacular, traditional, semi-staged and confined to the better known works such as *Carmen, Madama Butterfly* and *Nabucco*. Turning to the issue of technology, Classic FM in the UK has been enormously successful in building a large middle brow audience for classical music and opera, albeit broadcast almost entirely in bleeding chunks. This sort of presentation may not be to everyone's taste but it has undoubtedly been successful in achieving high audience figures. In the face of the reduction of formal music education in schools, some hope that this sort of exposure will mean that some listeners will find their way to live performances of opera. Classic FM has now launched a version of their channel on satellite TV.

Innovation and NPD

Companies have launched initiatives to address a whole range of perceived and actual barriers to access. Others, such as outreach programmes, are touched on elsewhere in this volume.

Higgins describes Welsh National Opera's new taster version of *Carmen*, designed to run for just 1 hour rather than its full three and introduce new audiences to opera. Its brevity is not the only unusual thing about this touring production. Price has been considered and tickets are intended to be cheap at £5 and £10. More striking perhaps are the unfamiliar times. Performances are at 2.30 p.m. and 6.15 p.m. Offerings are designed to allow visiting parties of schoolchildren to be back at their school by the normal finishing time, and the early evening performance is aimed at an after-work segment.

> ... the seats are cheap, and the length undaunting, the idea is that the curious will be tempted to take a chance ... The short duration of the show has advantages from WNO's perspective: apart from fulfilling the principle of giving people a taster it also means that two performances can take place each day.
>
> (Higgins, 2003)

Though the offering includes full chorus and orchestra, the plotline is inevitably distorted. The theme here is the issue of time and consumer investment. A similar concern has resulted in one company reportedly considering mounting a season containing more double bills. *Cavalleria Rusticana* and *Pagliacci* or 'Cav and Pag' as they are known, is an example of a traditional 20th century opera house staple. The twist in this new idea would be that customers would be allowed to choose to buy tickets for only one half of the pairing, rather than attend for a full evening. This would at least have the merit over the 'opera cuts' approach that each work would be seen complete.

Niche marketing or creating scarcity is a weapon that has also been used. A related approach occurred some 20 years ago when ENO launched a series of opera productions of opera rarities, including Wagner's early *Rienzi*, but announced beforehand that these would never be revived. Niche companies operate with a policy of presenting say, only Handel operas or baroque rarities. Alan Sievewright, commenting that if opera is dead then 'the corpse won't lie down' produced starting in the 1960s and throughout the 1980s and 1990s a successful and starry series of rarities, albeit in concert performances (Inverne, 2000). There is a huge variety available in a capital city like London.

Thinking of ROH or the Metropolitan Opera House, star singers and exceptional voices may come to mind. Yet the starriest of singers such as Pavarotti gain their highest fees not singing at such opera houses but in the large open-air concerts (Padmore, 2002).

Public would include not just those who attend or indeed the performers themselves. Stakeholders include government agencies, commercial sponsors, advertisers and for all companies in receipt of government funding, those who pay local and central government taxes.

The challenge of sponsorship and fund-raising

One of the more interesting issues in a sector which has difficulty when faced with the 'market test' is fund-raising. Here as in so many other ways, the UK might be considered to be located somewhere between the US and European Union countries such as France and Germany. With some exceptions already noted, UK companies seem to find the climate something of a challenge as for many the assumption is that the government will provide, attitudes, perhaps reinforced by the temporary success of the National Heritage Lottery Fund (Fraser and Fraser, 2003). The traditional view that what arts companies need to find is an indulgent chairman no longer holds. Companies that sponsor nowadays do this as part of a well thought out branding proposition (Broomhead, 2003). The role of the marketing director therefore can be seen as raising the profile of the organisation thus facilitating the task of the fund-raising or development people.

But some of the attractions of the UK system may be at least partly illusory. Elliott Carter who wrote his first opera when in his 80s, was once interviewed by John Tusa, managing director at the Barbican, London. Tusa commented how, on trips to America, on a visit to a gallery, a concert hall, or an opera house, 'we're amazed by the long lists of major supporters and we think this is a terrific strength'. Carter's response was more measured. 'Well it is a real strength except that they approach the arts, and in particular, music as if it were entertainment and not as education. While with state support it's assumed that this is more of an educational thing than we consider it' (Tusa, 2003: 93).

Michael Kaiser, one time boss of the ROH, holds the rare distinction of having managed the challenge in two dramatically different cultures and would never say the US funding system is better than the British one.

But there needs to be a societal discussion about how to fund. In the UK, there is no acceptable model. If there were, arts administrators would not have to spend so much time taking hits for raising money. After all, I wasn't doing anything evil.

Michael Kaiser, former head, Royal Opera House, Covent Garden
(Higgins, 2002: 11).

Vignette – ENO

ENO is the latest of the UK opera companies to encounter serious financial problems. Newspaper reports suggested that the company was £1.2 million in the red, only a short time after receiving from the Arts Council a 'once and for all' lifesaving grant. There are not many votes in opera, and ENO has been bailed out by the British Arts Council twice in 6 years. ENO, originally founded by Lilian Baylis in 1931 as Sadler's Wells Opera, relocated from that theatre to the Coliseum in 1968 and changed its name to ENO in 1974. Also founded in 1974 was a spin off company, initially ENO North and now the autonomous Opera North, based in Leeds. The aims espoused by Baylis included opera sung in English, the language of the audience; an emphasis on accessibility partly through low prices, and on education.

Its home, the London Coliseum, a 1904 grade 2 listed Edwardian building, is currently undergoing a £41 million restoration. The 2-year building programme provides a range of significant improvements to enlarge public spaces and generally bring its standards of the theatre building up to those of the new century. In the first place, its location just off Trafalgar Square close to restaurants, bookshops, art galleries and transport links, seems close to ideal. The renovation however is long overdue as the building had become increasingly shabby. The limitations of the Coliseum had been all the more evident since The ROH at Covent Garden had undergone renovation several years earlier. For much of its time at the Coliseum, the building had simply been leased, becoming increasingly dilapidated. ENO continued to lobby for support to enable it to upgrade the building and eventually in 1992 the government paid for the freehold on behalf of the company. The Coliseum, as its name might suggest, is renowned for being one of the largest theatres built. Its capacity even now is as much as 2358 seats. However this background is important for a number of reasons. If not quite 'arena opera', the size means that the auditorium is best suited to performance on the large scale, with implications for staffing, production values and of course resources. Not all voices suit such a large space and indeed some of the more intimate operas do not normally sit well there.

A new strategy document issued in 2003 by the ENO board set out management proposals for action including a reduction in the number of performances by 20 per cent and a loss of 70 jobs. This represents an apparently constrained future. While the details as reported were unclear, major changes seem likely. In terms of business development, the plan included also proposals to have big screens broadcast performances, and to market its own label ENO CDs, following the examples of the London Symphony Orchestra, Royal Philharmonic and Hallé orchestras. Newspaper reports suggested that the ENO tradition of performing opera in English might also be dropped (Morrison, 2003). While this has been the practice since the formation of the company, board members are no longer in favour of maintaining this tradition. Sponsors, it is suggested, do not find this attractive.

A more general issue might be that of brand image. How should ENO position itself in relation to the competition? What is its image other than simply being 'not the Royal Opera'? (Morrison, 2003). Perhaps best known for performing in English, its brand values, arguably, are 'quality, innovation and accessibility' (Alberge, 2003). What is the ENO brand? At present, it would incorporate several layers – the company and its history, the particular opera and its companions in the season's programme, and the venue itself. Other resonance may be provided by the company's performers and guest artists, the artistic policy and so on. In the relationship between the 'house styles' of ROH and ENO there are echoes elsewhere, for example, in New York between the Metropolitan Opera and New York City Opera. One is the city's upscale house specialising in prestige international productions, the other a 'poor cousin' operating in English with perhaps a more adventurous house repertoire and production style, and more accessibly priced.

Vignette – Birmingham City Opera

Faced with extremely demanding redevelopment problems, many industrial cities and regions seek success in rebranding themselves with the aid of the arts. One such UK city which made dramatic strides in this way over several decades was Birmingham, at least partly through the success of Simon Rattle and the City of Birmingham Symphony Orchestra. Birmingham City Opera (formerly City of Birmingham Touring Opera), on the other hand has radically different aims. 'Led by Artistic Director Graham Vick' states its website, 'Birmingham Opera Company will be a new kind of opera company. Community involvement and involvement in the community is at the heart of Birmingham Opera Company. Local people now have the chance to observe, comment and question the whole process of creating an opera production. The productions will be specifically conceived to involve members of the community at every level, including performing alongside the professional singers and musicians.' Artistic Director, Graham Vick, is the driving force behind Birmingham Opera Company. In demand by major opera houses all over the world, he brings a special flair, passion and commitment to his work in Birmingham.

What approach do they adopt? Performing always in English, Birmingham Opera Company started with Berg's *Votzek*, which took place in a warehouse in Birmingham during February 2001. This highly successful production then toured to Sheffield, Liverpool and Portugal later in the year. The second production in March 2002 was Beethoven's only opera, *Fidelio*, which provided evidence of its links within the community. For this large-scale production over 200 local people were involved in the project. The setting was an enormous Big Top within the grounds of Aston Hall, Birmingham, in the shadow of Aston Villa FC. The South Bank Show also filmed a documentary about the making of *Fidelio* which was screened in October 2002. Birmingham Opera Company's production for April 2003 was Bernstein's *Candide*. 'I think one of the things that puts new audiences off new opera is theatres themselves and the existing audience,' Vick told the BBC recently. Speaking of *Votzeck*, he said 'I wanted to do a project that was well away from the glamorous West End or city centres or big plush theatres – somewhere where people live.' 'The piece has an immediacy, an emotional power that goes way beyond the word understanding,' he added. 'It is easy to relate to and the music has immediacy and power.'

One of the remarkable features of the Birmingham approach is that a local community cast is recruited in each city. The Birmingham cast includes members from the Birmingham Rep's youth company, a young Asian theatre company and unemployed youngsters who are doing apprenticeships in the creative arts. Just as distinctive in comparison to conventional presentations, the spectators are mobile. The audience wanders around, following the scenes, as there was no seating, something Vick sees as a real advantage. 'You could be two feet away from an opera singer singing in full voice and really understand the physicality and effort and emotional intensity that gives. You cannot fail to be affected and fascinated.'

Also with an eye to access, prices were kept low at £10 (£5 for concessions). A free bus was laid on to take people from Birmingham city centre to the location.

Conclusions

Opera provides some of the greatest creative and cultural achievements of the human race. However it also presents the marketer with many challenges, not least that of its future survival. The issue here is of ensuring that existing demand is met, that latent demand is identified, and that a balance is maintained between popular works which probably do not need subsidy and the sort of work that does and for which it is given. But it is an area which is extremely difficult to research, not least for the reason that it deals with emotional and unconscious issues outside rationality and analysis. The cultural and educational context is of course critical.

Promotion can be carried out on behalf of the sector as well as by individual companies.

As this chapter was going to press, media stories highlighted again the financial challenge facing opera houses. ENO's financial difficulties have been touched on. Scottish Opera are said to be in a very precarious position. Frank McAveety, Culture Minister, has written to the company turning down their request for an additional £1.5 million in funding, on top of its current annual £7.5 million. There has also been a call for them to sell the Theatre Royal, their base since 1975 (Cornwell, 2003).

Marketing is not simply a matter of focusing on consumers buying tickets but on negotiating and engaging with a whole range of other relationships. These include companies in the media, and those on the governmental bodies providing subsidy as well as co-operation with opera and other related companies in the sector. A key issue must lie in trying to influence the educational curriculum so that schools incorporate the arts and arts appreciation at all levels. Companies the world over have been active in experimenting with a wide range of presentation modes to try to engage more with their communities, reduce costs and manage without subsidy or sponsorship. Arena opera, concert performances, opera cuts and opera accompanied by piano or reduced orchestra only, provide a range of solutions each with their own advantages and disadvantages. TV, video, theatrical and internet distribution of filmed performance offers another route, perhaps better considered a distinct and separate product.

Acknowledgements

Thanks to all those friends, colleagues and relatives who have supported and encouraged my interest in opera over the course of my life. In particular to those who have granted valuable time for interview, conversation and discussion: Sue Broomhead of ETO, John Calder, Sheila Colvin, Ken Fitzhugh, Iain Fraser, Stephen Fraser, Dianne Grieg of Scottish Opera and many others.

Chapter 6

Marketing and jazz

Dorothea Noble

Introduction

One of the most successful jazz organisations outside London, the Anglia Modern Jazz Club, celebrated 25 years of high quality jazz in 1997. The Club's founder and animateur had worked for a county council for several years, promoting jazz in the region. On the basis of her demonstrated success in these two ventures, jazz lovers from the club's committee joined her in preparing an Arts for Everyone (A4E) proposal in May 1997 to create an integrated jazz service for two eastern counties. As a result of the success of that bid, a new organisation – JazzAce – was established to promote and produce jazz activity in that area. It would be a small entity, with a chief executive, an administrator and great ambition.

I was introduced in early 1998 to JazzAce, and the organisation shared my life for the following 4 years. I had rather lost contact with Carole Franks but she had approached me at a jazz club gig saying 'You're something to do with business, aren't you? We're looking for experienced people to help with this new jazz organisation'. I received a two-page introduction to the project by post a few days later. I joined the next meeting of the steering committee which had been gathered to set up JazzAce.

All the stakeholders were there, except perhaps the professional musicians. The various funders were represented – county councils, and the Regional Arts Board for A4E – various amateur and professional jazz organisations, and local jazz supporters, promoters and patrons. Carole was probably the only one there to know everyone. There was quite a buzz; locally, jazz had not received such an official boost for a long time and everyone was hopeful and keen – until, that is, they asked for volunteers to become members of the Board. I was one of the four who finally agreed to stand.

I am going to draw on this experience to write this chapter. In research methodology terms I am a participant researcher, reflecting on my experience with others as I sought to fulfil the responsibilities of Chair of the Board of Trustees, and the aspirations of a jazz fan working to share the excitement of that music, and to make the skills of its musicians known to a wider public.

Jazz: what is the story?

According to Shipton (2001), jazz was by far the most significant musical form that emerged during the 20th century. In its early years it spread like wildfire throughout the US, and then quickly to the rest of the world:

> where its combination of syncopation, unusual pitching, vocal tones and raw energy touched the hearts and minds of people across the entire spectrum of social and racial backgrounds. Its message was universal, something risqué that overturned the old orders of art music and folk music alike.
>
> (ibid.: 1)

Jazz has always had a mixed image, with many fiercely contested variations; few can agree as to what is and is not real jazz music. Emerging in the black communities of New Orleans these bands quickly gained enthusiastic support in Chicago too. With those associations of poverty and hardship, jazz arose in 'conditions likely to nurture a new musical form' (ibid.). Shipton's narrative story of jazz reveals, however, the complexity of the genre's roots, and its development, as well as the range of associations it still recalls. Its disreputable image has never entirely disappeared; in the 1920s – the jazz age – it stood for decadence and the range of dubious pleasures indulged in by societies recovering from the trauma of World War I. For a white public it represented something daring, exotic, while for a black public, it represented unity and aspiration. In the 1940s, ideas of political and racial revolution were associated with its music, with a more genuine political revolution emerging in the 1960s, to foster the arts as a unifying social influence.

Jazz music nowadays has a more intellectual reputation than pop, but not the mainstream, educated image associated with classical music. It remains a subversive form, despite audiences ranging from inattentive wedding guests, and restaurant and bar customers for whom it is merely ambience, to attentive listeners in cellar venues demanding quiet from those around them. Jazz fills large venues when one of the few bands or musicians whose name is widely known performs, but it is more widely associated with smaller club venues. Here, the music still raises the hope that something extraordinary may happen between the audience and the musicians, an expectation based on the potential of improvisation among experienced, risk-taking musicians. Perhaps because of this tradition of improvisation, and the limited take-up in the UK of free jazz, a public performance based on improvisation, jazz tends to remain on the periphery of musical attention, thriving in these clubs and among small audiences, with few musicians and bands attracting mainstream attention. Cleo Laine, writing in *The Observer*, commented that the previous focus of attention in the UK on foreign names in classical music was now a thing of the past. However, in jazz it remains the case that British musicians receive little attention, despite a history that goes as far back as the early 1920s, and despite having built over the years an audience equal in number to that of so-called classic music:

> the art of this classic music is still struggling to be acknowledged, even though many of our musicians have proved they are world class.
>
> (Laine, 2000)

The popularity and authority of classical music lies in the continuity of its history, in its acknowledged European masters and their compositions. Jazz by contrast 'has always been obsessed with the new, with experimentation, and the result has been that it has rarely paused to exploit its discoveries before leaping out to make fresh ones' (Collier, 1978: 497). Shipton (2001) has a different view, recognising at the same time a continuing tradition in jazz's history until the 1970s. The fragmentation of musicians' lives since then, the growing tendency to play with whichever group or band needs their instrument, rather than developing in the tradition and style of just one, means a loss of continuity in rich understanding of both the tradition of the form, and its subversion. He quotes T.S. Eliot (1919: 874):

> Tradition cannot be inherited, and if you want it you must obtain it by great labour. It involves, in the first place, the historical sense ... and a historical sense involves a perception, not only of the pastness of the past, but of its presence.

These complex associations of tradition, subversion and revolution, of continuity and experimentation, along with its roots among marginalised black communities, are paradoxically the features that make it most attractive in education and in policies of social inclusion. These same characteristics however, make it a marketing nightmare: no one can agree what the product is, and if they did it would have to be subverted to retain consistency. The contrast between the music and its associations, and the public funding bureaucracies attempting to justify giving the art form financial support, could hardly be greater.

Policy background

A4E was one of the lottery-funded initiatives, designed to fulfil a government undertaking to bring the arts to groups perceived as gaining little from them under earlier legislation. By the same token, jazz, as a significant source of new music, was identified among neglected areas for funding:

> The Arts Council and Regional Arts Boards have always maintained that new music is a funding priority. However, historical commitments have made it impossible to dedicate the necessary resources to this area ... lottery funding for the arts promises to alter the way in which the arts are funded.
>
> (ACE, 1996)

The Arts Council of England (ACE) published its policy document for support of Jazz in England in November 1996. Its stated objectives included the intention to support initiatives to generate new audiences for jazz while sustaining the interests and commitment of existing supporters. The network of promoters and producers was to be strengthened with a commitment to supporting adventurous programming across new styles. Conditions for jazz musicians were to be improved, allowing for the artistic development of individuals and for proper rehearsal of bands. Opportunities for jazz musicians, producers and promoters were to be improved to extend and develop their skills and jazz musicians were to be more involved as animateurs in formal education. Partnerships with other areas of the music industry were to be encouraged to ensure that jazz is disseminated nationally and internationally through recordings.

JazzAce, a small organisation of two full-time employees and a Board of six to eight volunteer directors/trustees, was to be one of the means by which the government, through ACE, would seek to achieve these goals. Its bid for A4E lottery funding was designed to address these objectives.

The lottery had generated waves of change for the Arts Council during the 1990s, and once money from that source began to flow through its systems it ended up working two funding streams. Witts (1998) reports how the 'old' Council received about £190 million from the government to spend on the yearly work of clients. The 'new' Council, the Arts Council lottery unit, received one and a half times as much to spend, but with the proviso that it could only be spent on buildings, films and puny schemes for amateurs:

> It's staggering to think that anyone could conceive of bolting on a unit sometimes twice as rich as its presumed boss, but what has transpired will either transform the Council into a revitalised mechanism or the Council will buckle and collapse from the weight of its conflicting responsibilities.
>
> (ibid.: 396)

Talk of a restructuring of the Arts Council and its regional offices began in the late 1990s as its role as the vehicle for control by the Department of Culture, Media and Sport (DCMS) in lottery disbursements developed. Within 6 months of setting up JazzAce, I was reading the DCMS *Comprehensive Spending Review, a new approach to investment in culture*. This envisaged structural change which would give an increased role to regional bodies, and establish a tough new watchdog to monitor efficiency, financial management and compliance with objectives – familiar language now to the public sector. Moves to decentralise and transfer more authority to fewer regional boards began in 1999/2000. Uncertainties as to what was to happen, which offices would be affected and which jobs would go, amplified during this time and affected the working environment within which JazzAce was operating.

It was also becoming clear that funding priorities would change. In the summer of 2002, ACE published their new ambitions for the arts, after a period of radical reform and in the confidence of receiving a substantial increase in public investment. Their ambitions included the intention to give priority to individual artists, to work with funded arts organisations to help them thrive rather than just survive, to place cultural diversity at the heart of their work, to prioritise young people and to maximise growth in the arts. An impressive injection of cash has been implemented, increasing the £189 million allocation for the arts in 1998 to in excess of £410 million in 2005. This expansion in funding is a challenge to the performing arts – 'here's the cash: spend it so we know why you wanted it in the first place' (Hytner, 2003). It is accompanied by policies that justify it politically – 'we are being asked to paper over the cracks in education policy' following the abandonment of arts education in state schools in the 1980s (ibid.). What in the 1980s was the economic justification for public funding of the arts – its invisible earnings, its significance in regenerating inner cities – had taken a new turn by the late 1990s, the focus turning to access, diversity and inclusion, laudable ideals. Their translation into strategic objectives and often clumsy performance targets has expanded with the funding. In the arts as in education and health, the target driven culture is stifling the personal enthusiasm at the heart of great learning (ibid.). I would suggest performance as well as learning, and performance in all its associations in the arts and in management. This background, I feel, sheds light on the experience we had as a funded organisation (a puny scheme for amateurs?) dealing with arts policy and bureaucracy from 1998 to 2001.

All in the same boat

A thought recurs as I try to think through this chapter on marketing and jazz, for a book about marketing the arts: we are all in the same boat, whether we were talking about jazz or opera, theatre or dance. There are legion interested parties with competing aims, all dealing with bureaucratic public funders, idiosyncratic patron funders, image-conscious corporate funders, volunteer and professional staff, inspiring and not-so-inspiring artists, intermediaries of various kinds and a range of providers of essential resources – venues, ticketing, and the like. There are therefore myriad stakeholders, a raft of competing interests and a complex political context. Marketing is not straightforward, nor is it clear what the term is meant to cover; hence the nature and role of marketing is continuously negotiated as part of the power dynamics among the groups as they all work to achieve their own ends. After all, if public money goes to galleries or dance, there is less to go to jazz. Decisions to charge, or not to charge, for entrance to museums has implications for all involved in the public funding of the arts, as the champions of the various arts compete to attract funding to their own preferred sector. The same might be said regarding audiences; if more go to orchestral concerts, does that reduce the jazz audience, or can the whole arts audience be expanded?

So in one sense these chapters could be all the same, a plea for each of the arts represented in each chapter and their greater worthiness in comparison to the others. Equally, they could each be an account of the struggle of each sector to survive and manoeuvre their path through the conflicting interests of stakeholders, in an educational context which seems to be transferring responsibility for arts training to the voluntary and private sector. And this despite such declarations as:

> It is our central belief that the arts have power to transform lives, communities and opportunities for people throughout the country.
>
> (ACE website, April 2003)

However, in the context of this book, I have gradually come to take heart from these thoughts. Despite similarities the underlying processes and conflicts, we will each produce a different and unique story from our own arts niche. At the same time, we will be saying something that is relevant to the whole sector, about the dynamics and politics of the whole sector. The sociologist, Norbert Elias (1983) felt that the investigation of any social grouping, large or small, existing or long defunct, must contribute to our understanding of how people are linked, intellectually, emotionally and in all their situations and activities:

> The variability of these human connections is so great that … one cannot conceive of an objective study of a hitherto unexplored human figuration and its evolution that would not bring new understanding of the human universe and of ourselves.
>
> (ibid.: 9)

I expect therefore that the account of my experience with JazzAce will say something of relevance about the whole situation of the arts, their funding and the role of marketing for the various stakeholders and their manoeuvrings.

Marketing jazz

There is an immediate contradiction in that title: how can jazz, that wayward and subversive music of the periphery, be constrained into becoming a marketable product? If there seems to be a dichotomy between the classic definition of marketing and the widely accepted independence of the artist to define what the product might be, how much more can this be true of jazz? Classic marketing indicates the ideal of researching the market in order to then define and provide what the market wants. Gander (1998) stressed that the product takes precedence in the arts, and arts marketers have to go out and find the appropriate market. Yet he finds people who advocate the establishment of common ground with more mainstream forms of consumer marketing, transferring many of the techniques used (ibid.).

Much has happened recently in arts marketing which proves that there is some truth in this. Crossover use of mailing lists gets information about modern dance to known jazz attenders, for example, having found a link between these interests from box office records. Bundling of tickets for different kinds of performance with differing concessions draws audiences to attend events they might only have mused about otherwise. Extensive use of IT makes all this widely accessible to affiliated venues and intermediaries. But it requires co-operation and the conviction that there is mutual benefit in sharing information and resource. It has to be believed that audiences will attend more events, not attend your event instead of mine, a jazz gig instead of a classical music concert.

With the policy focus on access, diversity and inclusion, participation was to include not only attendance at events, but also performance, education, promotion and administration, encompassing marginalised communities and groups and the mainstream of society. Marketing came to be seen as having an essential role, a role particularly emphasised by policy makers and funders. Part of my interest in making sense of my experience with JazzAce was related to understanding the role marketing seemed to be playing in all this.

Early meetings

I attended that first meeting of the JazzAce steering group, as naively as the other jazz supporters present, with little thought as to what might be a useful outcome of the event. Carole, as Arts Development Officer, was effectively to be the chief executive of the new organisation we were there to form. She had done little to ensure that her 'friends' volunteered as board members, to secure the support she would need. It was unclear what the Board could and could not do, and what its responsibilities were; the only ones with apparent experience were the county council funders, and the ACE representative, so they had the most to say.

One suggestion they made was that the salary, indicated and accepted in the A4E bid for the chief executive, was excessive and not standard for the sector. I had assumed that this would be negotiable, despite a specific salary being stated in the bid, and that talks would be developed by the funders with Carole, the proposed CEO, before the next meeting. This would be the first formal meeting of the Board of JazzAce, and the first day of the CEO's contracted employment.

The ACE representative turned up for that next meeting with a table of comparable salaries, but had made no contact with Carole. So on her first day of working for JazzAce, she attended a meeting where we were bending over backwards to appear equitable in recruitment, even though we were not going to advertise the job. Since the bid had been awarded on the basis of Carole's extensive experience as a jazz animateur, originally on a voluntary basis and more recently as a county council employee; she was the history upon which this new organisation was to be founded. We could hardly advertise the job: she was the organisation at this stage. She was asked to leave the room while we discussed her conditions of employment, and was recalled to be told that the salary would be lower than originally proposed, her contract would be for 1 year only, and would be renewed only if the objectives stated in the bid were achieved to a satisfactory level. I had got so caught up in the power of the funders present, and their equal opportunities speak, that I had not spoken up for Carole in her absence and neither had anyone else – hardly equitable.

A growing sense that we had not gone through a fair process developed following the meeting. An unhappy CEO was not going to be a major asset to this infant organisation, so the decision would have to be raised again. It was beginning to be evident by then that a lot went on via conversations between individuals, rather than openly in groups. Carole had spoken to us all separately by the weekend following the meeting. I had been clear that we could change things if she was not happy, and that anyway we should at least make her a formal offer so that she was given the opportunity to respond in her own interest. The other directors seemed mainly concerned that she should not rock the boat with the funders, and that we would have to find other ways of making sure she could benefit legitimately from the activities of the organisation. For example, we could pay rent for the office accommodation which was to be in her home, initially at least. I was not happy with this obfuscation, but also realised that I was taking on these issues as my own, when in fact there was no reason why Carole should not make her own case, given the appropriate opportunity. I took a new approach with her: you are the boss though it might not seem like it at present, so decide what you want and prepare to fight for it.

Later that week she had a meeting with the representative of ACE and then the Chairman of the Board of JazzAce, supposedly to finalise her contract. I encouraged her that it was not too late to say her piece, and that we could go back on any ill-advised decision we had made. So she did just that, having first spoken to one or two of her own contacts at ACE, reinforcing her own resolve before the meeting and gathering some powerful backers of her own.

Soon after this the directors and Carole met to progress operational matters – her contract, recruitment of her assistant, the setting up of an office and the official launch of JazzAce. This meeting overturned most of the decisions made at the earlier meeting attended by the funders. We ran through a couple of existing contracts and very quickly finalised an appropriate version for Carole. Again it was suggested that she should leave the room while this was discussed, once she had stated her position. I said I had nothing to say that I was not prepared to say in her presence, which made it hard for others to say that they had. So we all had to say what we thought in front of her and had a certain amount of difficulty in doing so, even though most comments had already been made to her in the individual conversations she had had. Justin suggested that there be a performance-related portion, but could not identify the performance it would be based on. Andrew suggested we extract maximum benefit from other justifiable sources of income, such as rent. I told him that this sounded a very accountant thing to do, and that we should stick to what the bid had proposed as her salary level. Tony suggested that we find a range on the scale that would average the bid amount over the 3 years of the funding. (He was sympathetic to her sense of being undervalued, as his public sector pay did not represent his own worth in his view, but he was also aware of the low rates many people in the sector have to live with.) No one would support my suggestion of going along with the bid document – the first time its terms came under negotiation. Tony's idea was passed, with Carole's full acceptance. She had been party to the discussion, had seen the concessions made, and had been able to concede something herself. But these all came after some pretty difficult ideas were expressed, difficult to say in Carole's presence, and hard for her to hear too. Despite this I felt that the outcome was good; we had said what we had feared to say and the sky had not fallen in, we were all still speaking to each other; and the Chairman commented that this was the highest salary that he had ever heard of in jazz! He subsequently resigned as Chairman, because we had allowed this best-paid job in jazz to be allocated and not competed for in accordance with equal opportunities principles. I was appointed to the post shortly afterwards.

A strategic management approach to making sense of this process might start with a consideration of the stakeholders and their power and influence

(Johnson and Scholes, 2001). Because the funding for JazzAce was from lottery and public sources, the activities of the organisation had to comply with government policy and contribute to achieving the strategies devised by the public bodies who were the mediators of that policy. For JazzAce there were two pathways: one was the arts link, from government policy for the arts, via the Department of National Heritage through the Arts Council and its regional board, to their representative as observer on the Board of Trustees. The other was through the funding received directly from local government councils, whose representatives were also observers on the JazzAce board of trustees. For these bodies, policy is translated via outdated business models into a hierarchy of strategies, each with specified outcomes which feed into the next level of strategy making. The achievements of one level, for example the county councils, feeds into the achievements of the appropriate section of the DCMS, later the Department of National Heritage. Performance is measured against targets for each level of this hierarchy with ongoing monitoring being the pre-requisite for the receipt of the next tranche of funding. For JazzAce this meant reports to two county councils and the regional office of ACE every 6 months, against all targets detailed. The ongoing threat of loss of funding meant that compliance with the wishes of funders was a clear priority.

The final judge of performance cited by the government and their representatives is the taxpayer: all the details gleaned from these various strategic reports feed into government statements about the results achieved by spending in each area; everything has to be justified to the taxpayer. Of course, the taxpayer is also a participant and beneficiary of government policy. Stakeholders in jazz include musicians, audiences, promoters, producers and the various owners of venues – taxpayers all. These are fragmented groups however, often with little power. Although represented by the Musicians' Union, for example, musicians frequently accept fees below the Union's minimum level, for a range of reasons including the need to earn whatever they can, and the need to remain in the public eye. Intermediaries like JazzAce are developed and funded in order to draw these fragmented local groups working in their own interests, into the control model of performance measurement and thus under the policy umbrella.

The results of this focus are conversations of conformity and stability, of anxiety to please and a search for blame (Stacey, 2003). The control model in the case of JazzAce was articulated constantly through a marketing discourse about what we should do, and our non-conformity with marketing standards, our absence of marketing skills and our non-compliance with the aims of the organisation or its funders.

If we now consider the 1996 policy for jazz again, we find objectives such as supporting existing audiences, and finding new ones; adventurous programming, expanded opportunities for promoters, producers and musicians; drawing musicians as animateurs into educational environments.

These are the kind of aspirations you would expect for jazz, one of the least orthodox of the creative 'industries', and the one most identified with passionate creativity through its practice of improvisation. How does this reputation, this requirement for adventurous offerings and unstructured demands to educate, fit with a reporting model of control and conformity? And how does a chapter about jazz reach this stage without any mention of musical performance.

Music: a wing and a prayer

JazzAce was creatively successful, due to the inventiveness and imaginative way in which Carole made connections between places, musicians and target audiences. A good example of this was the Andrew Milne Jazz Award project, which took place in 1999. The purpose of the award was to encourage the composition of major new jazz works by British artists. For JazzAce, competing for it also had to address strategic aims such as drawing in new audiences and regions, and fulfilling an educational purpose. In conversation with established musicians, and with the district and parish councils responsible for local youth music and the proposed venue, a bid for the award was devised. The project was given the title 'A Wing and a Prayer', evoking associations with the location chosen to inspire the composition, a 15th century church in a Fenland town not usually involved in jazz events. This church has a remarkable wooden ceiling, dramatically embellished with carved angels, which surmount every pillar, and adorn the whole roof. The composer who agreed to work with this location as a theme was Julian Arguelles, one of Britain's finest young musicians. The joint bid was successful. The result was a major new jazz suite for jazz quartet and classical orchestra, which was performed to sell-out audiences at its full premiere in the church and its second performance in Norwich.

The orchestral parts were written with the local youth orchestra in mind; the Julien Arguelles Quartet rehearsed with them, teaching them the basics of jazz and giving the young musicians the experience of playing a new type of music in a world premiere, in the company of world class musicians.

The first concert of the project took place in a nearby prison with just the professional band. The full inaugural performance of the new composition was held in the church during November. I found the whole evening a truly 'fen' experience, travelling through slight mist, locating the venue from some distance away by its lofty tower, shivering at first in the chill of the old church. The music was glorious, the young players delighted and delightful in good spirits and proud of the event they were creating; the audience, which included many proud parents, were captivated and forgiving. Professional and amateur musicians alike were enjoying themselves, playing with skill and good humour. The music in two sets was well received, with the youth orchestra playing well with some complex musical patterns in support of the quartet's confident performance. The second performance, in Norwich in January, and featuring the same musicians, was *The Guardian*'s choice for jazz concert of the week. It was once again a sell-out and enjoyed a rousing reception.

The role given to marketing

Early in the life of JazzAce, the funders stressed the need for strong marketing skills, though they never articulated this in terms of JazzAce's need to market itself to the funders themselves. We knew our audience figures through box office records, and the profile through data cards available to jazz fans at all jazz gigs. We published a quarterly gig guide covering our funders' regions and gigs easily accessible from those regions. We developed a website also publicising all jazz events, not simply those related to JazzAce. We initiated several musicians' co-operatives supporting them through their early days and helping them establish ways of working that suited their particular members. We organised workshops for singers, and for promoters, always with the participation of experienced practitioners. In a sense our product was information as we had a generic responsibility within our region to promote all jazz and its range of venues, musicians and promoters. Part of this was our links with education, supporting and training existing practitioners, as well as participating in the development of jazz awareness and basic skills in schools, both with pupils and teachers.

We also put on our own gigs, usually associated with workshops and master classes, like 'A Wing and a Prayer', so that novices had the experience of working with established performers. We produced striking promotional literature, distributed it throughout our regions and usually gained good coverage in the relevant press. The choice of musicians was based on Carole's experience of them; she tracked both established and new performers and sought to bring a wide range of quality music to the region. All of this was reported in narrative form and verbally to the funders, supported by brief financial summaries.

Moving the goalposts

In July 1999, 15 months after the setting up of JazzAce, there were hints of discontent from the funders, which came to a head when we were invited to a meeting with them. The meeting had been called to correct a misperception that JazzAce may have about the county council's role in relation to JazzAce – that they are not policing the organisation but seeking to ensure that the aims of the councils are met in some way, through the activities of JazzAce and in the form of reported outcomes' (JazzAce internal document).

I knew that the councils had recently come under pressure to reduce spending in anticipation of a cut in funding from central government, but this insight into their motives for concern, their anxiety, did not help me cope with my own anxiety at that meeting. It seemed to us that everything we had achieved was seen as unimportant, misconceived and was no longer being accepted as complying with our aims, never mind theirs. A year ago, they had been concerned that we establish an identity for JazzAce that was distinguishable from the reputation of Carole, the CEO. Now JazzAce should be supporting the local enthusiasts in their work, not developing JazzAce. Where was the infrastructure for jazz, they challenged? Which local groups, trained and developed by JazzAce, would subsequently work independently with the local community to develop local capacity? The musicians' co-operatives that we already had established in the two counties were a start, yes. The workshops we had planned for new promoters would be useful too. The projects in schools may well be generating interest in the music among young people, yes. But why did we insist on putting on big name gigs rather than working with local musicians, promoting local bands?

Gigs on their own do not meet the needs of funders in the counties. They should be only the tip of the iceberg, with workshops, educational work, local participation in concerts, and a raft of training and development of local promoters and organisers supporting this peak less obtrusively.

(Notes taken at the time)

We were given 10 days to respond to their concerns in writing. Our response took the form of a memo stating our achievements in terms of the aims for the organisation as declared in the original A4E bid. That document was once more re-interpreted in the light of more recent events. We could justify our achievements in terms of those aims just as forcefully as the funders could use them to justify our non-compliance with those same aims. In addition we wrote a letter covering points made by the funders which did not relate directly to the terms of the original bid. This included our continuing intention to bring the so-called 'big names' into the communities of our region, and our reasons for doing so. After all, it had been envisaged as part of our role in the A4E bid, and it acknowledged the region's position and role in the wider UK jazz infrastructure, which needed our support too. The performers were not expensive, they brought good quality performance to our venues, which might be matched or aspired to by local musicians, setting them standards to assess themselves by. Audiences were attracted by even some slight familiarity with the name to attend gigs they might otherwise have overlooked so their experience was extended. They would also feel that the region was on the national jazz map and not constantly overlooked as insignificant by better known musicians.

We also pointed out that these big names frequently gave workshops or master classes for local musicians when they attended to do their gig, so in this too they did not represent only the tip of the iceberg of benefits the community receives.

The minutes of the Board meeting, somewhat unusually, recall the feelings of the members and staff of JazzAce and evoke the contradictions we were experiencing:

> Andrew expressed exasperation that funders had not attended this meeting to hear in person what JazzAce was doing. Justin stated that they seemed to be picking holes in everything we were doing. He was particularly incensed by criticisms of the website – a modern, up-to-date site up and running before any of the longer established bodies in the arts had made such a move. Andrew commented that all the funders seemed to want were analytical and numerical statistics to illustrate what JazzAce had done. Carole drew attention to our successes; I pointed out that what they would want to know is why it was a great success: what made it a success? How did we define success? Who was it a success for? Feedback from participants had been good, but what had we done with that? We needed testimonials from all stakeholders – venues, council officers involved, participants, tutors, musicians, everyone.
>
> (JazzAce internal document)

I had become the voice of the funders, an irony that was not lost on me. I had been drawn to JazzAce by the music, yet was finding myself trapped in those same business theories that in my academic work I contest fiercely. I was trapped in the sterile conversations of control; the formal responsibilities of the Chairman role and the pressures for compliance were taking over my conversations.

This exchange of letters and meetings continued into October, taking up considerable time, over a period of 4 months, for both paid staff and volunteer board members. I remember it as a very anxious time, which sapped my interest in attending jazz gigs as this brought me in contact with my JazzAce colleagues and simply reminded me of the endless reporting and defending processes that we were caught up in. Ultimately, the funders were either satisfied with our efforts on their behalf, or their attention had been diverted onto other public sector crises. For whatever reason, we secured our funding for the following year. We also collected 'evidence' of success at every move, and built up a standard format report which allowed for both the narrative accounts of events that we had always produced, and detailed numeric calculations of attendees, audience growth and other indicators. More and more scarce time had to be dedicated to this kind of activity.

JazzAce: a second phase

The July meeting with the funders mentioned above came as a shock to us, and marked a new phase in our interactions with them. It coincided with our own realisation of mistakes on our part, but these alone did not seem to justify the changed attitude of the funders. Around this time there had been reports in the media of high profile failures with some large lottery projects, notably the Royal Opera House, and the Arts Theatre in Cambridge. Both of these found themselves millions of pounds in deficit, and had to be rescued with additional funding. Boards were sacked and new reporting and auditing requirements were imposed. The impact of these events rippled throughout the arts funding structures. As board members we felt that, as small players and easily dispensed with, the scrutiny we were put under was excessively intense. At the same time government policy regarding the Arts continued under review, with jobs under threat as re-structuring was planned. With budget cuts to local government too, all JazzAce's funders felt under threat and were looking for ways of saving money. This anxiety translated into a close scrutiny of everything related to JazzAce, a questioning of our fulfilment of our role, and demands for highly detailed reporting, addressing the continuously changing policy aims of the funding bodies themselves. The term 'best value' entered their discourse at this time (DETR 1999; see Speller, 2001). We were not really aware of the situation in all this detail at the time, and felt that what was being demanded of us was excessive, and restrictive of what we could achieve for jazz.

The inadequacy of our marketing was a constant theme and it was suggested that we buy in some expertise from Business in the Arts, an organisation of contributing individuals and institutions offering their skills in support of arts activities; grants were available to pay them. We gained the support of an excellent marketing specialist, who remained with us for at least 2 years, for much of that time working on a voluntary basis. All her efforts were devoted to establishing a better relationship with the funders, through detailed reporting, follow-up market research and the completion of strategy documents, and business plans. These had existed in some form before but not with the investment of time and effort that they now received. They took hours of her time, of the two staff members' time and much effort from board members. It seemed like we received funding in order to report back to funders, with no time for anything else; music had become an extra-curricular activity. Despite this, we continued to work creatively, with musicians, schools and venues throughout the region, guided by the aims of our core funders, and of other funders who supported specific projects. But we were still achieving what we achieved through an intuitive capacity to bring together elements in a novel way, not based on consumer research but on discussions with alternative funders, musicians and many other fans and practitioners in the region. There were two parallel lives, one of paperwork, counting and reporting, and of seeking out and bidding for alternative sources of funding; the other of talking, getting varying groups together, of identifying stimulating projects and novel ideas. One time, we did gigs around the theme of travel, with performances in airport, railway station and transport museum, of music specially composed around this theme – a year of the artist project. And we handed out questionnaires to listeners, coded their responses and added numbers to our reports.

So marketing had become a theme that explained our 'failure' to our funders, despite the success of most of what we did in musical terms and in terms of attracting expanding audiences. The term had such wide application that however successful our marketing in one area might be, it served to focus criticism elsewhere. Market research, difficult at all times as it reveals only what is within the range of the imagination and language of those questioned, is particularly interesting in terms of the arts. It will reveal what may be supported by audiences sufficiently to provide a reliable income; but it will not give insight into what is 'adventurous' in programming. That is down to the creative capacity of motivated groups prepared to take some risk in what they present. The most useful research we did was the work in schools, which addressed perceptions of jazz among teachers, and young people, and barriers to music-making in schools, relevant to all kinds of music. This was basic research from which more market-oriented investigations might arise and prove useful. It also highlighted how differing strands of government policy could not be considered separately. The same bureaucratic approach we were suffering, of defined targets and performance measurement, was depriving schools of the capacity to attend to teaching or participating in the arts. These are non-priority areas in education policy, so the foundational learning and playing processes are squeezed out of the timetable. Strange that they are now a core part of many management training courses (Noble, 2000), just as jazz improvisation has been considered as a model for management (Barrett, 1998). It is these early activities (ironically based on improvisation and play) that establish the appeal of music and the arts among children and motivate them to taking a continuing interest in their preferred area. Our research highlighted this.

Mapping the music and plotting a course, and the jazz generators

JazzAce developed an ambitious project for the foundation responsible for the stimulation of music among the young, with funding from one of their grants. The scope of the project was wide, taking in research into the regional provision of music education particularly jazz, the provision of an interactive website, and a 3-day programme of workshops and performances with young and elderly people in a community characterised by higher than average poverty rates and high incidence of social exclusion. Local schools, community centres and pubs were the locations for various activities, led by the musicians from a 10-piece band with a great deal of experience in leading participatory music projects. The musical brief was to develop a programme that would allow non-instrumentalists to participate, and that would allow the old and young to create music together. From a slow start, gradually more and more young people joined the workshops, learning to sing, play basic instruments and themes, and becoming performers in the final gig. The reverse happened with the elderly people invited; a few came to start with and gradually faded out. For a few days there was great delight for the youngsters. Some adults were heard to comment however, on these '3-day wonders', where a lot of attention is focused on the community for a short period, then disappears leaving no lasting trace. Some of the reasons for this can be detected in the conversations held for the research part of this project. The local partners were the schools and community centres, both with limited resources and relying on volunteers for extra-curricular activities like music and sport.

The research

The research brief was to find out what teachers, young people and education professionals thought most important about music education and its provision in the region – what exists, and what would benefit and appeal to them most. Music teachers, including peripatetic staff, and young students were approached via postal questionnaires or focus groups. The responding sample size was 115 teachers, and 89 students. Rather than report on findings (Somogyi, 2001), I will highlight how the issues raised reflect some of the points already illustrated in this chapter.

Participating schools used a wide range of music in some form – jazz, world music, pop, rock and the traditional western-classical style, with the choice very much dependent on the interests, skills and confidence of teachers and supporting enthusiasts. The emphasis was on playing and composition, giving young people 'hands-on' skills and supporting their enthusiasm. Many were using jazz with particular emphasis on improvisation skills as a highly relevant part of any musical training, and from an early age:

> … the echo work you might be doing, questioning and answering, the building up of phrases, … is very easily manageable by primary school teachers as long as there's a coordinator who understands how to use it. …

Jazz was acceptable to the children too; while not as cool a style as pop and its variations, it had higher street credibility among their peers than other music forms.

But the comments of others noted earlier in this chapter were supported by this investigation. While policy exists for music education, priority under performance indicators goes to formal skills and subjects – reading, numeracy and writing for example. No relationship is acknowledged in policy between the creative and technical aspects of all subjects, so music and its related skills are devalued and left to 'special projects' funded from outside the education budget – like this one.

So, whatever the musical value of jazz, it faces the same curriculum pressure as music teaching in general:

> … music was always the thing that got pushed out, even more so than R.E …

and

> time available for music is very small – ever shrinking – because of national numeracy/literacy strategies. We try and fit it in by having singing assemblies and snatching half an hour of the day to do rhythm games and that sort of stuff … but it needs to be time-tabled more.

> Some schools try and cram in extra lessons which squeeze the amount of time for music … a particular problem for primary schools, where there is no music specialist, and the staff do not feel confident about teaching it.

Secondary schools are under similar pressure:

> I think the pressures of the timetable are such – the pressure on schools to increase results, to increase the academic component of the timetable, key skills, literacy, numeracy – that's all impacting upon music education generally …

Extra-curricular slots in the day, so valuable to musical activities, are coming under the same kind of pressure:

> … the students and staff are doing so much that to get them to take part in a rehearsal is very difficult … the amount of time you've got for rehearsal and performance is again becoming more and more limited. You'll find schools where they haven't got the resources to perform, put on concerts, do gigs, except at certain, fairly controlled times of the year … rather like sport – what's happened to cricket – everyone's taking exams.

So although the focus has moved to performance, composition and a valuing of improvisation, the academic focus of the national curriculum leaves no space for these creatively valuable developments:

> Music has lost out with the restrictions of the National Curriculum. The pressure on students to perform (academically) has made a lot of students,

particularly as they get further up the school, reluctant to join in extra-curricular activities.

The distancing of children from live performance was considered to have further effects that bring a new dimension to the idea of audience development:

> A lot of children don't know what an audience actually does. … You and me take that for granted but they still think they can yell out and it's a bit like watching a video.

Participating both as performer and audience allows them to understand the significance of enthusiasm for both, and that the relationship between these two is what creates the success of the experience for both. Also, the impact of live musicians working among them was great:

> The impact of that on the whole school is enormous. One of our feeder middle school heads attributes that sort of experience to the fact that he has increased his music take-up by 50% in the last two years.

If music education is to be predominantly extra-curricula, children will need to be inspired by live events if they are to dedicate their time to it.

Closing thoughts

I look back over what I have written and pause to consider how the themes generated around marketing can be so diverse. I have written at some length about the equal opportunities themes associated with the chief executive's appointment, but what has that to do with marketing? And why do I say relatively little about the successful marketing of most of our gigs?

As I think about this I realise that a unifying theme is about rules. Good equal opportunities policies require access on equal terms to all – yet Carole was unique in providing the experience that was to justify the establishment of JazzAce. Advertising the post would imply that the job was available to others, but it was not. Equal opportunities practice can therefore, like the law, be an ass. Good marketing has rules requiring research to establish what the market wants, yet JazzAce's job was to promote jazz and was therefore product led. Its market however included the various public sector arts officers, promoters and venue owners, and its product varied with each of these groups. A sophisticated marketing portfolio would be required to identify a theoretically thorough approach to each for each group. And in the meantime the things that matter get lost.

I talk throughout this chapter about stakeholders, their range, variety and power in the situations as we experienced it. Orthodox strategic theory places stakeholder analysis at the heart of strategy development in the not-for-profit sector. Except as public relations spin, marketing theory in general does not seem to attend to stakeholders, focusing mainly on the concept of customer. Customers are given the rights of demand, which generates a particular attitude with few responsibilities. Stakeholders attain rights mainly through their responsibilities, whether these are imposed in some way (as with funders) or adopted (as with music enthusiasts).

JazzAce was a very small enterprise, and 100 per cent public-funded. The smallest funders, the councils and the regional arts board, were appointed as watchdogs for the largest, the government and ACE. Their responsibility for public answerability almost overwhelmed the creative and developmental role which was at the heart of JazzAce's work. This creative work was sustained by the passion for jazz of the two staff members and the hours they put in to make the events happen, and the willingness of the volunteer trustees to shoulder a lot of operational and administrative work alongside the full-time staff.

Our opposition to reducing Carole's salary probably did rock the boat of our relations with funders in a way that impacted on us later, as reporting demands grew. We also lived through a transition in espoused theories in the public sector: from internal markets to best value. Under the first we had won in winning the lottery bid, and our role was to fit within the hierarchy of strategies and policies of the various funders. By the time we were half-way through our 3-year funding period, best value demands were being placed on us – for example to benchmark against similar organisations. In our case the proposed comparison was with a dance charitable trust with 10 full-time staff, more extensive funding and a different role. While talking to them was useful, a formal benchmarking would have been very time-consuming, largely meaningless and would divert yet more attention away from jazz itself.

Our most powerful stakeholders therefore were undergoing changes in perspective and adapting their views of us accordingly. Our ongoing failure in marketing was to do with their perception of how things ought to be if we would only do the right things. And while the mechanisms changed, the underlying beliefs were the same: that we could work in a predicted way, planning or emulating success, and by doing that, we could ensure the achievement of specified desirable outcomes. It matters little whether that is termed a strategic plan or a marketing strategy. Satisfying these stakeholders meant complying with these beliefs, at least on paper.

Our gigs and projects worked out quite differently. Carole and her assistant talked to their many contacts in jazz – musicians, promoters, bureaucrats, friends. Carole seemed to be able to evoke unusual relationships among places, themes, jazz styles, and performers and in talking about these, a proposal for some kind of event, whether gig, workshop, festival or composition, would arise and develop. Policies clearly influenced these, through conversations, board meetings and policy documents we had written, but it was in formal reporting that overt links with policy were exploited, to show how the event – what we wanted to do – fitted with strategy – what we were supposed to be doing.

Our marketing of jazz in conventional terms was successful; in the main we reached our audience and 'grew' it. The belief persisted with key groups that our marketing was poor, because we failed to appreciate at first the extent to which it would have to be marketing of ourselves to our funders. Indirectly this meant marketing ourselves to representatives of the arts in the various bureaucracies throughout our region, because they had the ear of the funders. Musicians, educationalists and music teachers that we dealt with were happy with our work. Promoters and music officers were less happy, mainly because they saw us as prospective competitors so were wary, or funders so were disappointed. I think the situation changed for us in JazzAce when themes of conformity and control began to dominate our conversations with funders (with the July meeting mentioned above), and our relationship with them came to be expressed only in formal exchanges, meetings and memos. The public funding bodies were in the throes of learning a new language of control, 'best value', and a period of comfort, familiarity, within the old control discourse was over. Their 'competent use of a given set of rules … founded upon their practiced grasp' of how to work with them to achieve a reasonable state of affairs (Boden, 1994) had been undermined by the imposition of the new rules of 'best value'. The tone of board meetings changed, though we retained our conversational minutes of them. And the contradiction we lived between what we believed we were there for, and what we found ourselves doing became very difficult to hold. The marketing that we did easily to draw in our audiences was one side of this. The reporting we struggled with, our marketing of ourselves to our funders in their terms, was the other. The creative did not get lost, but against all the odds and at great emotional cost to ourselves.

Chapter 7

The theory and practice of visual arts marketing

Ian Fillis

Introduction

The author recently attended two plays in London: *Vincent in Brixton* (Wright, 2002) and *The Shameful Death of Salvador Dali* (Sewell, 2002). The former was a West end production of Van Gogh's early years in London and the latter an avant garde interpretation of Dali's dreams, philosophies and outrageous behaviour. The insight into creativity, use of imagination and innovative marketing obtained by watching these plays was invaluable (Fillis and McAuley, 2000). The art world is full of creativity and yet existing art marketing theory, such as it exists, continues to prescribe formulaic, stepwise processes to art marketers who struggle with their artistic ideals as they attempt to develop a marketing orientation.

This chapter examines visual arts marketing from critical, theoretical and practitioner perspectives. To date, little or no attention has been paid to the philosophical clashes of art for art's sake versus art for business sake when constructing visual arts marketing theory. By understanding how visual arts practitioners creatively combine artistic and business expertise, the marketing researcher can then construct a more appropriate form of marketing theory. The existing theory versus practice gap is in line with other areas within marketing where what is actually carried out does not match the formulated, theorised version; for example, there has been an increasing call for more critical thinking in terms of how successful the marketing concept is in explaining actual behaviour of the firm and the consumer (Brown and Patterson, 2000; Schroeder, 1997, 2000), the smaller firm in domestic and international markets (Fillis, 2001) and, of particular relevant to this chapter, the artist and arts organisation (Butler, 2000; Fillis, 2002a, b; Gainer and Padanyi, 2002; McDonald and Harrison, 2002; Meyer and Even, 1998; Rentschler et al., 2002).

Defining the art world, art and the artist

Calling art an industry has resulted in considerable debate, with some believing that it is no more than an industrial product, while others view it from a semiotic perspective where the art work possesses an aesthetic sign which is culturally defined (Anderson, 1991; Barrere and Santagata, 1999; Parsons, 1987). Panofsky (1940) distinguishes between practical objects which do not demand to be aesthetically consumed, and works of art which do. Both types of product are communication carriers and it is difficult to determine precisely when a communication carrier or utilitarian object becomes art. Baumol (1986) notes that a collector of art looks for aesthetic pleasure in the purchase, as well as, or instead of a financial return. Honig (1998) defines painting as the practice of representation, the finished arte-facts as visual products and paintings as commodities.

Barrere and Santagata (1999) use the sculptor Brancusi and his court case against the Customs Administration in New York in 1927 in order to demonstrate the difficulties of defining art and non-art. His sculpture *Bird in Space* which was to be exhibited in New York caused confusion upon arrival at the port: All art in the US had been exempt from import duty since 1913 but many argued that it was actually a manufactured item and therefore attracted the relevant tariff. Brancusi won his case but this ultimately served as a stimulus to a much wider discussion of defining art. Factors considered at that time included the originality of the art work, whether or not it was hand manufactured, the utilitarian value of the work, as well as consumption related issues.

Defining an artwork as an original can be problematic, as with Duchamp's ready-made objects (Judovitz, 1993: 76):

> ... I had in my studio a bicycle wheel turning for no reason at all. Without even knowing whether I should put it with the rest of my works or call it a work.' Duchamp's interest in the double status of the bicycle wheel suggests that it is this paradox whose potential as a work of art began to intrigue him. Many industrial prototypes are also original pieces but they are not seen as art. Given that the boundaries of art are dynamic and that much contemporary art is temporary in nature and may draw on mass produced technological

factors, then physical originality is often superseded by the original idea and the value of that idea.

Art has been used to describe the representation of the underlying nature of reality, the manifestation of pleasure or emotion and direct intuitive vision (Chartrand, 1990). This last interpretation mirrors the thinking of the author in terms of the importance of understanding how the artist uses their sets of creative competencies to develop and market their art. Chartrand (1984) distinguishes between non-profit and commercial fine arts, considers the role of the amateur artist and notes that the three types are ultimately interrelated: The fine arts are assumed to be a professional activity which serve art for art's sake and are the fountain from which flows the creative waters of artistic expression. The dominant organisational form of production in the fine arts is the individual professional artist, and the non-profit corporation. The commercial arts place profit before professional excellence.

Drawing on the work of Galbraith (1973), Chartrand (1990) views the artist as a risk-taking entrepreneur who is unwilling to conform to organisational thinking. This interpretation matches the author's conceptualisation of the artist as owner/manager of a micro-business. As such, there are a number of shared opportunities and barriers to growth (Fillis, 2000a, b). Hirschman (1983) cites Becker (1978: 864) in distinguishing between the artist and the craftsperson who produces functional products, but his interpretation of craft focuses on the vernacular tradition rather than embracing a wider perspective where contemporary craft objects as art are also part of the sector: A craft consists of a body of knowledge and skill which can be used to produce useful objects. The organisational form is one in which the worker does his work for someone else who defines what is to be done and what the result should be. Artists, conversely, wish to free themselves from the requirement of creating to fulfil others' needs.

Functionality or utilitarianism is often cited as the main differentiator between craft and art, but much contemporary craft is exhibited and sold as art. Becker (1982: 1) also grounds the world of art in a sociological networking context: All artistic work involves the joint activity of a number of people. Through their co-operation, the artwork we eventually see or hear comes to be and continues to be. The existence of art worlds suggests a sociological approach to the arts. It produces an understanding of the complexity of the co-operative networks through which art happens.

The development of the art market

Works of art are economic goods, whose value can be measured by the market, sellers and buyers of art are people trying to obtain the maximum benefit from what they own (Grampp, 1989: 8).

The marketing of art and artists has formed part of art history and practice for centuries and yet it is only now emerging as an avenue for investigation with the discipline of marketing. Honig (1998) identifies the 16th century in Antwerp as an important era in the development of the visual arts market. Understanding of the market mechanism is obtained by examining the Antwerp paintings and the pictorial representation of products, consumers and producers. At this time, painting of the physical marketplace was common and so there is a rich visual source of data from which to draw. Honig (1998) defined the market as the practice of exchange, the site where daily marketing occurs, as well as a wider social notion of commerce and the values it produces. These factors form part of today's formal marketing concept, which can be defined as involving individual and organisational activities which facilitate and expedite satisfying exchange relationships in a dynamic environment through the creation, distribution, promotion and pricing of goods, services and ideas (Dibb et al., 2001: 7). Honig (1998: 3) identifies the emerging role of painting in the wider marketplace in the 1500s: Painting was engaged in constructing new systems of understanding in a world where perception was being reshaped by the values generated by the market in its broadest sense. And through its engagement with the market, painting was constructing its own place within the changing society.

If painting was viewed then as possessing such qualities and impact, then it is a wonder that we are only now beginning to investigate and understand its implications for visual arts marketing theory. Analysis of the expansion of the marketplace through painting offers an understanding unhindered by conventional thinking. The merchant, who was the main handler of the artwork, was viewed as someone with a social conscience, rather than as an individual with a profit orientation (Honig, 1998: 6): Words such as buying and selling scarcely arise in positive discussions of his activities. If by chance he should acquire extra funds, they were of course to be given to the deserving poor.

As market systems became more complex, the social aspect of marketing was superseded by notions which we recognise today as 'shopping'. The growth of painting as a commodity resulted in it being traded domestically and internationally Honig (1998: 13): No longer did artists need to rely upon employment by the court or on commissions; instead their challenge was to produce works that would attract the eye and open the purse of some willing buyer.

Rather than continue to produce art in the conventional manner of the time, the Antwerp artist began to experiment with a variety of styles of expression. The growth in artistic genres was in part in response to demand by the buyer (Honig, 1998: 13–4): The Antwerp painters worked in an entirely unprecedented variety of styles and experimented with new modes of painting. The open market was a place where novelty was demanded by buyers and where competition determined the strategies of sellers.

Honig (1998) acknowledges that the commercialisation of artistic production did not begin in the 16th century and that the 15th century contains many elements of visual arts marketing practice. However, it was the scale of the artistic exchange process and how this was paralleled in the wider marketplace that changed markedly. This in turn impacted upon how people interpreted commodities with consumer necessity being superseded by consumer choice. By painting a marketplace scene, the artwork symbolises the production and marketplace conditions and provides a framework in which to position the transactions taking place (Honig, 1998: 18). Using the artist Pieter Aertsen as an example, Honig (1998) notes that his paintings of the marketplace involve not only visualisations of goods, but that the paintings themselves are commodities.

Montias (1994: 57) describes the mechanisms of the art market in the Netherlands in the Early Modern period (1501–750) and identifies the ways in which the consumer could make choices:

1. direct interaction with artists, who could be employed or given commissions to produce what consumers wanted and
2. the choice consumers made from among the ready-made objects offered by artists ... ; artists ... could hardly overlook these market signals ... Dealers acted as intermediaries ... either employing artists directly or ordering from them works that were readily saleable in the market place.

The art market was ultimately shaped by customer wishes, and the intermediary (Montias, 1994: 69):

... as market relations became more complex, there was an increased demand for the services of intermediaries ... [who] helped bring together artists and consumers ... The intermediary could be an independent dealer buying from established artists and selling to clients. He could also be employed by a patron ... He could also hire artists directly to paint pictures for which he had a demand.

Anderson (1991) understands the philosophical and practical difficulties many artists have with the notion of a market for the artwork but that, in the majority of cases, artists will need to finance their living expenses through their painting or by other means (Throsby and Mills 1989; Throsby, 1994). The key to success is in understanding how the various players interact in the art marketplace. The problem for many artists is that they do not earn a living from their primary artistic activity. Whatever the case, a significant amount of work needs to be done to develop a clear understanding of both the social and economic structure of the cultural sphere, and the place of individual practitioners and consumers within it.

Cowen and Tabarrok (2000) see the choice artists face in marketing their work as between wishing to secure pecuniary, or monetary, benefits from selling to the market or to acquire the non-pecuniary outcomes of following their own tastes in creating what they want. Withers (1985) identifies the importance of understanding the non-pecuniary aspects of an artist's life and the reasons why they enter the industry. The concept of the consumer in art must be reinterpreted to also include the self as producer (Cowen and Tabarrok, 2000).

Non-pecuniary benefits often outweigh any financial returns on artistic endeavour. Even the well-known Renaissance artists Donatello and Michelangelo were prepared to abandon financially rewarding projects if they did not have overall say in how the project developed. Artists either firstly seek artistic fame or financial rewards and this behaviour choice is grounded in early economic trade theory (Cowen and Tabarrok, 2000: 244):

> Adam Smith saw the search for approval as the end of half the labours of human life … Artists therefore pursue artistic styles that are favoured by the most prestigious critics … they pursue high art … artists generally will face a trade-off at the margins between pursuing fame and money … For this reason, they also face trade-offs between pursuing high and low art.

For some working in the art sector, recognition and reputation are more important than selling the artwork. Becker (1982: 352) interprets the concept of reputation:

> Art worlds … routinely make and unmake reputations … They single out … a few works and a few makers of works of special worth. They reward that special worth with esteem and, frequently but not necessarily, in more material ways too. They use reputations, once made, to organise other activities, treating things and people with distinguished reputations differently from others.

This then raises sector specific issues relating to reputation and image where idealism clashes with commercialism. If a gallery exhibits work to a specific narrowly defined audience, overall image and reputation may be just as important as any conventional form of promotion. Word of mouth activity among the artistic community is perceived to be equally important as promoting the gallery to the public.

Art for art's sake, art for business sake and the avant garde

Art for art's sake philosophy is often positioned alongside the notion of the avant garde (Harrison et al., 1998: 37). Victor Cousin (Harrison et al., 1998: 192) is credited with developing the foundations of the doctrine of art for art's sake, or l'art pour l'art, which promotes the belief that art must remain independent from utilitarian, religious or political purpose. Cousin's view is confusing since much avant garde art is grounded in political concepts centred around the manifesto (Caws, 2001). Barrere and Santagata (1999: 35) distinguish art versus market orientation. They highlight praise for the creative over the commercial depicting the artist as indifferent to commercial success. The notion of the avant garde focuses on the ability of those artistic individuals and groups who attempt to change societal thinking (Harrison et al., 1998). The avant garde utilises creativity to shape future thinking and practice, while also having a central role in defining culture Chartrand (1984). Examining the differences between financial and non-financial returns helps to explain the reasons and motivations behind popular and avant garde artistic production (Cowen and Tabbarrok, 2000). The market disciplines and forces the artist to pay a price for producing the art most desired. Artists typically feel that market incentives lower the quality of art.

Art for art's sake orientation is seen as a 'romantic attitude' by Belk and Groves (1999), but this philosophy has shaped and given direction to the art world and its history for hundreds of years. Gustave Courbet (Harrison et al., 1998) dismisses the notion of the avant garde, instead drawing on the importance of individuality mixed with tradition. Proudhon (Harrison, 1998: 407) is also critical of the avant garde stance, believing that it results in the separation of intuition from reason. Instead, art is viewed as having a much wider impact on the self and on society than previously imagined. Diego Rivera (Harrison and Wood, 2000: 405) views the art for art's sake philosophical stance as elitist, calling it the typical theory of 19th century bourgeois esthetic criticism. Rivera also raises purchasing and consumption issues which are of particular interest to the marketer and uses the term in connection with the over-riding artistic rather than business orientation in visual arts organisations:

> ... this theory serves to discredit the use of art as a revolutionary weapon and serves to affirm that all art which has a theme ... is bad art. It serves ... to make art into a kind of stock exchange commodity ... bought and sold on the stock exchange, subject to the speculative rise and fall which any commercialised thing is subject to.

This interpretation is somewhat at odds with the author's thinking. Avant garde art can be viewed as challenging the boundaries of convention, and therefore a potential strategic weapon for change in the industry. The lesson for visual art marketers is to use their creative, entrepreneurial marketing competencies in order to establish competitive advantage in the crowded marketplace. Avant garde status does not necessarily mean that popularity and financial rewards are minimised. In fact, art history is full of examples of one-time avant garde artists who, through their creative entrepreneurial marketing activities, attract a following and create success and market demand in the longer term.

Visual arts marketing theory and practice

Artists' principal reservations towards marketing are mainly due to their reluctance to make concessions to consumers' expectations. In their view, this cannot and must not be part of product policy. The artist can adopt a marketing approach by defining himself as a target group and thereby improving the creative process of fulfilling his personal, artistic expectations (Meyer and Even, 1998: 282).

The height of research into marketing the fine and performing arts in the USA was in the late 1970s (Thomas and Cutler, 1993). However, this is a growing area in the UK and Europe, with the recent formation of the Academy of Marketing Special Interest Group in Arts and Heritage Marketing and a special edition of the International Journal of Non-profit and Voluntary Sector Marketing dedicated to arts and cultural marketing in 2002. The author has investigated the use of the promotional mix by both non-profit and for profit visual art organisations in Glasgow, Dublin and Northern Ireland (Fillis, 1993). At that time, the number of academic art marketing publications was minimal, with little attempt to apply marketing beyond the $n \times p$ perspective to a more critical approach which accounts for the art for art's sake and avant garde factors (Hunt, 1976; Kotler, 1979; Shapiro, 1973). One of the key findings of the study was that in terms of marketing competencies at the organisational level, few galleries had progressed beyond the 'marketing as advertising/promotion' stage, with many tasks being carried out intuitively with little planning. Those formal marketing roles, which had become established, were derived from the publicity or public relations function.

Today, it is optimistic to suggest that the state of critical knowledge has improved while the practice of marketing beyond advertising/promotion has expanded within the visual arts industry. Thomas and Cutler (1993) identify only 31 articles in mainstream marketing journals spanning a 20-year period focusing on fine and performing arts. None of these articles offer a critical perspective on visual arts marketing but instead focus on audience analysis and segmentation, marketing mix issues and marketing planning and policy issues. Bates (1983), for example, investigated the market mechanisms used to develop international sales for oil paintings, concluding that there was a lack of research in the area, coupled with poor statistical information. They found it puzzling that there was a dearth of material, given the growing interest in non-profit organisations generally. However, visual arts marketing occurs in the profit sector also and therefore the lack of research is even more intriguing. Holbrook (1980) was surprised by the lack of studies of high involvement artistic consumption compared with low involvement behaviour. Bourgeon-Renault (2000: 4) notes that the consumption of cultural products involves a much higher degree of subjectivity than any other product type. Unlike consumer behaviour studies in mainstream marketing where customer orientation is central to marketing practice, artistic consumption centres around the artist and the product. Each time a painting is 'consumed' by a different observer, a different subjective experience occurs. The meaning assigned to the painting changes, although its physical composition remains constant. Ultimately, each cultural consumer obtains a unique set of intellectual and emotional reactions from the experience.

Andreasen (1985: 11) confuses product- and artist-centred marketing (Fillis, 2002a; Hirschman, 1983) with a selling orientation:

> the selling orientation ... starts with the product or service ... consumers ... will ordinarily not buy enough of the organisation's products. The organisation must therefore undertake an aggressive selling and promotion effort ... marketing is ... the task of persuading people to do things they might not otherwise do. This is a definition of marketing that is a very comfortable one for most arts administrators to adopt.

Creative visual arts marketing puts the artist and the product at the forefront of planning, unlike conventional marketing activities centred around the customer. Andreasen's (1985) assertions that art marketers must be committed to reaching consumers on their terms, not the organisation's, and that conventional marketing is the best way to develop interest, are fundamentally flawed. They take no account of the strong art for art's sake and avant garde philosophies which prevail across the sector and which can result in profitable outcomes.

Several researchers offer alternative conceptualisations of the adoption and practice of marketing in the visual arts beyond the formalised, prescribed approaches of the textbook. Jyrama (2002) adopts an integrated institutional, network and sociological approach to examining contemporary art galleries and their publics. The artistic creativity found within the network relates to the shared interest in art and also relates to common beliefs, norms and values. Existing visual arts marketing theory does not acknowledge the contribution of innovation and creativity in formulating more appropriate and actionable forms of marketing, despite the very industry it claims to fit being full of creativity and innovative thinking.

Hirschman (1983: 46) suggests that the marketing concept does not match the behaviour and philosophy of the artist as a producer of products because of the personal values and the social norms which impact on the production process:

> ... artists ... do not bring forth products according to ... the marketing concept [which] holds that products should be created in response to the ... desires/interests of their consuming public ... creators of aesthetic ... products frequently exhibit exactly the opposite pattern. An artist ... may first create a product that flows from his or her own internal desires ... and then present this product to consumers who choose to either accept or reject it.

Artists create mainly to express their subjective conceptions of beauty, emotion or some other aesthetic ideal (Becker, 1978; Holbrook, 1981). Aesthetic creativity is the central influence in the process, rather than responding to customer demand (Hirschman, 1983: 46; Holbrook and Zirlin, 1983): Typically, the artist is motivated by the need to achieve self-fulfilment via his/her creativity. That is, the creative process itself is intrinsically satisfying. Artists differ from creators of utilitarian products in that their creativity is valued for its expressive qualities and not strictly its functional utility or technical competence.

Hirschman identifies three possible audiences for the creative producer: The wider public at large; peers and industry professionals; and the self. Hirschman distinguishes between artistic and commercial creativity, since the values of the individual will ultimately determine creative orientation. These differences can be compared similarly to the philosophies of art for art's sake versus art for business sake. Byron (1981) believes that, because there may be little overlap with consumer wishes, artistic products may fail commercially but there are certainly high failure rates at product and business level in industries which do follow marketing orientation. Hirschman (1983: 48) considers the implications of adopting a product-centred marketing approach where self-oriented creativity dominates behaviour:

> Self-oriented artists ... do not purposely design products that are at odds with peer and mass market consumer values ... [they] create to communicate a personal vision ... they follow their own inclinations ... [they] hope to achieve peer and mass audience approval of their products ... they believe that by creating something that vividly expresses their values and emotions, the audience will be moved to accept their perspective.

Hirschman (1983: 49) considers altering the marketing concept in order to incorporate self-oriented creativity and a wider variety of audiences where the artist/creator is seen as the initial consumer, with exchange relationships occurring internally. Within this view, marketing exchanges include transactions that are initiated on a producer as consumer basis and then extended to multiparticipant exchanges, as the creator makes his/her product available to others. Meyer and Even (1998: 271) critique Hirschman's interpretation of the limitations of the marketing concept in describing how artists develop their work. They believe that art is not just a matter of the artist's creativity, but is also related to how the work is received once it is completed. The notion of reception is intertwined with interpretation and realisation (Eco, 1977) and is distinct from other types of products and services:

> The usual separation of manufacturer and consumer is ... not applicable to artworks. It is replaced by a unique form of collaboration ... that ... includes all those involved in activities – from the inception of an idea to the public

reception thereof – carried out according to a certain pattern of rules and practices – mutually attuned to the production, distribution and reception of works of art.

Within the network of forces impacting on the artwork, the gallery owner is seen as having an important part to play, with interpretation and mediation impacting on the process of converting art into product. Other contributing factors include the way in which the art product is exhibited and the amount of recognition given by critics in terms of style, quality and suggested interpretation. The exchange process within peer-oriented creativity identified by Hirschman is viewed as a type of non-profit marketing by Meyer and Even. This seems to fit, but the notion that the artist is actually a non-profit organisation (Loock, 1988) is a state of abstraction taken too far. The author does view the artist as an organisation, but mainly within the realms of the micro-enterprise where the majority of such businesses are operated by one or two people at most. Profit is an important element which must be incorporated in any conceptualisation of the process: This can be in monetary terms or in the more intangible form of fame and reputation. Meyer and Even (1998: 273–4) suggest that product-centred entrepreneurial creativity is really what occurs:

> ... the artist does not find products for the customer, but seeks customers for his products ... art becomes a traded good once it is brought to the marketplace which, however, may not be the objective during the process of creation ... the contemporary artist would assume the role of a financially dependent innovator and entrepreneur ...

Butler (2000: 344) also critiques the limitations of the marketing concept, noting that conventional arts marketing texts tend to promote the adoption of the marketing mix approach to 'doing arts marketing' which is of limited use to the arts marketing practitioner:

> ... they tend to outline ... why arts marketing is different from consumer goods marketing, and then proceed through the standard series of textbook marketing topics ... What is required is a more advanced model or representation of the arts that would enlighten marketers already au fait with marketing theory and practice, but with limited knowledge of that business or context.

Butler (2000: 355, 359) also discusses the merits of product-centred marketing and notes that the discovery of new art conveys the notion of something much more than development:

> ... artists feel they must shun the notion of following ... artists are the ultimate manifestation of that absolute insult in the marketing schoolyard, namely

the 'product orientation'. But their internal focus … is what makes them artists … This may not be anti-marketing though.

Botti (2000) analyses the role of marketing in the process of artistic consumption and the spreading of artistic value among the various interested publics. This diffusion of value is seen as a result of the interaction of product-centred and consumer-centred perspectives. Botti believes that marketing only becomes involved in the process once the artwork has been produced. This mirrors the conventional marketing concept where communication, publicity and public relations are traditionally seen as assisting the arts marketer to develop sales and inform audiences. However, marketing begins at the initial construction of the artistic idea. Understanding how creativity interacts with entrepreneurial marketing behaviour is the gateway to understanding marketing's role in art. The artist should be viewed as the owner/manager of the art product, where internal marketing processes have been operating long before the artwork is produced. Creative marketing behaviour is ultimately driven by a set of competencies linked to the personality of the individual artist. Subsequent construction of visual arts marketing theory must therefore consider and incorporate these factors. Given the existence of the two competing schools of thought (art for art's sake and art for business sake), the continual promotion of customer orientation in art marketing is surely futile. The author's research identifies artists who have successfully followed the former orientation and, by exploiting their inner creative entrepreneurial marketing competencies, development of consumer interest and market development will follow naturally. So product-centred marketing can and does create demand and profitability over time. Also, if fame and celebrity status are part of the aspirations of the artist, then exploitation of a unique set of product-centred competencies will result in competitive advantage.

If artists always responded to the wishes of the marketplace, there would never be any meaningful progression of artistic thinking, new schools of thought, movements and development of theory. Evrard (1991) notes the importance of understanding the inner personality of the artist and how this affects the process of artistic creation. The role of marketing involves locating a public for the art-work, rather than in following market demand. Analysing the creative behaviour of entrepreneurial artists results in the identification of sets of key characteristics which are central to successful performance. Although it is unlikely that the majority of art organisations will be able to reach such creative heights as those reached by Picasso and Dali, there are valuable lessons contained in their oeuvre, and their everyday lives, practices and philosophies which can then be readily translated into actionable visual arts marketing theory. Marketing gurus such as Kotler and Hunt are now calling for more creative ways of interpreting marketing and deriving more meaningful theory. By investigating biographical evidence of visual artists and their artwork, this creative process produces additional data from which to construct more appropriate art marketing theory.

The biography of the artist as source for visual arts marketing theory

Since artists and the works of art they create often consist of intangible factors and abstract concepts, they do not lend themselves well to conventional marketing research procedures. The author recognises this and has promoted the use of alternative, more creative modes of enquiry such as the adoption of the marketing/entrepreneurship paradigm of investigation (Carson and Coviello, 1996; Hackley and Mumby-Croft, 1999), and more particularly, the biography and other historical methods in order to better understand how the artist as creator and owner/manager achieves success (Fillis and Herman, 2003). The artist is the central biographical subject where facts can be collated from a range of primary and secondary sources (Carson and Carson, 1998) and then combined with conventional marketing thinking in order to construct a more appropriate visual arts marketing theory. These may include a documented or filmed interview with the artist or their paintings, journals, diaries, correspondence, autobiography and biography. Evidence can be grouped into a number of clusters including the written record (e.g. biographies, memoirs, diaries), artistic elements (e.g. portraits, sculptures, films, photographs) and relics (e.g. letters, public documents, receipts). One criticism of the biographical technique is that the author may bias the process by writing an over exuberant, idealised version of the truth (hagiography). However, bias also occurs in other, much more common management research techniques (Gill and Johnson, 1991).

The artistic biography is not a recent phenomenon. The earliest artistic biographies related to artists as gods. The reason behind this elevated thinking was that art was thought to be divinely inspired. In ancient Greece, when artists respected the gods and acknowledged them as sources of artistic inspiration, they were allowed to pursue their creativity. Early accounts of artists and their patrons appeared in Ovid's 'Metamorphoses' and Pliny's 'Natural History' where the artist Zeuxis adopted an early form of advertising, helping to promote his value as an artist (Barolsky, 1995). In 1550 the first meaningful artistic biography appeared. Giorgio Vasari's 'Lives of the Artists' was commissioned by Bishop Paolo Giovio in an attempt to record a 'Who's Who' in the arts (Vasari, 1998). Vasari's biographical work was constructed without the aid of written reference materials, relying mainly on oral accounts. Therefore some mistakes were inevitable but as a major biographical work, it is not disputed. Since the Renaissance, the artistic biography has grown to include a number of related genres, from short anecdotal commentaries, autobiographies, notebooks, poetry, memoirs, journals, letters, fictional biographies to multimedia output such as videos of artists at work, taped interviews, film biographies and use of the Internet to disseminate pertinent information.

The following section focuses on the examination of Vincent Van Gogh, Salvador Dali and Andy Warhol as creative, entrepreneurial art marketers. Biographical evidence of how they established new ways of thinking and, to varying degrees, created demand for their products, is then incorporated in a framework of visual arts marketing theory.

The passion of Vincent Van Gogh

An in-depth appreciation of the artist's daily thoughts and deeds can be readily gained from the incredible amount of communication by letter between himself and his brother Theo (Hanson and Hanson, 1955; Roskill, 1967; Sweetman, 1990). However, a more creative insight is obtained by examining the play which the author recently attended (Wright, 2002). Although artistic license has been used in the writing of the play, much of the source material is drawn from an accurate account by Bailey (1990) of Van Gogh's time in London. His early attempts at drawing reveal insecurity and lack of conviction, which are later to be overcome by his artistic passion and directness (Wright, 2002: 18–9):

> VINCENT … Some months ago I did a sketch of my room to send to my parents. They thought it was good … the urge to draw is curbed by modesty. One of my uncles has a fine collection … I've seen at his house, originals by … Hals and Rembrandt. With such magnificence in the world, what is the point of adding one's own pathetic scribblings? …

Wright (2002: 23–4) uses the imagery of a chair, later to become a well-known Van Gogh visual cue, to convey the notion of identity and reputation of the individual as creator:

> VINCENT … at Goupil and Company we sell a copy of a drawing which was done in Broadstairs. It's the chair in which Charles Dickens wrote David Copperfield … and The Old Curiosity Shop … It's called 'The Empty Chair'. That is all you notice in the picture. Just the chair. But when you look, you see the character of the man who sat in it …

A picture is formed of constructs a picture of how Van Gogh may have thought about his early technique as a mixture of convention and experimentation (Wright, 2002: 44–5):

> VINCENT … This is the one I like … That's a kind of ditch we have at the side of a field to drain the water away … I'd been reading a book about perspective.

Thinking, oh, who cares about ridiculous old-fashioned nonsense? Then I saw this line of trees, so I thought I'd follow the rules for once, and guess what happened? It worked!

Van Gogh's passion is central to his artwork and without this energetic input, his paintings would lack meaning Wright (2002: 57–8):

URSULA ... you told about the way you felt that day ... all that fury, all that anger and confusion ... and I looked at the drawing again and I couldn't see any of that. That was the most important thing that was happening at that moment, and you left it out.

Van Gogh adopted a novel and adventurous approach in his painting which won few admirers outside his own social and artistic circles, yet he still persisted with his individual style. His use of strong brushstrokes differentiated his work from others by indicating his desire, motivation and ambition (Ehrenzweig, 1970). As his interest in painting developed, Van Gogh became aware of an avant garde group of artists working in Barbizon, near Paris (Adams, 1997). They held a particular interest in nature and painting en plein air. In line with other emerging groups of nature painters at that time, the Barbizon group had rejected the classical and religious subjects promoted and exhibited by the art establishment of The Salon. Van Gogh's main influencers included the artists Millet and Mauve (Murphy, 1999) and this motivated him to pursue new ways of seeing and embracing alternative concepts. There are a number of lessons to be learned, one of which must be his never-ceasing drive and self-belief.

The ambition of Salvador Dali

Salvador Dali is one of the greatest self-publicising marketers of all time, an ability which allowed him to grow into a commercial success through his art and other forms of creative production. An analysis of his characteristics reveals the notion of acute observation and seeing what others cannot see. This ability to identify and exploit new opportunities resulted in a competitive advantage which he used in his efforts to move his painting forward and profit from creating demand for his art. An example of Dali's unconventionality was in his early interest in the practice of automatic expression, later adopted by the Surrealists (Dali, 1993). There are also a number of lessons to be taken from Dali's sense of ambition: 'At the age of six I wanted to be a cook. At seven I wanted to be Napoleon. And my ambition has been growing steadily ever since' (Dali, 1993: 1).

Obviously not content with the status quo, Dali continually pushed the boundaries of convention as he searched for new challenges. He was a successful risk taker and was also very good at shaping and evaluating the market and predicting future directions of consumer demand (Ades, 1988; Dali, 1993; Gibson, 1997). Graham (1997) observes that Dali was perhaps the best known of the Surrealists, deliberately interpreting reality and dreams in a way never seen before in order to court controversy and then revel in the publicity received. Graham (1997: 95) summarises Dali's approach: 'Dali creates an alternative experience rather than capturing the visual in our normal experience, and at the same time his creations can be seen to be explorations of that experience'.

Dali was careful to build up a network of patrons throughout his life to ensure a steady income. He used such technological inventions of the 20th century such as film and television in order to generate publicity and ensure that his reputation continued to grow. An example of his joint work with Louis Bunuel, the Surrealist film-maker, Un Chien Andalou, is still viewed by many today as groundbreaking and challenging of existing thought and practice (Evans, 1995). Dali's wider competencies outside painting included the creation of the dream sequence in Hitchcock's film Spellbound (Condon and Sangster, 1999), designing jewellery, furniture and a lobster-shaped telephone. Another example of Dali the self-publicist and commodifier can be seen his setting up of the Dali Museum in Figueres, with members of his own Dali Foundation employed to manage it. Ultimately, Dali exploited his artistic and business competencies very successfully in order to create demand and maintain patron loyalty in the longer term (Gill, 2001).

The commercial success of Andy Warhol

Warhol successfully differentiated himself from other creative practitioners, attracting individuals who were drawn by his ability to successfully differentiate his artistic message from the crowded marketplace (Warhol, 1975). His 'pop art' was strategically developed to exploit a consumer counter culture, in a deliberate attempt to deviate from established and accepted codes of behaviour. On the one hand rejecting mass production and mass consumerism, and on the other using multiple production techniques such as the silk screen process, Warhol combined these skills with his marketing competencies gained from working in the advertising industry in order to generate large amounts of self-publicity. His eccentric personality and creative ability resulted in an offer by a company, not to buy his work, but to instead purchase his 'aura'. Warhol believed in the merits of manoeuvring his 'freelancers' into 'superstars' or 'hyperstars' with difficult to market skills. Over time, this awkwardness in the marketplace then served to stimulate demand for the artistic product. Over 30 years later, this status can be compared similarly to the approach adopted by Charles Saatchi and his Young British Artists (Barnbrook, 1998).

Warhol developed a particular form of marketing philosophy derived from his observations in 1960s New York, an era in which bad taste abounded among the expanding consumerist society. Rather than attempting to compete openly in the mass market, he thought that it was sometimes preferable to examine the reasons behind why some products are badly produced. In doing so, niche market opportunities are created, turning bad practice into good by targeting the alternative consumer. Warhol also provides an insight into the type of employee preferred in his business. Ideally the individual should exhibit some degree of misunderstanding of Warhol's philosophy, not major discrepancies, but certainly a small level of misinterpretation. During the communication process, the ideas expressed by the other individual sometimes interacted with his own in order to create a unique solution to the problem so that: 'when working with people who misunderstand you, instead of getting transmissions, you get transmutations, and that's much more interesting in the long run' (Warhol, 1975: 99).

Warhol (1975: 92) also encouraged the proactive interaction of artistic creativity and entrepreneurial business practice, successfully mixing the art for art's sake and art for business sake philosophies:

> Business art is the step that comes after art. I started as a commercial artist, and I want to finish as a business artist ... Being good in business is the most fascinating kind of art ... making money is art and working is art and good business is the best art.

Warhol used naked, overt imagery in order to convey his artistic message. A further insight into Warhol's philosophy is shown in the way in which he survived financially while working on shoe drawings for magazines. Since payment was based on each drawing, he counted up each individual drawing, working out how much he would then get paid. This suggests that, at least during this period, he was living on a day-to-day, down-to-earth basis with not much security. He prescribes this practice for every creative practitioner (Warhol, 1975: 86) where '... an artist should count up his pictures so you always know exactly what you're worth, and you don't get stuck thinking your product is you and your fame, and your aura'.

Recommendations for visual arts marketing theory and practice

Critical examination of the literature has identified the need for the development and incorporation of creativity, imagination, innovation and insight as core visual arts marketing competencies. The formulaic, linear, prescriptive form of marketing clashes with the creative, often avant garde nature of the visual arts. At the moment, there is a wide theory versus practice gap, which fails to account for the art for art's sake philosophy which is often at odds with the art for business sake thrust of marketing orientation. Defining the visual arts industry has shown that there are non-profit and for profit factors which must be considered when attempting to practice marketing; for example, non-profit dimensions range from publicly funded art museum issues to the fact that many artists view their art as an extension of the self, where marketing begins from the initial conception of the idea to the construction of a market for the product.

Historically, the marketing concept did fit the art market with rich patrons commissioning the artist on their terms but today artists are also seen as consumers of the art work as they produce art on their own terms. Consumption of art differs from many other products, with aesthetic pleasure playing a large part of the process. Art is seen as a communication carrier of a variety of qualitative, intangible messages which conventional marketing frameworks cannot interpret. Another differentiating factor between the visual arts and other market sectors is that art as product has little or no functional or utilitarian value. Some commentators frame the development of the art market in economic terms and differentiate between the pecuniary, or monetary, benefits of being an artist, with reputation, fame and image sometimes seen as more important than financial returns. There is a close link between artistic practice and entrepreneurial thinking, with some commentators, including the author, linking art with intuitive vision and visualising the artist as a risk taking entrepreneur or owner/manager. It is important to realise that art continually impacts on society and changes the way in which we think. This being the case, then art should impact on how marketing is practised and theorised. Avant garde art has continually challenged convention: Avant garde visual arts marketing should be used to challenge conventional marketing which continues to be applied to the art sector. There is still a lack of research on art marketing, and a severe lack of critical research, which seeks to promote and construct alternative methods. New art marketing theory needs to be constructed around the following: The realisation that the artist and the artwork are the focus of consumption, and not the conventional consumer as modelled in marketing frameworks; a variety of internal, qualitative, intangible exchange relationships occur within the persona of the artist as creator and marketer and that these cannot be interpreted using conventional marketing research techniques; future art marketing research should focus on the product-centred nature of entrepreneurial creativity where the personality, attitudes, beliefs and behaviour of the artist as owner/manager are central to 'doing visual arts marketing'. Future research should focus on alternative methodologies such as the biography as a stimulus for uncovering the realties of art marketing in practice and in constructing more actionable theory.

Marketing has had a number of set rules and regulations, embedded ultimately under the guise of formal marketing planning and strategy (MacDonald, 1999; Wensley, 1999), but which are today sometimes deemed no longer relevant or useful in their current form (Carson et al., 1995; Gummesson, 2002). Those working in art management can take valuable lessons from those artists whose work they exhibit. Confidence, motivation to succeed and the ability to express industry specific viewpoints can ultimately influence the way in which marketing is practised in the sector. Much in the same way as avant garde artists have been able to theorise about and then implement creative, entrepreneurial marketing practices, visual arts managers should be encouraged and enabled to derive a more appropriate brand of marketing within the sector. Instead of continuing to manage in a curatorial way, with little creative marketing input, art marketers should adopt a proactive stance, challenging established practices, when needed, in order to identify alternative and more appropriate mechanisms and processes within which to develop creative marketing. The philosophical clash of 'art for arts sake' versus 'art for business sake' should not be viewed as an inhibitor of visual arts marketing progress, but rather as a catalyst for creative change. Instead of perceiving philosophical clashes as problematical, they should instead be viewed as opportunities for developing new solutions, feeding into a more meaningful and appropriate theory and practice of art marketing.

Following in the footsteps of the Surrealists and the Italian Futurists, the author has formulated a statement, or proclamation, of how to achieve creative visual arts marketing in response to the often ineffective, conventional formalised marketing as prescribed in textbooks. This statement takes into account the art for art's sake philosophy and the avant garde thinking in the visual arts.

A proclamation of visual arts marketing

- Visual arts marketers must foster an environment where self-belief is encouraged and sharing opinions and developing alternative values are used to shape future thinking.
- Visual arts marketers should exploit new ideas and innovative thought and practice as a response to prescribed, formalised ways of 'doing' marketing.
- Instead of attempting to preserve existing working conditions and patterns, the visual arts marketer should encourage change and work with it, rather than against it.
- Creative entrepreneurial marketing should be promoted as the alternative, more effective response to customer-centred marketing.
- Creative entrepreneurial marketing should be visualised as a strategic choice in a similar fashion to existing marketing strategies.
- Creative visual arts marketing should be seen as a new school of marketing thought.

- Challenging conventional thinking should be continually encouraged if existing marketing practices are viewed as ineffective.
- Visual arts marketers should utilise creative clashes of ideas to stimulate future thinking.
- Visual arts marketing researchers should utilise alternative sources of data to help construct a more meaningful framework of visual arts marketing.

Acknowledgements

I would like to dedicate this chapter to Adelina who rekindled my interest in art, as well as to my mother and to my late father. And to Vincent and Salvador!

Chapter 8

Museum marketing: understanding different types of audiences

Ruth Rentschler

Introduction

This chapter examines the relationship that museums have developed with their audiences, and undertakes a brief history of the development of that role. It draws examples from museum marketing in four Commonwealth countries: the UK, Australia, New Zealand and Canada, which have a similar history and funding approach. One of the most serious issues facing museum marketers today is the erosion in the proportion of revenue provided by government, which needs to be supplemented by audience revenue and giving from individuals and trusts. This tripartite funding model – government, audience and 'sponsor' income – is essential to museum sustainability. The erosion of government income gives marketing a boost, as it becomes an important tool for helping to fill the funding gap left by declining government revenue. This chapter contributes to understanding the relative value of different types of audiences to museums. Audiences are important, especially when government support is reduced and the arts are both pressured to be more business-like and more attune to the needs of diverse audiences.

The last two decades have seen considerable debate and significant change in museums. First, there is a shift in government attitudes to funding, access and diversity or distinctiveness, which led to a need for increased marketing in museums. Second, there is a shift in interest from the individual artist to the industry, which in the mid-1990s led to recognition of the importance of new marketing approaches for the development of museums (McLean, 1995). Government initiatives have encouraged creative industries development, with a shift in focus to the importance of marketing for artistic success and sustainability (Johanson and Rentschler, 2002). Creative industries demonstrate a move away from 'art for art's sake' and towards an acceptance of the economic, social and aesthetic value of culture, where the arts are treated 'as ingredients in a new cultural mix' (Volkerling, 2001). While specific categories vary slightly from country to country, creative industries embrace activities which have individual creativity, skill and talent as their origin as well as the potential for job and wealth creation through the generation and exploitation of intellectual property (Volkerling, 2001). In general, creative industries incorporate categories that embrace literature, multimedia, music, broadcasting, films, computer games, and even extend to craft, fashion and town planning, as well as including the traditional performing arts and museums. Museums are placed as part of this larger industry mix, which has been controversial. Some see the new industries model as giving museums more political clout in the wider framework. Others see the model as a betrayal of the hegemony museums held in the high arts, where economic values are seen to outweigh intrinsic cultural value.

Despite these initiatives, evidence shows that audience numbers are declining in some museums (Museum of Victoria annual reports, 1997–2002). With the threat of Disney-style theme shows and blockbusters, the need to review museum approaches to marketing is urgent (McLean, 1995). Museums are exhorted to adopt audience techniques that are related to the accountability factor. The key is striking the right balance between finding new audiences and nurturing existing ones. This chapter offers three perspectives on marketing for museums that present a solution to these issues. The first perspective is evident in the arts marketing literature, where it was demonstrated that marketing as a concept has only been considered in the last 20 years maximum and has undergone a change in orientation from a product focus to an audience focus in that time. Scant attention has been paid to segmenting audiences beyond 'goers' and 'non-goers' in the literature examined. The second perspective links museum viability to government policy: that less money is available in government coffers for each museum and that commercial approaches to generating income need to be undertaken. Despite this economic pressure, museums also recognise the social requirement to ensure access to audiences across the community. This third perspective is of crucial concern to museums. Traditionally they have focused energy and effort on development of their product to the exclusion of development of their customer base and audience activities. This approach is rapidly changing. Improved audience research is seen as an opportunity to increase long-term museum viability, and to enable them to meet social and economic obligations.

Museums need to rely more heavily on marketing in this climate. Understanding audiences is an important part of museum marketing. Audiences are analysed using audience studies. DiMaggio et al. (1978), Thomas and Cutler (1993), Kawashima (1998) and Rentschler (1998, 2002) have all reviewed audience studies in museums. Their work showed overwhelmingly that audiences were well-educated, professional and predominantly white. While these studies were conducted over several decades, during which significant demographic shifts have occurred in the population, there has been no change in the profile of museum audiences. This fact has lead those interested in audience research in museums to conclude that there is one audience for museums. These reviews indicate that audience studies have rarely segmented audiences. Most audience studies compare users and non-users, with a small number of studies more recently researching audience diversity (Bennett and Frow, 1991; Robertson and Miglorino, 1996). Because of the demographic homogeneity of museum audiences, it has become politically necessary for governments to insist that non-profit organisations which receive at least part of their income from government, try to broaden their audiences. However, the relational marketing needs of the organisation may not align with this social and economic imperative. How can non-profit museums both meet their social and economic marketing needs? If most studies treat audiences as one audience, despite the plethora of audience studies, what knowledge of audiences are museum marketers lacking?

Museums defined

This chapter discusses museums and argues that they have changed. 'Museum' derives from the classical Greek word 'museion', a place of contemplation, a philosophical institution or a temple of the muses (Lewis, 1992; Murphy, 1993; Piggott Report, 1975). The first recorded instance of the use of the word 'museum' to describe a collection relates to the de Medici material at the time of Lorenzo il Magnifico (1449–92) (Lewis, 1992).

The word 'museum' is chosen in this chapter in preference to the word 'gallery'. This choice is in accord with the international preferred usage of the word and a sense of change (Murphy, 1993). Non-profit museums can no longer remain static places of contemplation, tied to attitudes opposed to a general diffusion of knowledge. In considering the change in meaning of 'museum', it is contended that it applies equally to 'art museum' and that the term 'museum' refers to those organisations which operate *both* as a museum and art museum (Australia Council, 1990, 1991, 1992, 1993, 1994, 1995; Hancocks, 1987; Hendon, 1979). Museums hold art works in their collections. Museums and art museums combined hold art works and other objects in their collections. The approach taken in this chapter is supported by the Piggott Report (1975: 16) which states:

> the border between the themes of an art museum and a general museum is often blurred ... [which] encourages us to see these institutions as variations of the one species.

Museums have traditionally been defined by function rather than by purpose (Thompson, 1998; Weil, 1990). Functional definitions relate to activities performed in the museum and are object-based: to collect, preserve and display objects. More recently, there has been a shift in definitions. Purposive definitions now relate to the intent, vision or mission of the museum where the focus is on leadership and visitor services: to serve society and its development by means of study, education and enjoyment (Besterman, 1998). These definitions are illustrated in Figure 8.1.

As museums themselves are changing to meet the needs of a changing world, so too important concepts change. Change has led to an increased interest in researching museums and to a reappraisal of their purpose, evident in the changing definition of the word 'museum'. The change in definition has been gradual and has been influenced by prevailing social and philosophical attitudes.

Noble's (1970) five basic responsibilities of a museum represent a groundbreaking definition that has proved enormously useful as an evaluative tool for judging a museum's functions (Weil, 1990a). The functions (acquisition,

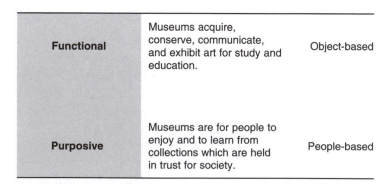

Figure 8.1 Shift in museum definitions.

conservation, study, interpretation and exhibition) form an entity. Noble stated:

> they are like the five fingers of a hand, each independent but united for common purpose. If a museum omits or slights any of these five responsibilities, it has handicapped itself immeasurably.
>
> (Noble, 1970: 20)

More recently, Noble's definition has been organised around three principles:

> to preserve (to collect is viewed as simply an early step in that process), to study (a function that remains unchanged) and to communicate (this third function being a combination of Noble's final two, i.e. to interpret and to exhibit).
>
> (Weil, 1990: 58)

The American Association of Museums' definition is in similar vein:

> … [a museum is] an organised and permanent nonprofit institution, essentially educational or aesthetic in purpose, with professional staff which owns and utilises tangible objects, cares for them and exhibits them to the public on some regular schedule.
>
> (Weil, 1990: 45)

In the 1990s the discussion of definitions introduces a new point of emphasis. The emphasis shifts from objects to leadership and visitor services (in the service of society and of its development) which has particular relevance to this chapter. The International Council of Museums (1995) definition establishes the pattern:

> A museum is a nonprofit making, permanent institution in the service of society and of its development, and open to the public, which acquires, conserves, researches, communicates and exhibits, for purposes of study, education and enjoyment, material evidence of people and their environment.
>
> (International Council of Museums, 1995: 3)

Besterman (1998) develops the pattern, clearly putting people first in the *draft* definition of museums for the Museums Association in the UK:

> Museums are for people to explore and learn from collections for understanding and inspiration. To do this, a museum collects, safeguards, researches, develops, makes accessible and interprets collections and associated information, which it holds in trust for society.
>
> (Besterman, 1998: 37)

More recently, the Museums Association (UK) definition of museums enhances the point about the transformation of museum definitions from functional to purposive: 'museums enable people to explore collections for inspiration, learning and enjoyment' (2002).

The increasing recognition in this definition of people, society and the contextual pressures impacting on museums, raises important questions concerning the museum's audiences. The order in which attributes appear in museum definitions reflects the development of the museum's role from an inwardly-focused concentration of resources, to an outwardly-focused distribution and dispersal of resources to the community, to audiences and to the wider public (Besterman, 1998; Murphy, 1993; Weil, 1994). The common ground of all definitions is that they consider the collection central to the museum's function. However, more recent definitions focus increasingly on museum leadership and the importance of visitor services. Further, they focus on the non-profit nature of the organisation.

Museum marketing then and now

It was not so long ago that Alan Andreasen in the *Journal of Arts Management and Law* wrote about the confusion in arts organisations between marketing and selling (Andreasen, 1985). In this first special issue on consumer behaviour and the arts, a lead was taken by an academic journal as to the importance of marketing for the arts. In Australia, museum marketing, particularly increased audience participation, has been the primary objective of arts organisations since the 1994 release of the cultural policy statement *Creative Nation* (Commonwealth of Australia), where a shift in emphasis from supply to demand was highlighted. Attendance levels, venue occupancy rates, subscription purchases and the number of members have become important performance measures for arts organisations (Kotler and Kotler, 1998; Kotler and Scheff, 1997; Radbourne, 1998). Marketing research, marketing strategies and marketing plans have become commonplace management activity. However, studies in 1996 (Radbourne and Fraser), 1998 (Radbourne) and 2001 (Rentschler) show that the costly marketing effort for current patrons is not increasing frequency or attracting new patrons sufficient for organisations to develop without ongoing high levels of subsidy and corporate and private philanthropy. Research shows that museums in Commonwealth countries rely on three sources of income: government income; audience income and sponsorship/philanthropy. For example, in Australia, longitudinal analysis of museum income streams shows their dependence on a balance of income sources for survival. In this environment, museums are at risk (Rentschler, 2001). This highlights the need for greater emphasis on finding out more about attracting new and retaining existing audiences.

The adoption of marketing methods by museums, then, is of recent origin and their applicability to museums is still debated. For example, in 1979–80 a 'broad marketing plan' was drawn up by the National Gallery of Victoria in Australia and specific tasks relating to the marketing of the museum under-taken. Increased attention was being given to activities that not only attract visitors to the museum but also encourage them to return on a regular basis. This seems to be a shift into viewing the museum more as a commodity or product in the marketplace, not as something existing outside the needs or wants of the public. This is very early to consider marketing matters in museums. Similarly, in the UK, arts marketing awareness has increased from the 1980s. According to the International Council of Museums, it is now accepted that 'political, social and economic development cannot be divorced from the human and cultural context of any society' (International Council of Museums, 1997). Therefore, while transformations in museums aim to realise equity in access to resources and opportunities, the fundamental objective is to attain higher levels of excellence in all areas of life by involving the entire population and drawing on the broad diversity of local culture, heritage, experience and knowledge. The Australia Council's recent discussion paper, *Planning for the Future: Issues, Trends and Opportunities for the Arts in Australia*, highlights an awareness of this international development, arguing that 'advocating for the arts in the public policy arena is not inimical with the notion of an intrinsic value for the arts. On the contrary, it reflects the diversity of values within the arts sector and beyond' (Australia Council, 2001: 4).

Reflecting the stated concerns of arts representatives, this chapter ack-nowledges the dependence of the maintenance and growth of the nation's artistic resources upon marketing. Marketing requires innovation and renewal and that:

> innovation [is] dependent on diversity, creativity and the interaction between the two, and the connection of new products with new markets.
>
> (Australia Council, 2001: 14)

Concern about government funding for innovation and diversity is at the forefront of the report. Community ownership and fostering a connection with local communities is a challenge for Australian arts organisations, which see the strengthening of community support for the arts to be a key factor in increasing box office income, corporate and philanthropic support and political will (Australia Council, 2001). Although there is no central body responsible for cultural policy at the federal level in Australia, established statutory authorities operate as agencies responsible for cultural affairs in different cultural areas. Arts organisations report that increased leadership is required in order for them to enter more fully into the nation's political debates and to counter anxiety that:

> Art ... is being seen as increasingly redundant in a materialistic society. Artists are part of the culture but artists and scientists do not lead the culture.
>
> (Australia Council, 2001: 17)

According to arts leaders involved in the Australia Council report, in this country the arts have not yet succeeded in seizing the agenda outside the arts policy area (Australia Council, 2001).

New Zealand sentiments mirror those expressed in Australia:

> How can the true extent and value of creative activity be determined? Not all cultural activity can be measured through the production and consumption of goods and services, and not all cultural output has a dollar value. However, quantifying the economic features of cultural activity through a statistical model may help provide an insight into the larger reality that is 'culture'. The ability of statistics to 'quantify' is their greatest strength.
>
> (Statistics New Zealand, 1995: 15)

This approach has been extended and confirmed in more recent reports on government intentions to back a strong creative industry sector (Heart of the Nation Project Team, 2000), although the thorny issue of indicators for both economic and social value of arts and culture remains to be resolved. In the UK, Australia and New Zealand, creativity is prized, but within an industry framework, which focuses on access to economic resources through a diverse funding base.

In Canada, contemporary questions regarding museum policy centre upon access and participation, particularly how to encompass all ethno-cultural groups (Weppler and Silvers, 2001). Museums are looking to define their wider sense of purpose, making museums an integral part of their communities in the new pluralist society (Goa, 2001). During the last decade, Canadian arts organisations have relied increasingly on private support. Corporate sponsorship of the arts in Canada has increased dramatically during the last two decades, and the demand for support continues to grow. The interest of the Canadian private sector in the arts is primarily associated with the sponsorship of productions of performances, the purchase of visual arts and the provision of operating or acquisition funds for public art galleries and museums. Canada still has relatively few foundations with extensive programmes to support and develop the arts and the humanities. Corporate awareness and its potential role in this area is also relatively recent, although it has been greatly increased by the efforts of the Council for Business and the Arts in Canada (Culturelink, 2001).

The rhetoric associated with marketing sees the arts as industries, which can be classified and outputs measured. In Canada (Standing Committee on Canadian Heritage, 1999), the notion of creative industries is seen as interdependent with the arts. The same emphasis is seen in New Zealand cultural reports (Heart of the Nation Project Team, 2000), as well as UK and Australian cultural policy development (Kawashima, 1998). Museums, where they are specifically mentioned, help define national identity, are examples of innovative practice and must increase access, diversity and distinctiveness, while diversifying their funding sources. Striving for national symbols and linking culture with industry resonates with politicians who have to divert funds to non-profit organisations and justify the expense.

The increasing globalisation and internationalisation of cultural activities has had an isomorphic effect on museum marketing in developed nations. Most prominent has been a shift in emphasis from development of the artistic product to a focus on organisational marketing culture and visitors that comes from intellectual enquiry into the nature of cultural production that has been emerging for two decades or more. Overall, there has been an increasing emphasis on audiences as a means of achieving both greater museum development and greater income security. Increasingly, it is impossible to rely on government income alone in a changing environment. Certainly, the reality is that museums operate within a tripartite income structure, seeing income being derived from government, audience activities and individual or group giving. Museums from the four countries discussed in this chapter have characteristics in common due to their shared cultural heritage. Here the philanthropic role is one for government, as well as for sponsors and individuals. Previous research has shown a gradual scaling back of government activity in many areas of public life, with a new focus to cultural policies and a changing financial environment, which affects museums (Rentschler, 2002). Ideologically, there is a move away from elitism and connoisseurship to community access and audience development, with an increasing focus on diversity of income but maintenance of the income mix. The most significant problem in museums has been income uncertainty and the increased complexity in the context, which has seen volatility in funding over time.

This shows a strategic response to change in museum marketing (see Table 8.1). Marketing is approached positively, even in an environment of change and resource-scarcity, as marketing initiatives are often funded from grants. This is a sign that museums are undergoing a paradigm shift towards a stronger organisational marketing culture and focus on the audience. Considering the often-limited resources for marketing that restrain possibilities, it is even more remarkable that museum marketing has changed so much in a short timeframe.

Table 8.1 shows the evolutionary stages of museum marketing, culminating with a post-modern focus on audience deepening and diversification as part of organisational philosophy. Inspiration for a museum marketing approach is found in sources which extend beyond traditional marketing theory. It has already been mentioned that non-profit museums lack marketing capabilities. As a consequence, very little of the marketing literature is directed to them. Instead, a new literature is developing led by theorists in entrepreneurship and post-modernism, but with an appreciation of marketing and its shortcomings for museums (Brown, 1993; Fillis, 2002). What such authors recognise is the need to base the marketing concept both on satisfaction of wants and the process of economic change that better fits with the idea of entrepreneurship and the small organisation. This is leading to a reorientation of the marketing concept, so that it adjusts to the needs of the smaller organisation (Blenker, 2001). The current author has developed this process further by linking these new concepts to the non-profit museum (Rentschler, 2001).

Marketing and the non-profit museum

In the new century of competitiveness and globalisation, non-profit museums are as concerned with marketing as are their for-profit cousins. However, marketing is complicated for the following reasons: the non-profit nature of the 'business'; its non-financial objectives; the necessity to cater to multiple publics some of whom pay and others who do not; the necessity for collaboration as well as competition with competitors; and the need to foster identity as well as education, research and entertainment for visitors. Further, in the recent past museums regarded marketing with suspicion. Not any more.

Marketing is defined as a social and managerial process by which individual paying and non-paying visitors obtain what they need through creating, offering and exchanging with others' products and services of value. As far back as 1969, Kotler and Levy identified marketing as concerned with how

Table 8.1 Museum marketing then and now

Evolution of museum marketing	Product focus	Selling focus	Marketing science focus	Post-modern marketing focus
Product	Object-centred	Need effort to sell	Enhance with services	Differentiate audience segments
Marketing function	Data gathering	Sell benefits; build brand identity	Promote as means of communication	Shared service philosophy across the museum and with its people
Marketing position	Low resources; low status	Increased resources	Management status	Strategic integration
Market knowledge	Irrelevant	Need to locate	Profile	Needs; wants; attitudes and behaviours
Segmentation	General, socio-demographic	Visitor studies	Geo-demographic	Attitudinal and behavioural change

Source: cf. Morris Hargreaves McIntyre (2002)

transactions are created, stimulated, facilitated and valued, the main purpose of marketing being to create and distribute values among the market parties through transactions and market relationships. Carson (1985) has pointed out the characteristics of small firm marketing, such as limited resources, lack of specialist expertise and limited impact. These characteristics manifest themselves in non-profit museums, as they are mostly small to medium-sized organisations. Further, museums are resource-scarce, impacting their ability to hire specialist marketers of the highest quality and expertise and hence limiting their ability to make an impression in a competitive and crowded marketplace. This view is consistent with studies of small entrepreneurial firms (Blenker, 2001).

Marketing in small firms needs to be relevant, appropriate and relative to the position of the firm in its life cycle. As many museums are older organisations, with limited resources and marketing expertise, marketing in these organisations needs to be change-focused, opportunistic in nature and innovative in approach. This approach aligns with Carson's (1985) view as to the central focus of marketing in small firms. Accordingly, marketing in museums exists between the museum and external social entities. The notion of museums as social entities is not a new one (see, e.g. Bhattacharya et al., 1995; McLean and Cooke, 1999). It sees museums as consisting of salient group classifications, which may be based on categories such as demographics, gender, or race as well as membership or values. These categories create social identification such as the perception of belonging to a group. It is a concept which helps to make sense of change in our social, cultural, economic and political context, which has either a fixed notion of identity or a fluid and contingency-based notion. Thus, identity can change as circumstances change. The latter view sees identity as a social concept which forms links with society. It is therefore important to manage the marketing and social interface by overcoming some of the barriers mentioned above and including the identity factors important to museums' social role.

The museum experience

Museums offer a diverse range of experiences to the people who visit them. Museums deal in ideas, objects and satisfactions not found elsewhere. Ideas and experience derive from natural and human-made objects and sensory experiences. The presentation of these ideas, objects and satisfactions is founded on research, scholarship and interpretation. Museums are engaging in wider self-assessment of their programmes and projects, due to changing contextual circumstances. In Australia, *A Study into Key Needs of Collecting Institutions in the Heritage Sector* (Deakin University, 2002) identified the transformation which has occurred in collecting institutions in the last decade in terms of access and preservation, but that this 'needs to be coupled with the need for quality visitor experiences' (p. 9). This has led to a reassessment of the importance of marketing to museums.

Over the last 20 years, marketing has become one of the most important and exciting components of management strategy. Marketing was once considered a 'dirty word' in the arts, seemingly incorporating all that was 'commercial'. Now, however, marketing is recognised as a legitimate tool for enhancing the visitor experience, the product portfolio and assessing the organisational marketing culture. This tripartite relationship is illustrated in Figure 8.2.

From research conducted in museums (Deakin University, 2002; Rentschler and Gilmore, 2002), it is clear that they are developed in two of the three elements illustrated in Figure 8.2. The attitude towards visitors and indeed non-visitors has developed over the last century until now people who work in museums understand the importance of visitors from a marketing perspective. Traditionally, museum people have focused on the product portfolio, such as collections, research display and objects. Indeed, museums are institutions which collect, research, display and interpret objects. It has been argued cogently that their very existence depends on the possession of a collection (McLean, 1994). While collection care and interpretation are acknowledged as basic museum functions, declining public funding and accountability pressure have led to the discovery of museum marketing as an important contribution to museums' viability (Rentschler, 1998). This discovery has led to changing behaviours in museum personnel, so that the beginnings of an organisational marketing culture are created. The total reinvention of Museum

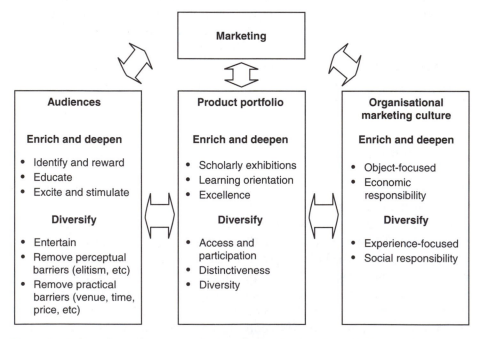

Figure 8.2 Tripartite audience, product and organisational marketing model.

of New Zealand Te Papa Tongerewa (Te Papa) in Wellington, New Zealand is a case in point. Its transition moved from being part of the national museum and art gallery, as two separate institutions, to flagship national museum. Te Papa expresses New Zealanders' national identity, biculturalism,[1] customer orientation and positive commercial focus in a time of economic restructuring. Total reinvention occurred in the 1990s. Its success is a result of breaking with tradition and taking risks: its popularity – more than 2 million visitors in the first year of operation – is a consequence of the fact that, while serving visitor's needs, it is also something new for New Zealanders. Positioning the museum within an organisational marketing culture has been central to its outlook.

It has been argued that museums need marketing, and especially so when understanding their audiences, in order to be competitive in the future and achieve their mission. Countering this is an environment poorly suited to the introduction of marketing initiatives. Apart from the small firm capabilities mentioned earlier in this chapter, there is the traditional curatorial focus of key staff in museums, which by training and preference focuses on the object. However, marketing is increasingly being seen as an essential museum activity by museums themselves (Kelly and Sas, 1998). Hence, marketing serves the museum's mission rather than compromises it (Reussner, 2002). Part of this change is reflected in a better understanding of what marketing is and what it can achieve. Marketing provides opportunities for creativity and imagination in expanding the visitor experience through a wide range of activities, with the foundation of that expansion based firmly on an understanding of visitors and the organisational marketing culture.

Post-modern museum marketing: an argument for segmentation

The conventional view of museum marketing is that it should be formalised, comprehensive and linear. This approach is epitomised by the textbook approach to marketing. Here the argument is that this is an inappropriate model for museum marketing. In fact, a more informal, creative and flexible approach could be adopted which suits the service environment of museums and the policy framework (cf. Brown, 1993). This approach makes considerable demands on the museum organisation in time, commitment and focus. The model illustrated in Figure 8.3 suggests that museum marketing can be introduced sympathetically without destroying the cultural values which represent its strength. It allows for sectional implementation of marketing, so that success in achievement of results is demonstrated progressively.

---

[1] Biculturalism is policy recognition of the two peoples of New Zealand, European settlers and the indigenous Maori inhabitants of New Zealand, who signed a treaty with the settlers.

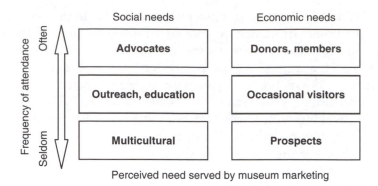

Figure 8.3 Types of audiences by needs served and frequency of attendance.

A purposive museum meets the audiences' social needs through the type of exhibitions they put on, programmes and activities they offer, ancillary programmes and events, and relationships they build with potential or traditional audiences. On the other hand, the economic needs come from the museum, so audiences (including donors and sponsors) can be seen to meet the museum's needs. Within those categories, there are the subcategories of prospects, occasional visitors, members, donors, educational visitors, multicultural visitors and advocates – akin to O'Riordan's (2002) 'mosaic of minorities'. The recent census in Australia mirrors a country in which we are moving towards a more multicultural society (Cleary and Murphy, 2002). The results make it difficult to describe what is typical in Australia as increasing diversity is driven by immigration. It is clear to most organisations that quality and sustainability are best achieved by focusing on what matters most to the audience. Understanding attitudes and characteristics of the potential and actual audience through audience research is the most important precondition for being responsive to their needs. This has become more urgent in the latest snapshot of the Australian population that identifies consumer trends and provides a window on the consumer mind (O'Riordan, 2002). However, the recent National Museum of Australia Review (DCITA, 2003) highlights the political climate in which museums operate, which may constrain them in fulfilling such a mission.

Audience research that looks at the specific profiles and needs of the subcategories within an existing audience body is scant (Johnson and Garbarino, 1999). Urgent economic and social questions for museums and for the society whose needs they meet can be answered by appropriately understanding audiences. As audience research requires an investment of time, money and staff, it is important that audience studies are conducted effectively, understanding whether they are conducted for social and/or economic purposes. Nonetheless, the lines between the two types of marketing research are blurring as population shifts occur. Traditionally, for example, the function of multicultural audience research has been perceived as meeting *social* needs. However, considering the multicultural nature of western democracies, it can be argued to be of *economic* benefit as well. An effective use of audience research is strategically important to museums in this changing market place.

The goals of inclusiveness, accessibility and use by a broad range of people are acknowledged as primary public duties of museums. The emphasis on accessibility implies a change of attitude towards the museum audience. Only by understanding how to offer a valuable, enjoyable experience to a greater diversity of audiences and thus gain their support can any museum increase its accessibility and audience base.

Customer orientation does not necessarily force museums to meet demands of a prospective audience that compromises their mission and their integrity. On the contrary, museums are balancing their aims and duties on the one hand and the preconditions and needs on the part of the audience on the other (Rentschler and Gilmore, 2002).

To combine the organisational and creative aims of museums with the expectations of customers, museums may develop in two directions simultaneously:

(a) Invest in audience research to crystallise the important attitudes and characteristics of their members, non-member visitors and non-visitors; and, on this base

(b) Develop the attracting power to retain and build on the current audience base by providing a service that satisfies a multiplicity of audiences and potential audience needs.

Understanding diverse audiences

Recently, articles on the arts have appeared on diverse audiences and relationship marketing (Bhattacharya et al., 1995; Johnson and Garbarino, 1999; Rentschler et al., 2002). An underlying theme in these publications is that such programmes enable consumers to identify with the corresponding organisations: in the case of museums, drawing infrequent visitors inside their doors and making them regular visitors, members and donors. Research shows that different audience segments visit for different reasons (Wiggins, 2003). This is often discussed in conventional marketing but less often in museum marketing. It also relates to the drivers of visitation, what causes repeat visits and how to understand visitors.

The notion of a ladder of customer relationships, ranging from transactional at the bottom to relational at the top, is a formative concept in marketing. It is argued that organisations can analyse customers on a continuum of exchanges, pursuing both transactional and relational marketing simultaneously as not all customers want the same relationship. In museums, it is possible to segment the visitor base into groups that vary in their responsiveness to transactional or relational marketing (cf. Garbarino and Johnson, 1999 in performing arts organisations). Not only can different types of visitors be separately identified but they also interact differently and can be treated differently. Hence, Melbourne Museum greatly increased its youth audience when it exhibited 'body art', an exhibition on tattooing and body piercing, just as the Powerhouse Museum in Sydney, Australia, increased its youth audience when it held an exhibition on the history of contraception. Both exhibitions generated much publicity in the media and drew large crowds from niche target groups. However, an exhibition at the Art Gallery of New South Wales on Indigenous art drew the young professionals as well as the traditional 40+ audience. Lumping audiences together as 'goers' is of limited use. Segmenting them on a ladder of opportunity makes more sense.

The problem in museums is that publications on relationship marketing often are based on anecdotal evidence rather than on research. Surveys in performing arts organisations suggest that major audience groups have relational differences (Johnson and Garbarino, 1999). Similar findings are known in museums (Falk and Dierking, 1992). For example, low relational visitors are driven by overall satisfaction, and can be irritated or dissuaded from repeat visits by poor facilities, displays or services such as in restaurants. However, committed visitors, such as members, have a relationship with the museum and seek something different from their visits. They seek trust and commitment rather than satisfaction, suggest Johnson and Garbarino. These implied differences suggest that transactional marketing programmes focused on managing satisfaction are more successful with low relational visitors, while relationship marketing programmes focused on trust and commitment are more successful for high relational visitors.

Museums routinely incorporate visitors as members, however, they often know little about them and create even less leverage from that membership. In academic terms, there is little literature on museum membership. In practical terms, understanding museum members helps managers and curators develop ideas about how identification can be used for visitor retention (Bhattacharya et al., 1995). While other work has focused on alumni and identification, there has been less analysis done on museum members and identification.

Why has there not been more interest in the relational marketing opportunities of museum members? A review of visitor and non-visitor studies suggests they rarely look at member differences. If researchers focus on demographic or lifestyle factors, members appear not to differ from occasional visitors. Because of the demographic homogeneity of high culture, marketing managers have tended to see them as one audience (Johnson and Garbarino, 1999). Based on theories of relationship marketing, members are more relational than occasional visitors, but even within the member grouping there are differences between members. Members often provide volunteers to the museum as well as patrons, donors and advocates, who provide their time, talents and money to sustain it. A member base is also an indication of community support that is vital when arguing for government funding.

Research shows that the identification of members leads to increased loyalty to the organisation. In the case of visitors, this has the desirable consequences of high brand loyalty and positive word of mouth, an aspect of museum marketing that has constantly been identified as a means of spreading the word about product efficacy. The benefits of increased loyalty and positive word of mouth are well known (Bhattacharya et al., 1995). For cash-strapped museums, understanding the benefits of identification can lead to sustainable competitive advantage and improved financial results. Identification is defined as creating an interface with the causes or goals that the museum embodies and espouses. Thus, when a museum stands for specific causes, visitors are loyal because they identify with the museum mission.

Museums often have categories of membership, ranging from individual to family and higher contributing levels of membership or patrons. All membership categories offer benefits such as special viewings of exhibitions, guided tours, monthly newsletters and a calendar of activities, plus discounts of purchases in museum shops. Higher level members such as patrons are given additional benefits such as free guest admission to receptions and recognition in the museum annual report.

At the top of the ladder are patrons. Patrons are motivated by the social relationship and the satisfaction it engenders. The donor receives an intangible satisfaction that relates to their personal motivations: an enhanced degree of self-esteem; a feeling of achievement; a new status or a sense of belonging (Mixer, 1993). The social exchange relationship contains some expectation of continuity.

Businesses and foundations interact with museums as patrons too. They provide services, personnel and gifts-in-kind, as well as money. For example, the National Gallery of Victoria, has a successful partnership with the Ian Potter Foundation, which invested $15 million in the new art museum on Federation Square, Melbourne. In other cases technology has been provided to museums by computer companies. However, different motives drive the exchange processes of businesses and foundations. Many large foundations fund innovative projects that individual patrons shy away from. However, their interest in innovation is generally confined to fields linked to company strategic direction. In other words, businesses have health, education and cultural needs to satisfy their employees. Museums, as non-profit organisations, have financial, personnel and management needs that corporations can provide. Thus the two types of organisations enter into exchanges in order to ensure both organisations' functional success. Social exchange is more open, less contractual and less bounded by time commitments than commercial exchange, but there is an implicit assumption that benefits will accrue to each organisation. In fact, one of the areas researchers grapple with is how to evaluate social exchange transactions, so that returns and benefits can be quantified.

Marketing can be considered as those museum activities that pay tribute to museums' social *or* economic mandate and responsibility by broadening access, not only through increasing visitor numbers, but also by increasing the variety of audiences reached. Bennett (1994) picks up these arguments in his study of non-goers to South Australian history museums and art galleries. He argues that for a mixture of economic and political reasons, museums and art galleries are increasingly dependent on the number of visitors they attract, either directly (through entrance fees) or indirectly (through diverse public use) which ensures continued public funding. To quote Bennett:

> the dynamics of access policies and the requirements of effective marketing are really the recto and verso of the same set of issues.
>
> (Bennett, 1994: 6)

Museums need to find a balance between their object-based focus and market awareness, brought forward by visitor orientation.

Cause related marketing (CRM) picks up this notion. It is generally defined as joining a non-profit and commercial organisation in order to raise funds and awareness for a cause while building sales, awareness and corporate image (Rentschler and Wood, 2001). Hence, museums can benefit from liaisons with commercial interests. The customer can purchase at their discretion and they may, by their continued use of a product, donate on more than one occasion. Thus, museums can get more hits per visitor for a limited ongoing work input and limited intrusion into the lives of the audience.

CRM enables consumers to identify with the museum. By aligning themselves with worthy causes or implementing policies that are radically different from standard practice, museums enable visitors to identify with what the organisation represents (Bhattacharya et al., 1995). For example, the new-age cosmetic companies support natural ingredients which shy away from animal testing, while universities have alumni to encourage a sense of belonging to the organisation. Museums use these strategies to ensure identification on the part of visitors by linking exhibitions and research to social issues and by drawing visitors 'inside' the organisation by making them members, volunteers and patrons. Research has consistently shown that members identify with the organisation. This leads to increased loyalty to the organisation, high brand loyalty and positive word of mouth (Bhattacharya et al., 1995). Increased loyalty provides benefits. For example, some studies show that retaining existing customers is up to six times less expensive than luring new ones (Rentschler et al., 2002). High brand loyalty is seen as different from identification: loyalty is necessarily tied to causes or goals an organisation embodies. In other words, a museum can foster visitor identification with its social mission by linking with other social causes. Brand loyalty is a deliberate choice to purchase a brand stemming from past positive experience with its use. Positive word of mouth is most important to museums: it builds visitor numbers, visitor retention and social identity for visitor identification.

Conclusion

This chapter investigated the consequences of museums becoming more oriented to their audiences, while at the same time recognising the importance of their product portfolio and organisational marketing culture. Over the last quarter century, museums have recognised the need for changes in marketing to be met by moves towards greater management and financial autonomy (Rentschler and Gilmore, 2002). In the past, being successful in a museum meant focusing on cultural heritage collection, preservation and research. For a long time this focus went unchallenged. Although marketing has become more important to museums, there is still only fragmentary knowledge on visitors and non-visitors. A better understanding of audience profiles is still needed, particularly concerning segmentation, so that targeting of visitors can achieve greater benefits for museums.

The need for decreasing reliance upon government income has seen each museum move from an attitude of dependence – bemoaning the government's abandonment of the organisation – to an increasingly positive attitude in which innovative post-modern marketing has become central to museum operations. This needs to be achieved in unique ways, according to each museum's individual strengths and means – the Art Gallery of New South Wales in Sydney, Australia, never wavers from its central focus upon diverse and engaging public programming, maintaining effective publicity and harnessing its popular profile to attract sponsorship; while Canterbury Museum in Christchurch, New Zealand has recently adopted the notion of 'total visitor experience', reshaping its operations to embrace a whole new vision. In these ways, museums are recognising audience differences, encouraging governments to recognise the range and diversity of their product portfolio and developing their organisational marketing culture to reflect them.

Where should museum marketing go from here? There are three implications that emerge from this chapter. First, alternative segmentation approaches need development via psychographic and attitudinal measures, as they promise a more accurate picture of audiences and provide information that is of more practical use than mere demographics (cf. Schulze, 1992). There is also an opportunity to further segment the audience into occasional visitors, regular visitors and types of members, as performing arts research suggests that there is more variability in these groups than there is in visitors and non-visitors (Johnson and Garbarino, 2001). There is a danger in drawing too strong conclusions from performing arts research and its applicability to museums, due to differences in entry fee policies – no entry fee means audience is a drain on resources, whereas entry fee means it is 'box office' – unless museums also develop products and services within the museum for which audiences pay.

Apart from expanding their view beyond visitors and non-visitors, museums can consider a much larger group of *stakeholders* as communication partners and thus, as a subject matter for audience research, such as members and patrons. Second, the fear that a greater orientation on visitors will lead to a decreased concentration on the product portfolio is not necessarily the case. As Gainer and Padanyi (2002) found in a study on non-profit arts organisations, an increased marketing focus and greater popularity does not necessarily lead to decreased artistic reputation. In fact, growth in artistic reputation and audience satisfaction lead to increased resources, both at the box office and through higher artistic reputation. Gainer and Padanyi state that this is presumably due to the funding provided by public agencies and by donors, who want to support excellence. Finally, as Kotler and Scheff (1997) state, there is danger of competitive myopia where museums view their competitors as only museums: a segment that has too narrow a focus for instigating effective competitive marketing strategies. While there is verbal recognition of broader competition, an adequate strategic approach – entailing its closer examination and developing targeted strategies – is still in its infancy, even though, for example, it had been stated as important by the McKinley Douglas (1995a, b) report on the New Zealand museums sector. Conventional marketing concepts are often seen to fall short of museum marketing needs, most of which are small, non-profit organisations. But if museums can adapt and adopt the innovative, flexible principles which are applicable to them in a post-modern age, they stand to gain the opportunity of understanding the values of different types of audiences.

Chapter 9

Societal arts marketing: a multi-sectoral, inter-disciplinary and international perspective

Nil Şişmanyazıcı Navaie

(*Including a discussion piece contributed by Elif Shafak*)

Introduction

The arts serve various purposes in marketing: as a product, a tool of marketing communications and as a vehicle of social change. The previous chapters have already explored various forms of the arts in their commercial context. While the commercial role of marketing is widely accepted, the use of arts marketing techniques in changing behaviour and benefiting society is not fully acknowledged in literature. Therefore, this chapter will focus on the latter two purposes of the arts. It attempts to capture the multifaceted nature of the arts in the context of marketing and development. The first section of the chapter examines the historical use of art as a tool of marketing communications, and representing cultural identities as well as societal enhancements. The second section explores the role of the arts in social marketing, the application of marketing techniques in communicating social issues and affecting social or behavioural change. It incorporates the indirect marketing attributes of arts whence utilized as an education and therapy method in the development field.

The role of arts marketing in the realm of international development from a glocal and multi-sectoral perspective is discussed throughout this chapter. It also provides an exploration of the use of the arts as a social marketing tool in efforts to fight the difficulties of underdevelopment such as poverty, illiteracy, gender inequality and ecological complexities. This is demonstrated through a set of case studies.

We first examine briefly the concepts of glocalization, development, the arts and artwork, along with culture, and social and human capital. In a world which is seen as shrinking due to the increase in usage of new technologies and people's ability to travel, marketers have recognized the commercial value in drawing widely upon interdependent multidisciplinary influences. A succinct look into the arts and human history is followed by an examination of the marketing of the arts in the global–local development scene. The following section concentrates on cases which provide sound examples of where techniques of art, arts and social marketing have substantial influence in human development and youth empowerment; gender equality, community and peace building, health, economic and sustainable development. Almost all of the case examples used in this chapter are based on individual interviews, presentations, documents and reports provided by the project directors of those organizations. The overall aim of the arguments suggested in this chapter is to contribute to the free flow of ideas and visions between people in the arts, development, and marketing with a view to pave the way for more interdisciplinary learning.

The development of the arts in 'marketing' – a historical perspective

Early art forms began as forms of communication, story telling and record keeping, activities that are the fundamental tools of marketing. According to existing research findings, recognizable art dates back to at least 38,000 BC in Europe, Africa and Australia (Marceau et al., 1998). Pre-historic and pre-literate people often represented their world and possibly their beliefs through visual images and used mainly five motifs in their cave arts, crafts and tools design: human figures, animals, tools, weapons, rudimentary local maps (topographical compositions of the areas in which they lived) and symbols or diagrams. This can be seen as an early form of marketing as these communities used arts to communicate their identity as well as documenting and shaping their social life.

As people became settled they began constructing edifices not only for shelter, but also making these constructions architecturally eye-catching, painting the walls of their houses and their temples, therefore communicating their increasing social and technical sophistication to other civilizations. From the end of 4000 BC, farmers and traders living especially along the Nile, Asia Minor, the Middle East, eastern coastlines of the Mediterranean and Aegean Seas created highly developed social systems and advanced artwork. The grandiose pyramids, paintings of figurative scenes of earthly life on tombs, religious and magical texts on rolls of papyrus creating the 'Book of the Dead', the vases, bracelets, pendants and ornaments of the Oxus and Priam treasures, and brightly coloured frescos of the Knossos Palace, are just few of those incredible examples of exceedingly skilled artists and craftsmen from the pre-classical era. The Indus jewels and animal terracotta statuettes from Mohenjo-daro (around the 4th and 3rd millennia BC) used possibly as toys also give us a hint of how art was integrated in everyday life even in these ancient cultures. The Landscape of the Odyssey frescos in Rome and the 'Nile Landscape' floor mosaics from the 1st millennium BC which depict the transformation of the complex system of tribes into city-states and the development of sophisticated Hellenic and Italic cultures; the polychromatic ceramics of Nazca culture, the tall pyramids of Maya culture and the frescos belonging to the Teotihuacan civilization from the Americas are as well some examples of artistic representations of the indigenous people's beliefs and lifestyle.

From late antiquity up until renaissance Christian religion in Europe diffused into the arts. In Northern Africa, the Arabian Peninsula and Asia Minor non-figurative motifs of the Islamic religion were used on textiles, architecture, household objects (ceramics), metal works (weapons) and jewellery. In the Indian and Far East region, Buddhism influenced the arts especially in stone funerary sculpture, silk, bamboo-paper and canvas paintings, and two-dimensional rock carvings in cave temples (Marceau et al., 1998). In this way, art was used as a marketing tool in communicating religious identity.

The emergence of the Renaissance in Europe and an increase of population accelerated the development of architecture and city planning in the 17th and first half of the 18th century. Palazzo Barberini, the aristocratic residence in Rome, the Royal Palace of Versailles and Le Nain Brother's paintings of peasant life reflect some of the characteristics of this era. In 18th and 19th century neo-classicism, a greater interest in the arts and the philosophy of antiquity, became apparent in Europe and North America. During the same period orientalism began to spread in Europe, particularly after the British expansion in India and French conquest of Algeria. Exotic Orient trends not only influenced the European know-how in science, but also the literature, music, interior design and the visual arts. For instance, in the

18th century rococo architecture incorporated Chinese, Turkish and Egyptian tastes, at the time when rococo style reached its height. Similar to the emergence of nation-state the industrial revolution gave rise to a reconstruction of urban planning, with state buildings, residences, department stores, ports and railroads, as well as operas, theatres and museums. As the 19th century progressed, innovations in industry and the changing face of society brought a new look to the arts and artwork. William Morris' decorative wallpapers, the 1820s American pressed glass products, Luis Comfort Tiffany's lamps and the Nancy School furniture are again a few of those examples of how the arts have been integrated with technology and consumer goods production (Marceau et al., 1998). Changes in printing technology (such as engravings, etchings and lithography) had a great influence on all kinds of print materials, from books to mass-produced posters which at times promoted national unity. The invention of photography and thereupon cinematography gave rise to the beginning of a new industry in the visual arts.

From the turn of the 20th century in Europe and the US environmentally conscious (organic) architecture developed. Germany's pure Aryan art and Picasso's Guernica painting expressing solidarity with the Spanish Republicans, are again examples of how the arts especially during the early to mid-century in Europe was integrated with politics and also used as a tool of social marketing in its negative expression as propaganda to influence the masses. After World War II, which accelerated the technological advancement of industrial design and globalization of culture, artists themselves became interested in different cultures and started incorporating these differences in their individual art, such as Picasso's interest in African, Van Gogh's and Gauguin's in Japanese art (Marceau et al., 1998). Today the arts have become accessible to everyone. Artists' and designers' have sought to combine aesthetics and practicality in mass-produced goods, which became fundamental parts of our daily lives. Art, technology and production techniques have become increasingly entwined, allowing artistic articulation to be represented in myriad ways. For instance, the digital Swiss wristwatch (Swatch) uses designs of famous artists. The fashion industry has progressed immensely. Alongside video art, computer graphics in making animated films and video games have become a new medium to be delved into.

The intention with the above overview of the arts from early 4000 BC to the present day was to remind us of how the arts and artwork played a major role throughout history. It is important for us to understand the past and notice the relations of the arts with natural (engineering and ecology) and social sciences (politics, economics, sociology, psychology and anthropology). This interdisciplinary approach in reviewing the history and reconsidering the present will provide us adequate grounds for developing concrete strategies to accept the significance of the arts in effective social change, particularly with the use of social marketing techniques. In addition to the above-mentioned functions of the arts-search for beauty and individuality, expression of internal and external worlds – the arts have been about:

- communication, story-telling and record keeping;
- architecture and engineering resulting in commercial, residential and leisure artefacts (Howard, 1982);
- consumer products (from furniture to light fixtures);
- household goods (decorative as well as functional appliances);
- personal items (ornamental art of jewellery, toys, watches, fashion items);
- entertainment (movies, theatre plays, concerts, operas and ballets, computer games).

The diffusion of modes of life, hybrid civilizations and the emergence of global citizens with people-centred perspectives, which are all part of the glocalization process, have intensified the impact of the arts. Perhaps the Hellenic culture developed in the 1st millennium BC could be considered glocalization's first endeavour. The orientalism movement during the late 18th and early 19th century can be also perceived as an impact of glocalization in the arts. And today where our world has become more interdependent than ever, we now find ourselves discussing how we should position the arts in the private, public and the third (civil) sector, as a powerful tool in human, social, educational, economic and political development.

Glocalization and marketing of the arts

The utilitarian and humanist aspirations for the arts develop different sectors and support building capacities at individual, organizational, institutional, and local, national, and international community levels. These capacities include elements such as developing children's cognitive skills, rehabilitating traumatized or disabled people and reintegrating them to the workforce, and creating opportunities for organizations and institutions to empower and foster communities. Among arts and development advocates, it has become a fact that art is the most resourceful tool in addressing educational, social, cultural, political and economic development issues worldwide. The case examples, mentioned in section two of this chapter, are believed to support this argument.

Some historians go back to colonialism as the first seed of globalization and even indicate globalization as neo-colonialism. Braudel has argued that there have always been world-economies linked with world empires. Wallerstein, likewise has dwelled upon the balances between core and peripheral countries in a world system from a global perspective (Şişmanyazıcı, 1998). If globalization truly means anything, then the emphasis should be certainly on the worldwide pull-push forces. These arise in the political, economic, social and cultural spheres in addition to the synergies created between the public and private sectors as well as the third sector, that is civil, voluntary initiatives, non-profit organizations. Globalization is the strengthening of worldwide relations, which connect remote areas in such a way that local activities are shaped by events occurring faraway and vice versa (Giddens, 1990). Today quite often globalization is being perceived as the reason for the increased asymmetry of power in the contemporary world setting and vulnerability of local economies and cultures (Spybey, 1996). The influx of modern, western values and tastes into local indigenous cultures has been considered as a major rival that imperils cultural and national identities.

This chapter, instead of further discussing various perceptions of the emergence, existence or the destructive effects of globalization, will focus on the creative constituents and positive impact of 'globalization' converged with the forces of 'localization', referred to as 'glocalization'. Glocalization is neither an end nor a reason, rather a description of the modification process of the interdependent world composition and the strengthening of local and global relations that are voluntarily influenced within themselves and by one another. Glocalization exists in all spheres and directions, from North to South, East to West and vice versa. For instance, in production and management techniques the West already incorporates Eastern traditions (Lipietz, 1994; Şişmanyazıcı, 1998). Along with the changes in the global demographic composition, juxtapositions of modern and traditional, urban and tribal elements are increasingly taking place. The famous musician Sting has been lately fusing Arabic tunes into his songs; the teen idol Shakira likewise has merged Latin and Middle-Eastern flavours into her music; Afro-Celtic music, which is comprised of northern and southern rhythms and melodies, is quite popular among new age music lovers all around the world; some western classical ballet and modern jazz dance groups also amalgamate southern vibrant colours and ethnic characteristics into their compositions and choreographies. It is possible that these fusions took place to attract a wider audience, global customers with international preferences. Is it likely that they have also intended (indirectly) to familiarize people, lead them to take pleasure in those eccentric tastes and pave the way for indigenous artists to enter the global markets?

Glocalization in the development field has become the process of adoption, adaptation and diffusion of standards in segments and sectors of communities that transform the conditions of underdevelopment, which affect human existence such as satisfaction of basic needs, availability of universal access to education, and attainment of civil freedoms and political participation (Outhwaite et al., 1996). This is in line with the aspirations of international development, particularly when we consider the millennium development goals (MDGs) developed by the world leaders at the United Nations Millennium Summit in year 2000. These goals were concerned with alleviating poverty, hunger, disease, illiteracy, environmental degradation and discrimination against women. If we look at the subject matter from a purely commercial arts perspective, we may not see the relevance of the arts in fulfilling the MDGs. But, when we approach the subject with an inter-disciplinary mind-set there is a chance for the arts to be a part of it all. The arts, as a societal marketing tool, may help alleviate social exclusion, poverty and discrimination.

Today, in the process of glocalization, the role of the arts emerged as mul-tifaceted. Throughout history there have been open-ended debates over the purpose and nature of the arts. Arts experts and advocates discuss whether the arts should have a didactic purpose, or should simply be 'art for arts' sake'. What are the arts and its difference from crafts and culture? Where is the thin line that differentiates the arts from human inventiveness of means for existence? Do the arts create change or change creates artistic' styles? When we are especially talking about various types of modern art, it is very difficult to uncover the difference. How many people would agree that the 'Sensation' exhibition held at the Tate Gallery in London in 1997 was art (see issues of aesthetics as discussed by Davies (1995)? How many of us would consider an airplane statue created with recycled engine pieces art? How about the street performer who uses buckets and tin cans to make music? In the development field, the questions related to the arts are even more complex. In rural underprivileged communities, where farmers sing while collecting their crops, celebrate their harvesting by dancing around the fire, or make simple wooden statues that symbolize their spirituality, the arts might be perceived quite differently than in the western world. So whose definition of art counts? This is quite a challenging question due to our dif-ferent backgrounds and perceptions of art. Perhaps for now the best way to define art is to see it as a process of human creative effort which is intended to stimulate some kind of an effect in the artist's and public's eye and lives. Here we take the artist's perspective into account as well because not every-one may appreciate the creativity of one's work. Artwork could be described as the artistic result/product of the creative process that could be for instance visual, literary, symbolic, decorative, useful, or elitist. Furthermore, arts market-ing in the development field (societal arts marketing) can be briefly described as the direct promotion of artistic goods to generate income for under-privileged communities and compete in glocal markets; and the indirect consequence of an increasing utilization of arts via multiple disciplines and integration of deep social content, development values and principles in artistic performances to build capacities.

The arts and artwork are the key elements of culture. Culture, like the arts and artwork, is difficult to define. Culture encompasses every aspect of our lives, it is a description of a way of living, and incorporates elements such as learned social manners and interactions that are conveyed from one gener-ation to another. Whether it is high or popular, culture of any group in any setting has been in a constant state of change since the beginning of humankind regardless of various types of socio-economic statuses. The speed of change has increased as globalization intensified. People worldwide became aware of different cultures and started diffusing some of those characteristics into their own lives voluntarily (glocalization) or as a consequence of predetermined political and economic transformation (colonialism). It is difficult to imagine culture distinct from social capital (Sen, 2002), which is the glue that holds the different spheres of the society together. Social capital (Puttnam, 1993) includes the cultural norms, institutions and the vertical and horizontal relationships within the social structure, attitudes, folklore, shared values such as trust, common rules and regulations that emphasize the importance of societal responsibility. Acknowledging this powerful role of culture and the need to recognize and defend this in developing economies – as well as underprivileged groups in developed societies – must mean a recognition of the important social role of the arts. There are some debates on the negative and weaker aspects of social capital such as mistrust, corruption and organized crime that exists within a society. However, this chapter focuses on the positive aspects of social capital that contribute to development by facilitating coordination and cooperation for the mutual benefit of the society.

During the past two decades multilateral agencies have realized the importance of the human factor in overcoming economic challenges (Cornia et al., 1987). Human assets (Beer et al., 1984) are the sum of intrinsic abilities, learned knowledge (including the intellectual capital of the information era) and skills that individuals acquire, develop, and put into practice throughout their lifetime. The cultural (and artistic) dimension of development has been perceived inferior, worthy of consideration only when people have fulfilled their basic needs and have become part of the modern socio-economic and political institutions (Tucker, 1997). Besides natural resources, physical capital (such as technology and tools) and the geopolitical position of a country, the social and human capital are crucial in determining national wealth. Social capital and human capital complement each other. The social-external environment shapes the human effectiveness, and the human capacity creates and changes the social-external environment. Artists use their 'creative' intrinsic abilities, artistic skills and knowledge to stimulate the society for creating minor or major changes for themselves, or various other members of the society, and influence the relations among and between themselves. Thus, art in any form is a universal link in interconnecting the social, cultural, political and economic spheres at local and global scale and sustaining development.

The arts should not be perceived as a substitution for other development schemes. Private, public and the third sectors; cultural, social and human capitals along with disciplines of several sciences (natural, social and medical) as well as all aspects of the arts, are all linked to each other. The development of artistic expression and the promotion and marketing of the arts serve to strengthen societies in terms of their identity. The manifestation of glocalization is basically helping us to understand this interrelation.

The cases below focus on how the arts have been used in the development field within the glocalization process. While the more developed communities treasure the opportunities to employ their know-how and devices in the arts and derive some benefit from their skills, the underprivileged communities bestowed by those essential means are advantaged to voice themselves and exit the perilous conditions that they are struggling with. Some specific figures based upon United Nations Development Programme (UNDP) report are given henceforth. How much these distressing figures may be alleviated by the societal marketing of the arts is yet unknown, thus further research needs to be carried out to find the exact effect. However, the below case examples are proof of the arts' thriving input in development.

Case examples of arts marketing in the development field

Arts in human development and youth empowerment

Case one

According to the UNDP Human Development Report 113 million children do not attend school. Every year about 11 million children die of preventable causes, which can be solved by simple improvements in nutrition, sanitation, maternal health and education (UNDP, 2002). These conditions can be alleviated and children's survival and intellectual development can be maintained if there is political and economic will at international levels. The arts can also play a role in addressing the issues of children and youth at risk worldwide.

Current research on the arts and human development shows that deep engagement in the arts has significant consequences for intellectual development and has substantial cognitive, social and emotional benefits to children. Research conducted at traditional schools in more developed communities indicates that socio-economic status is critical in predicting the child's academic performance. Widening economic gaps within and among the developed and underdeveloped communities, mounting competition and stress have been increasing the number of students who need special educational services. Whether the children live in economically depressed areas of urban cities, shanty towns, refugee camps or temporary housing, the arts and arts-infused education worldwide is nurturing those young individuals' minds with creativity, originality, and analytical and universal thinking.

A Washington, DC, based non-profit organization, WVSA Arts Connection, has been serving children and young people with special needs through the employment of the arts for more than two decades. Among WVSA's effective programmes, the School for Arts In Learning (SAIL), which is a public charter school (from kindergarten to sixth grade, and serves a student body of more than 100 elementary aged children who are predominantly African American or Hispanic), uses non-traditional teaching and education methods to provide opportunities for students who have difficulties in learning, processing information, and demonstrating knowledge. The key idea behind SAIL is that the arts can be fundamental to academic and social learning, that individuals learn in different ways, and, despite differences, all children are capable of learning. At SAIL the arts are the core of the education that creates a bridge between all other disciplines, brings community resources (parents, staff, artists, dancers, photographers, musicians, physical and speech therapists) together, and increases partnerships. The classroom space and teaching methodology have been designed in a non-hierarchical way and are child and the arts friendly to promote cooperative, participatory and active learning. The arts-based and child-centred curriculum, which is aligned with the local school standards, has motivated children to learn, improved their verbal and non-verbal communication skills, and increased their attendance at school and community participation. According to the evolving evaluation model developed by Rollins et al. (2002), to measure the effectiveness of the arts as an instrumental element in overall academic and social development for students in an arts-infused elementary school, teachers, parents and staff have witnessed the steady progress of many children at SAIL who were previously considered failures in other/traditional school settings. Those students who had difficulty in concentrating, controlling their anxiety and frustration, or had problems with socialization skills, have progressed immensely within a year or two. The analyses of the Stanford Achievement Test, 9th edn, for instance, show that SAIL students have been progressing in reading from 18.5 per cent basic and proficient levels in 1999 to 27.3 per cent in 2001, and the math performances have increased from 18.5 per cent basic level in 1999 to 50 per cent in 2001 (Riccio et al., 2003).

Another effective WVSA programme is the ARTiculate Employment Training Programme, which prepares youth with disabilities to join the workforce. Artists and mentors work with participants to develop artistic, vocational, social and life skills. The participants exhibit their work in the ARTiculate Gallery six times annually and receive commissions from the sales of their artwork. By acquiring presentation, marketing, interpersonal communication, problem-solving, basic computer and information technology skills, these young participants are prepared to transition from school to work. For instance, one participant, Harold Witlow, a 22-year-old artist with autism, is successfully employed at the Department of Agriculture, USA.

Case two
The YouthARTS Development Project, similar to WVSA's programmes utilizing the arts, was initiated in 1995 by federal agencies, national arts

organizations, and a consortium of three local arts agencies (the Fulton County Arts Council in Atlanta; the Regional Arts and Culture Council in Portland and the San Antonio Department of Arts and Cultural Affairs in San Antonio) to support local art agencies in building internal capacities and developing effective programmes, establish efficient arts-based programmes that address delinquency issues, and publicize nationally the information on programme design, execution and assessment. Although these local agencies aimed at developing art, vocational, entrepreneurial, social and life skills in these after school programmes (Art-at-Work, Atlanta; Youth Arts Public Art, Portland; and Urban smarts, San Antonio) the targeted groups, the incentives and art-activities were quite different from each other. For instance at the Art-at-Work Programme truant youth, between 14 and 16 ages were targeted, who besides artists training focused on subjects such as child development, conflict resolutions, problem-solving, communication, socialization and marketing, and were exposed to career opportunities in the arts. According to the end-programme-assessments participants gained the skills necessary to produce quality arts, were publicly recognized through their creative work, and improved their attitudes toward schooling, drug usage, as well as the frequency of their delinquent behaviours. The Youth Arts Public Art targeted 14–16 years old participants who were on probation for any status except sex offences. The members of this group, who had considered guns and drugs as an escape from everyday violence, physical abuse, poverty, homelessness and fear, acknowledged these activities as wrong and illegal and felt comfortable and safe in this after-school art programme. The third group, Urban smArts, targeted an age group of 10–12 who had poor academic achievement and engaged in antisocial behaviour. They likewise, showed great progress in developing art skills, dealing with anger, improving communication, cooperation, participation skills and task completion.

The National Endowment for the Arts and the US Department of Justice's Office of Juvenile Justice and Delinquency Prevention joined the group as well to carry out a national evaluation of the project. The evaluation that was conducted between 1996 and 1999 showed that increasing number of arts organizations became more and more engaged in social transformation projects, most of which focus on reducing juvenile problem behaviours such as school failure, drug use, delinquency and teen pregnancy (Clawson and Coolbaugh, 2001). Although the projects lacked sustainable amount of quantitative and qualitative evaluation data, the individual cases showed that the young participants' involvement with after school arts programmes overall improved the children's self-esteem, attitude towards school, academic development and their future.

Case three

There are hundreds of local, national and international development agencies worldwide that support alternative and popular education with the arts for children and teenagers. In lowest income communities these organizations are producing documentaries, creating radio programmes and musicals that are sensitive to societal realities. They respond to the needs of the population, providing facilities for creative development as well as giving information on issues like child rights, sexual education, substance abuse, teen-parent and kid relations and coping with natural catastrophes such as wars and terrorism. For instance, in South East Anatolia and shantytowns around Istanbul, Turkey a consortium of a university, local NGOs and the municipality have been providing arts services at a community centre for children between 6 and 13 years of age. Most of these homeless, economically deprived children have been traumatized in some ways and are compelled to live in isolation. Arts programmes like these rehabilitate these young individuals and provide opportunities to develop their artistic skills (painting, embroidery and music), and reintegrate them to society as creative, self-determined, active and empowered individuals (Bigglook and Aktuel, 2001).

Arts in gender issues and the empowerment of women

Case four

According to UNDP figures two-thirds of the world's illiterates are women and 80 per cent of its refugees are women and children. Every year more than 500,000 women die during pregnancy and childbirth, with huge regional disparities. Mothers need to be supported so that they can support themselves and save their children's lives. Women in general need to be recognized as active participants of the development process. The arts in various forms has been helping women from self-recognition to providing opportunities for self-employment and economic independence.

From 1995 to 1997 Dr Flavia Ramos developed the FotoDialogo Method and helped elderly Latinas in Springfield, MA, USA empower themselves through this method. The method, which is based on the notion of participatory and qualitative research techniques and Paulo Freire's adult literacy method, is called FotoDialogo because it establishes dialogue generated by pictures. The FotoDialogo method includes drawings of people and scenes of life inspired by real stories of the participants. The facilitator/researcher uses these pictures to create dialogue between groups with cultural diversities, encourages participants to tell their stories, observes their responses to these drawings and analyses the correlation between the portrayal of their experiences and their socio-economic conditions within the society that they inhabit.

In 1995 Dr Ramos started her 2-year long research study in the north end region of Springfield where she piloted her study with a community-based organization that was committed to provide education, health and empowerment programmes to the Latino community. She organized weekly sessions for the Latina Dialog Group (LWDG) that mainly involved low-income elderly Latino women of colour and also a series of FotoDialogo workshops that targeted community health and human service providers. During these gatherings she used a series of 30 black-and-white pictures, just about 8" by 11" in size. Each of these pictures portrayed various facial expressions of people of various ages and genders and also images of life common to the target group. In these dialogue sessions the participants interpreted these pictures (arranged in mixed sequence) and created stories based on these pictures either as a group or an individual. After the dialogue session LWDG reflected on the storylines and the characters, found similarities between the fabricated stories and real life situations, examined the issues that became apparent in the stories within the given framework, voiced those most challenging problems in the stories, and discussed possible ways to create change.

The dialogue and discussion sessions helped participants listen to one another. It led to a process of self-discovery among the Latino women. Before the sessions some women considered themselves as ignorant, illiterate, irresponsible mothers and blamed themselves for the death of their relatives due to HIV/AIDs and the imprisonment of their children who committed a crime and were drug addicts. After the sessions some regained their self-confidence and instead of blaming themselves they started thinking of ways to be effective in creating change. The sessions helped them to help themselves in examining and valuing their experiences. The sessions also made LWDG fully participate in the social change of their own community. LWDG participants became aware of the external factors (such as the issues of migration, language, ethnicity and education), that affected their living conditions and started to become *active leaders/educators* in child care, and women's health particularly for their families and friends. It raised awareness among practitioners regarding cross-cultural communication.

The results of this study indicate that illustrations, drawings, pictures of people and scenes that reflect the fabric of the community can help building collective dialogue. This method could enable community-based organizations working together with all the stakeholders to collaborate and focus on social and economic issues mutually. It could be a powerful strategy for low-literacy level groups, minority groups and marginalized women to exit their individual experiences of repression. The use of pictures and storytelling not only creates opportunities to voice personal histories, it also provides a suitable environment to flourish tolerance and build collective understanding (Ramos, 2002).

Case five
Create Africa South, is a non-governmental organization that has been facilitating opportunities to restore South African history and cultural identity, particularly through the empowerment of women. Conferences, seminars and exhibitions which enable local women to communicate and network

with international organizations and women from all around the world, a literary archive to collect contemporary writings and encourage creative writing in African languages; and a creative and cultural library in the visual arts within South Africa are a few of Create Africa South's projects. Voices of Women (Amazwi Abesifazane in Zulu) has been one of the most internationally recognized and supported projects which brings women from the rural and urban area of South Africa together. The founder of this initiative, Andries Botha, is a sculptor who has been concentrating on the role of artists in society and has been convinced that South African black women are the greatest contributors to the South African democracy building process. According to him women are the most stable element of society. Even in the most unstable conditions they are the ones who are capable of providing emotional and physical shelter especially for future generations. Therefore, women's security, their rights and well-being need to be maintained for preserving their individual existence, recovering the indigenous South African social and cultural history and creating a South African archive that had been exposed to cultural negligence and historical exploitation.

The 'Voice of Women' project provides opportunities for hundreds of women, not only in overcoming traumas experienced during the apartheid era, but also recovering personal, cultural and political information, discussing and recording history, transforming memories into creative works, learning about health-related issues especially about cervical, breast cancer and HIV/AIDs and gaining basic business skills (micro-enterprising, skill upgrading and product development). At the beginning of the project the participating women are asked to create a record of their stories and experiences. Memory cloths are created once their stories are written and their photos taken so that they become representatives of women rather than just mere statistics. The Memory Cloths are pieces of cloth slightly larger than an A-4 size sheet of paper and incorporates embroidery, appliqué and beadwork. The method of creating these cloths in fact brought the European patchwork tradition and the Zulu love letter (a form of beaded broach which is usually given as a gift by a young girl to a young man) together. At the earliest stages of the project women first resisted the idea of sharing their personal experiences and creating artworks based on their stories, but later on they realized the importance of these in constructing individual and collective identities, restoring indigenous African creativity and repositioning their history. Today these works of art are exhibited in Netherlands and the US and from the sales of these Memory Cloths, a fund has been created for these women's children, and new opportunities have been created for women to develop self-employment industry that creates products for international market. Although the stories depicted are heart rending, the cloths in contrast are colourful, and lively. Creativity and projects like this have progressively played a valuable role in remembering and re-establishing South African identity.

The arts in peace building and community development

Case six

Even to this date, interstates and intra-national conflict unfortunately still continues to impair millions of lives. According to the UNDP Human Development Report 106 governments still restrict many civil and political freedoms. Beginning of 1990, 3.6 million people have died as a consequence of 53 major armed internal conflicts (civil wars and ethnic violence). Consequently, a myriad number of individuals and organizations worldwide not only started to focus on urgent humanitarian relief, but also on mediation, building peace among groups in conflict, and developing cross-cultural understanding through multicultural peace concerts and other arts projects that bring people worldwide together. For instance, a UK-based non-profit organization PhotoVoice teaches basic photograph skills for street children in Vietnam, and Bhutanese refugee kids, who have spent nearly half of their lives in the camps located in the south-eastern lowlands of Nepal. Such participatory workshops provide opportunities for these disadvantaged children to forget about their daily distress, gain self-esteem, be better understood by their communities, and make the local, national and international audiences aware of the human stories behind the statistics, and political-ethnic conflicts. The Rose Project in Nepal has been taking place since 1998 and during this time the participants have been gaining arts/photography and writing/journalism skills, producing a monthly camp newspaper, and even conducting peer education sessions by themselves for hearing impaired children in the camp. The workshops culminate in exhibitions in Kathmandu where a few of the participants are able to travel and talk about their experiences and learn the process of putting up an exhibition. Today, a couple of the participants have already gone on to study journalism in Kathmandu and write for Nepali newspapers.

Case seven

An international non-governmental organization, Search For Common Ground (SFCG), has been incorporating the arts into peace building for the last few years. Besides projects like the 'US film exchange with Iran' which was established to encourage tolerance and cultural understanding, 'Nashe Maalo' (Our Neighborhood) children's TV series in Macedonia that enhanced multicultural harmony, and the cartoon summit where Arab, Israel, Iranian and Turkish editorial cartoonists delved into issues such as racism and the causes of ethnic stereotyping; SFCG has been organizing radio drama programmes and music festivals to create opportunities for empathy and unity to mature among people in political, social and economic dispute. According to SFCG's participative evaluation report, the Studio Ijambo in Burundi, which broadcasts *Our Neighbours, Ourselves* radio-drama programme, facilitates Hutus and Tutsis to equally voice themselves, helps reduce misunderstandings in their ethnic differences, and focuses on creating resources for collaborative development (Abdalla et al., 2002). The programme brings Hutu and Tutsi families together and focuses on resolving their problems through tolerance, humour and communication. The two Sangwe Music Festivals in Burundi, held since the beginning of the new millennium, also strengthened the belief that Hutus and Tutsis, despite their ethnic differences, are all Burundians. Hundreds of performers and thousands of participants from various provinces of the country joined these festivals. Among the performers there were women dancers who were actually traditional farmers coming from different regions of the country. What united them was that they all enjoyed dancing and singing while working in the fields. Prior to the performance these women went through an extensive process of auditioning, and for 18 months they practiced dancing and were educated in subjects such as women's health, dealing with domestic violence and schooling of children. These festivals help in redefining impasses, producing new visions, and creating common ground and hope for collaboration among ethnically diverse regions.

The Angolan Peace Song, which was produced collectively by 35 popular singers, was also one of those effective arts-infused peace-building efforts led by SFCG. Despite the geographical and ideological division among the singers, the peace song was successfully produced subsequent to intense negotiations. These singers showed amazing collaboration in writing the lyrics, recording the song, and making the music video, which includes scenes of the production. The Peace Song became the number one song played on Angolan radio. After the first launch concert, 10 more peace and hope concerts were organized. Over 10,000 cassettes were distributed vertically and horizontally, from teenagers to radio stations and government officials, who played the music video during parliamentary intermissions. The SFCG film series in the US have been influential in raising awareness and stimulating discussions among university students, scholars and general public about violent political strife, vicious cycles of terror, war, genocide, racism, and societal responsibility and accountability. These provocative, intellectually demanding and informative films from across the globe produce opportunities for the repressed and silenced voices of people to be heard, present challenges to the audience to deal with preconceptions and hard to discuss issues, and incite viewers to evoke solutions from a multiperspective point of view.

Case eight

Another non-profit organization, Shared Vision, whose mission is to produce monumental public artworks in urban areas, worked in collaboration with the city and private associations in Frederick County, USA to transform a 100 feet long, plain concrete bridge into an illusion of an old stone bridge. The entire edifice was hand-painted by a muralist, William Cochran and his assistants, applying the trompe l'oeil, 'deceiving the eye' technique. Within this structure they created four major features (including a bronze gate, a sculpture in a niche, a marble fountain and an archangel with a perspective painting technique called anamorphic projection), 3000 stones, and over 160 symbols and carvings. These symbol and carving ideas used in this Community Bridge Project (like *infinite knot* symbolizing energy, *two hands* – one black and one white – one helping the other over the wall; *shooting star* that inspires hope and faith; and hundreds of others) were contributed by thousands of people from all over the community and nation.

The 5 year long Community Bridge Project was also effective in building solidarity within the conservative, largely middle-class ethnically diverse community that had high racial tensions and a significant gap in income levels. For almost a year, a group of 12 community leaders designed the outreach to contact every population segment (from urban disadvantaged youth to bank presidents, from elderly workers to children, from teachers to business people, including the homeless) and geographic area and finally thousands of people participated in this project, either in promoting the project or sharing creative ideas, and painting. The actual impact of this project is difficult to quantify because many of the effects are intangible such as community spirit and belief in the power of collaborative effort. The creation of Community Bridge has brought community focus to a declining industrial area of the town, created significant capital investment to areas surrounding project site, and helped tourism to revitalize in this area. Since the completion of the project, architectural, artistic and cultural development in this community increased while problems related to racial tension began declining. As a consequence, the concept of this initiative has been replicated by school and church groups nationwide for education, training and inspiration. Companies as well use the method for corporate training in leadership and diversity. Today the bridge has become a symbol for shared values all over the world incorporating creative ideas from Bosnia, South Africa, Argentina, Indonesia, Saudi Arabia and more. These community development, conflict resolution and peace building projects with the arts have been tremendously successful at uniting people, building a broad sense of ownership, creating synergies between sectors, redirecting public and private investments, and strengthening communities for change.

The arts and health

Case nine

According to UNDP Human Development Report (2002) by the end of 2000 almost 22 million people had died from AIDS, 13 million children had lost their mother or both parents to the disease and more than 40 million people were infected with HIV/AIDS – 90 per cent of them in developing countries, 75 per cent in Sub-Saharan Africa. People with physical, emotional, social and psychological disabilities or who are under hospital care, or are dying or dealing with a death of a relative, need psychological, emotional and spiritual support in addition to physical care. The arts have been recognized as a powerful tool – an effective means for coping with emotions such as pain, discomfort, guilt, confusion and anger as a result of life-threatening illnesses, disabilities, dying or death.

In the South and Central Asia Region there are organizations that explore the potential of theatre as an effective means of social mobilization, especially in health-related issues, like HIV/AIDS, abortion and general hygiene. Theatre production (from conceptualizing, writing plays to performing, advertising, coordinating music, song and dance) is used as a method to ensure that the people's voices and concerns are incorporated into the design and realization of programmes that impact their lives. Theatre increases the self-confidence of participants, encourages teambuilding and promotes community income generating alternatives. In Kenya there are educational puppetry groups that aim to raise awareness among adults and children about HIV/AIDS. Some of these puppetry professionals are from Europe, the US and South Africa. Some are local and give performances in public places like parks and lead workshops for puppeteers and teachers on scriptwriting, puppet making, and social and health issues. The groups perform in local languages and use local musical instruments to create familiar tones and rhythms to attract audience. There are also partnerships of local and international organizations that have been using photography to promote the understanding of diseases, especially AIDs. For example, in Congo, PhotoVoice, organized photo-workshops for women affected by AIDs. The participants of this Positive Negatives Project learned using manual advanced semi-professional cameras and the know-how to educate others. Besides documenting the lives of family and friends, and creating personal albums to leave behind for future generations, some women were also able to earn money through their photography by working for newspapers and magazines to document the effects of HIV/AIDS in their country and share the stories with the rest of the world. Their work has been exhibited in Kinshasa, Ireland, around the UK, Barcelona and New York.

Case ten

In the States, WVSA Arts Connection's *ART is the heART* programme places artists (including visual artists, dancers, story tellers and musicians) into the homes of children and families receiving hospice or home health care services. After a careful artist selection process, the programme provides training, internships and ongoing support to enable artists to become effective members of the health care team. Artists work with children who are ill, disabled, or dying, or who have a family member who is dying. It can be a difficult yet satisfying task to help people, especially children dealing with issues of grief and loss. Reports of the programme have shown that artists' artistic and therapeutic work (painting, music, dance/movement, poetry and storytelling) have promoted healing. For instance, an 8-year-old boy who complained of nausea during the final weeks before his death, did not have those feelings during *ART is the heART* sessions. Another child, a 16-year-old girl with a rare immune disorder, was brought out of her depression by a dancer who worked with her for final 6 months. Before her death, this young patient was able to perform at a WVSA event and enjoy an international performance at the Kennedy Center, Washington, DC. The *ART is the heART* programme has been acclaimed within the US and replicated globally (Rollins and Riccio, 2002).

The arts in micro-enterprising and economic development

Case eleven

In the development field, eradicating poverty is one of the ultimate goals. There are local and global organizations that provide financial services to the world's poorest families. Some provide grants and some offer loans to low-income micro-entrepreneurs, who use the capital to create their own jobs, raise household incomes and improve their standard of living.

There are international organizations that work collaboratively with grassroots organizations in Latin America, Africa, Eastern Europe, Central Asia and Far East especially in developing businesses such as arts and crafts production. Along with marketable good production, these organizations concentrate on fair trade, employment rights (addressing problems of work and income security, food and social security), women's leadership and so forth. The Internet infrastructure creates online markets where one has access to unique artistic items. Through such initiatives people have the advantage to purchase goods, from sculptures to rugs and ornamental art (jewellery) from remote locations and help restore civilizations. There are also those organizations that focus on preserving national, cultural and historical identities through tourism and hence provide job opportunities.

One of these active organizations has been US-based Anatolian Artisans (AnArts) working closely with the Southeastern Anatolian Project (GAP) administration, the community centres, local grassroots organizations and low-income artisans (ceramicists, carpet-weavers, jewellery designers and others) in Turkey. In order to preserve the rich artistic traditions and designs of Asia Minor for local and global markets, AnArts programmes provide opportunities for the participants to learn about product diversification and marketing skills. These trainings help the project beneficiaries to understand all aspects of business planning and management. During these participative courses participants discover basic business concepts through discussions and activities guided by work cards and business simulation exercises within a self-paced learning and support environment. AnArts also organizes seminars and exhibitions in the US and in Turkey to raise awareness and appreciation of traditional arts and crafts that are the symbols of cultural identity and a means of sustainable development and links artisans to various markets, including museum gift shops, retail outlets and the vast global market via the Internet. The outcomes of a recent training course show that participants developed their understanding of basic business concepts, gained confidence in their knowledge of business, at least three participants of 14 were motivated to start a business incorporating the lessons learnt from the course, and quite a few were able to deliver a business-training course to 48 other young artisans. A participant, from Mardin, a small town in the GAP region, says that the trainings were very helpful for literate women who were unable to work before. The trainings assist women to become economically self-supporting while contributing to the national economy through tourism.

The arts in urban and sustainable development

Case twelve

More than 1 billion people still lack access to safe drinking water (UNDP, 2002) increasing population, poor urban planning, air, water and noise pollution, and other environmental issues such as global warming, deforestation, erosions, extinctions, these affect people's lives and living standards in a myriad of ways.

In North America and Europe, there are organizations that provide opportunities for people to develop their communities and environments with the arts for themselves and for generations to come. School arts projects incorporate sustainable development issues, which aim at teaching pupils effective protection of the environment and prudent use of natural resources. In America, Europe and Africa recycle-artists have emerged who use recycled materials such as broken glasses, mirrors, tiles, china, plastic bottles, tin, foil and paper to make items such as statues, paintings, home accessories, theatre costumes, public murals and puppets. Mosaicists and recycle artists, like Shylene Calla in Victoria/Canada, work together with communities to enhance living spaces, recreational parks, community centres and children's play grounds, by creating environmentally friendly mural and sculptural projects.

Worldwide concerts, art exhibitions, street theatres and numerous creative festivals bring together a wide range of stakeholders from government to NGOs to the general public to raise funds to assist projects for the protection of natural and historical sites (support eco-tourism), increase awareness on ecological issues, and turn people into 'global citizens' who understand the social and economic implications of environmental concerns, both locally and globally.

What is next? Social marketing via the arts or arts marketing with a twist of social responsibility

The common link in the above-mentioned organizations and individual artists is the use of the arts for a cause. Art is not created and/or supported only for arts' sake, rather it has an agenda. None of the listed projects, which are based on the society's past, its social structures, necessities and cultural setting, should be evaluated in a vacuum, one has to understand that these and similar arts projects are results of ongoing change processes and are likewise stimulators for furtherance of change.

From the most basic, purely aesthetic motivation to the most commercial expression of the arts, it has been shown that the arts are part of all our lives. For a long time advocates have been inclined to focus on promoting the arts within itself. This may appear as plausible if looking at the subject solely from an isolated view and single discipline. However, if approached from a multidisciplinary and sectoral perspective the main concern for the arts and development advocates becomes 'what art is able to do'.

The arts can help build human capacity, and support social capital. It can nurture creativity, help educate, advocate issues concerning human existence and offer a catalyst for social, political and economic change. Given the 'suitable environment' the arts can build strong and lasting community bonds. And it is the top decision makers and stakeholders of the public, private (businesses, small-medium enterprises and trans-national corporations) and civil/third (non-profit and non-governmental organizations) sectors that create the suitable environment, through the policies that lay the foundation for a multisectoral collaborative environment.

In today's glocalized world setting 'sectoral synergies' appear to be inevitable and it has become more significant than ever (Evans, 1996). As Lipietz puts it, '. . . there can be no local development (development by local firms and NGOs) without national and international solidarity' (Lipietz, 1994). During the past decade concepts such as good governance (Leftwich, 1994) and social responsibility became the key principles for building collaboration at local and global communities, co-regulating and co-addressing the challenges of underdevelopment (from poverty to labour migration/brain-drain, wage disparities to intellectual property rights, from human rights and democratization to the liberties of child workers and environmental protection). Good governance incorporates the ideals of people-centrism, participatory democracy, transparency, accountability, ethics, and openness at micro- and macro-levels. And social responsibility focuses on the inter-dependencies of public, private and third sectors and their commitment to achieving societal good at national and international settings.

Social marketing (Kotler et al., 2002), turned into a major strategy not only in promoting health programmes, but also those common areas that concern everyone. Today informed national and global citizens want to know more whether organizations in private, public and third sectors fulfil their social responsibility and act upon the principles of good governance effectively. The arts have been an effective social marketing tool and as the above case examples have shown has helped those complex issues to be voiced, created awareness within the target audience and in some cases led to supportive policy making. Although currently there is limited information about what works and what does not, the above case examples substantiate the hypothesis, that the arts have created constructive changes.

Glocalization has helped the arts to be acknowledged worldwide to be one of the most effective means in showing us all that problems and questions from the simplest form to the complex can have more than one solution and answer. Despite cultural differences and cultural biases from organizational to community level, the arts do not limit our cognition with our language, ethnic origin, race, religion, etc. and quite the reverse it helps us understand and rejoice multiple perspectives at local and global magnitude. It is therefore crucial to understand the importance of glocalization and the arts in the adoption of universal codes (good governance and social responsibility) and their impact on creative capacity building in all sectors.

As many developmentalists assert, education lies at the heart of development and according to Robinson (2000) the arts should be in the centre of education. He claims that academic ability is not the whole of one's intelligence and states that most human culture would have never occurred if the human mind were limited to academic intelligence. The current education system in the developed world has been constructed on the industrial economic model, where the industrial economy necessitates a workforce that is for the most part labour intensive. In today's information age 'knowledge workers' have changed the fabric of the workforce (Castells, 1996). Although education systems worldwide go through considerable reform, these changes also need to incorporate the inventive and creative aspects (Robinson, 2001). As Michelangelo said, 'one paints not with the hand, but with the brain' (West, 1996). In multicultural environs, where 'knowledge workers' (Boyett and Boyett, 1998) have become critical sources for development, to advance the arts and its role in creative capacity building for today's and tomorrow's progress happens to be unavoidable.

The main question in this section of the chapter was 'What's next? Social marketing via the arts or arts marketing with a twist of social responsibility'. It would appear to be both. Whether the arts are effectively utilized in all the disciplines of marketing communications (such as advertising and public relations), and in social systems' collateral materials, or is integrated with social criteria by advocates of the arts whence promoting art within the arts, human existence and the arts is the ultimate purpose. Perhaps the easiest way to understand the synthesis of both of these marketing practices is by recognizing these as 'societal arts marketing' as mentioned above.

Consequently, it would be useful to consider various points when marketing the arts and strengthening the application of the arts within and between sectors. First, where applicable, the arts should be incorporated into education rather than merely trimmed down to education about the arts as elective classes. Issues concerning arts-infused education such as curriculum, pedagogy (Clark, 1996), infrastructure design and education materials should be addressed by all the related stakeholders. Second, policies that are necessary for creating an open environment which nourishes human capacity, social capital, extensive implementation of social responsibility and good governance for all segments of society, need to be decided upon collaboratively. The arts have been perceived to be secondary in the development field, however, we should not forget that it is the people themselves who create the arts. If key decision makers are concerned about human aspects of life as they claim to be and this current development trend with a 'human face' is truly genuine, then we cannot alienate arts from the development scene.

Third, current alliances of business, the arts and cultural organizations should be maintained and new ones should be cultivated to fulfil the needs of appropriate institutes and underprivileged communities. According to UNDP the number of international non-governmental organizations grew from 1083 in 1914 to more than 37,000 in 2000. The third sector is an engine in cultural (Fox, 1963; Furlong et al., 2000), social, political and economic development (Øyen and Atal, 1997). Decision makers should recognize the significance of the third sector, alongside private and public, as a key actor in the development field.

Fourth, in order to create sustainability within the third sector, mutual trust needs to be created between non-profit leaders and artists, who provide pro bono or reduced fee-work, in attracting the right audience for effective social change and supporting social marketing projects that convey and implement the messages of the organization (Holland, 2002). Fifth, although there are so many individual organizations and advocate groups that work in the creative sector, the understanding of the arts as a powerful means for creating positive change in our daily lives is still at its embryonic stage and has not received the basic support. Art's valuable input in society should be re-examined by policy makers and incorporated into relevant lines of work and development schemes. Arts is:

- an effective education tool particularly in issues like human development, youth and women empowerment, sustainable development;
- a communication and marketing medium that for instance is powerful in raising health awareness, fostering democratization and resolving conflicts;
- as Hubbard and Taylor (1976) suggest a therapy method;
- a key industry in maintaining cultural identities and heritage, generating opportunities for workforce (creating jobs), and subsidizing economies.

Lastly, involvement of the arts in creative capacity building should be respected and hence more detailed qualitative and quantitative research along with arts-infused project effectiveness and success assessments should be conducted.

In our interdependent world setting the world has become a global village creating 3rd millennium fusion civilizations and developing opportunities for mutual understanding and solidarity. The arts in any form and style has been the major common factor in linking people at any level, social, political and economic position, age, ethnicity, race, religion, gender, colour, etc., and glocalization in particular has intensified this phenomenon.

The glocal, multisectoral and multidisciplinary approach in development with the arts has focused on the importance of the arts (and anything that relates to the arts), and partnerships in sectors at local and global settings. According to this approach, the people are at the centre of each sphere (political–economic and social–cultural) and are the ones who create the balance (rules, regulations and relationships) within and among the spheres, which intersect, creating a common ground for a people-centred perspective. The social–cultural sphere incorporates the main ingredients of communal values such as social capital and key representatives of the third sector like the non-governmental, non-profit, voluntary and civil organizations. The political–economic sphere focuses primarily on the private and public sector actors like the military and technological initiatives. The components of each sphere should not be perceived as static and in a vacuum, rather there is an emphasis on convergence, interconnectivity and flexibility in the overall approach. People – the stakeholders themselves are the ones that create this bond – this interconnectivity. One should obviously not forget the effects of external factors like the natural resources and adversities, climate and geography on all decisions related to change. However, people worldwide do possess those attributes (to varying extent) to build capacities and make creative changes for themselves and future generations.

Box 9.1 **Discussion Piece by Elif Shafak**

WOMEN'S ART IN THE AGE OF THE MILITARIST MACHINE

In the age of military machine, neither art nor the artist herself should be romanticized. As numerous examples from various cultures, East and West alike, demonstrated, art in this age has been a constitutive element in fabricating nationalist ideologies, homogenous identities, cultural stereotypes and historical continuities. Too often, what was intended to serve the muses served instead patriarchies, nation-states and vested interests.

Yet, the good thing about art is its enormous potential to concurrently accomplish opposition through its innate Dionysian capacity to destroy and disintegrate, decentralize and liberate. As such, art can bolster what Althusser named 'ruptures in continuity'. If, as Milan Kundera maintained, 'the struggle of men against power is the struggle of memory against forgetting', then, art can be a struggle against collective manipulative amnesia.

This twofold nature of art has been acknowledged by the women's movement from the early periods onwards. Art has on the one hand, been questioned as an embodiment of patriarchal patterns and vested interests, but at the same time, art has also been, especially during the 1970s, perceived as a site of struggle, a means

Box 9.1   *(Continued)*

of resistance and a ground of opposition for not only feminists who were pushed to margins by society at large but also by those feminists who were pushed to margins within the women's movement itself. Women artists from the margins have seen art making as a way of interrupting the dominant hegemonic stance that silences and subdues ethnic, class and gender differences. Art in their hands has been a way of renaming those de-named. Despite prolific records in this vein, though, my contention is that to this day, the depth and complexity of the triple relation between the feminist world, the art world, and the 'real world' has been only dimly mapped. The 'politicization of aesthetics' is still a barely touched issue in the women's movement.

'Women and art' is a problematic matrimony. While the couple can be awkward, each partner is even more so. If as Judith Butler asserts all gender is drag, where women and men have an ideal that nobody inhabits, can we still talk then about an art unique to women? And if so, should that be necessarily concerned with female experience? If imagination is free but not the artist himself or herself, where does the artist stand vis-à-vis 'real life'? Where does the woman artist stand vis-à-vis the age of the military masculinist machine that we live in? Interestingly, it is not the answers, but the questions, or perhaps the very presence of the query as such that reverberates an essential difference. For across the world today, to theorize on the muses has been a practice confined to a limited circle. Is it a luxury to ponder these questions? Is art that is political but not necessarily with a concrete political end, a luxury that only a privileged elite of wealthy societies and the non-Western artists who are accepted to those circles can truly enjoy? For Marcuse, since the strength of art lied in its Otherness, the function of art as 'negation to the existing' was abandoned, if art came too close to reality. At the core of his theory of art lay the notion of Beauty. To be effective, he claimed, art must exert its capacity for estrangement. As Carol Becker pointed out, the Left did not pay due attention to questioning the bond between the muses and politics, but neither did the feminist movement so far. One barely touched question is, how incompatible are beauty and politics, in the mold of art making? And where and when these two may conflict, how free are artists of minorities or non-Western societies, especially where there is an ongoing political turmoil? Can the artist in these urgent circumstances find intellectual or artistic stimuli to ponder along the same lines, develop artistic genres, not for a concrete political cause but for other ends or simply for the sake of art? When Western feminists encourage women artists from other parts of the world to tell their story, this no doubt is a great contribution to voicing the hitherto unheard. Nevertheless, herein lies a masked danger. Here in the US, an Algerian, Palestinian or another minority ethnic woman writer, is expected to tell primarily her own story as a woman in Algeria, Palestine or of a specific minority. Her identity starts to precede her work. As the feminist movement in America channels

Box 9.1   *(Continued)*

non-Western or minority women to tell their story, it also deprives them of the right to infiltrate into the stories of others, or even stories that are not necessarily real, or political but essentially imaginary and creative. How concerned is the women's movement with the shifts of art making and the possible prospects of these, and how open is the mainstream/malestream world of art to women of different belongings?

Non-Western/minority artists are incessantly confined by two separate, yet interrelated forces at work. On the one hand the progressive groups herein the States constantly encourage them to tell their own stories, which is in itself of primary importance, but here in lies the danger of the artist's identity preceding her work. The artist is pushed and encouraged to remain in her identity. As a novelist I find this highly worrisome. Since I came to the US, I asked myself more often than ever how to define and identify myself? What is the category I should be located in? What kind of a novelist I am? I believe only my work, my writing can tell that, but the irony is that for my writing to be translated into the English language, I should be defined beforehand.

According to Jeanette Winterson, the truth of fiction is not the truth of railway timetables, for against daily insignificance art recalls to us possible sublimity. If the truth of art is not the truth of railway timetables, what about the truth of wars, nationalisms, fundamentalisms, and about the truth of the military machine? How are we going to define the relationship between art and politics in these specific contexts? Is it a luxury to bring forward the primacy of aesthetics and the concern for beauty at times of war? Is art without a concise or concrete political purpose a luxury that only or solely the educated elite of wealthy societies can truly enjoy? To rephrase Adorno's question: is poetry still possible under war conditions?

Today, what Terry Eagleton calls the split between fundamentalism and cosmopolitanism has gained speed both within and across nations, an inclination that was already present in the US, at times reflected in the move from crowded urban centres to homogeneous suburbs, as Richard Sennett points out in *The Uses of Disorder*. Fundamentalist discursive block desires to erect walls between distinct cultural practices, establish homogeneous identities and identitical human beings, extol family values, simplify and deny national, religious and ethnic differences. Sustaining communities of monolithic character being their credo, fundamentalists can be speaking in the name of various religions, nationalisms, or ethnicities, East and West alike.

Sadly, a similar desire for homogeneity is equally at work in the 'world of art'. The question to what is art, or which artwork should be brought to the fore is answered by the mainstream art world. Only a few token 'outsiders' are included, and even then, they and their works are neatly pigeon holed. Biracial, multicultural or omni-confused artists are left in an awry position. They are marginalized,

| Box 9.1 | *(Continued)* |

and their characterizations are based primarily upon race, ethnicity or national background. Categories like 'native American art', 'Latin American art' and likewise, 'feminist art' are one-dimensional. They dehumanize the artists by negating their individuality.

Art does not need categories. It needs the in-between-ness of belonging; as Elsbeth Probyn says, of belonging not in some deep authentic way but belonging in constant movement, modes of belonging as surface shifts. Art needs blurred boundaries and artists need ambiguities and sliding belongings. This I believe is not a luxury that artists from countries torn by war conditions can be deprived of.

For a variety of reasons, the age we live in compels artists to make a choice between the muses and politics, between having no story of your own and telling your own story. The women's movement should give more consideration, to the quest for possible means of congruency, rather than perceiving them as essentially incompatible, and thereby intentionally or not, forcing women artists of distinct belongings to make a once-for-all choice between the muses and politics.

Questions

1. How should women's art be marketed internationally? Explain this in the context of the above debate.
2. What role, if any, international marketers should play in the world system described above?

Conclusion

As William Morris, an English writer, artist and social reformer, mentioned in his book *The Arts and Crafts of Today* (*1889*) (Marceau et al., 1998) if arts were not applied to everyday objects, not only would products have no meaning but also there would be gradual deterioration of the human race. Throughout this chapter the main emphasis has been on people, local and global society and its needs, and the ways and principles of creating individual and societal prosperity at macro- and micro-levels. We need to understand that any type of art is woven strongly into today's complex social structure, and to fight against the challenges worldwide and build the necessary capacities, arts' role is essential.

Obviously art by itself should not be seen as the remedy for underdevelopment and overcoming the impediments against the continuance of humanity. The arts alone cannot help people in need unless the authorities create the necessary environment for innovative, productive and sustainable development. The political and economic will and commitment of national and international communities needs to co-exist. The degree of commitment within/among these spheres influence the quality and the stability of projects that are critical for overcoming crisis and developing individuals and societies.

The arts, marketed in the development field, are without doubt an effective catalyst in making a positive difference (for all of us). Art broadens our imagination, unties existing rigid beliefs, creates tolerance and instigates new paths to find alternative – balancing solutions.

Acknowledgements

The case examples in this chapter could not have been prepared without the kind support of many individuals and organizations. I am particularly grateful to Judy Rollins, Susan Coscis, William Cochran, Flavia Ramos, Yıldız Yağcı, Anna Blackman and Janine Zagel for taking time and providing information and insights on their projects.

Chapter 10

Key issues in arts marketing

Peter Fraser, Finola Kerrigan and Mustafa Özbilgin

While most marketing texts and articles incorporate examples from a wide range of sectors, it is increasingly clear that they do so either on a general or specialist case study basis. However, as soon as we try to consider the issue of marketing in a particular context, it is quite clear that the distinctive features of that particular sector or organisation demand a different local approach. When we look in the literatures for examples, we find it hard to identify these distinctive features. There are several existing texts on marketing in the arts. However, some of these have been criticised for the way in which they offer limited applications of traditional or generic frameworks and seem to contribute little in the way of new insights.

Principles of marketing seem to be modified or modifiable in relation to the arts. Why is this? Is this so any more than for any other activity as marketing generalisations and frameworks are always modified in their application? Or is this because the arts seem particularly different in some important respects? Before turning to examine marketing in the arts, it might be useful to reflect on the challenge in what we are doing. The first is the challenge of understanding the nature of the arts themselves. It is hard not to ponder their intangibility, the impossibility of conveying the central experience. Several authors have made the point that truly great art can only be understood or interpreted in its own terms. To put it another way, words are normally inadequate. The writer, broadcaster and musicologist Hans Keller took this to a logical development. In wanting to convey the nature of masterpieces for string quartet, he wrote musical analyses whereby his pieces foreshadowed and worked on the musical themes in the works he was addressing. You, as an amateur artist, may have tried to describe the qualities of paint handling that make a particular portrait, for example, special, but only by standing in front of it and experiencing the effect can its greatness be understood.

Culture is a term used for many things by many people. One definition has it as the body of the arts or general state of intellectual development (Chambers 20th Century Dictionary, 1983). Should subsidy be directed to 'high' culture – or to folk or mass cultures too? 'High culture is the term now used for much of this. Its sprawling, majority antithesis, oblivious of class pedigrees, is "mass culture" – an imprecise term roughly interchangeable with "popular culture" and not necessarily pejorative. Theoretically, high culture is acquired selectively and actively, mass culture passively, even unconsciously' (Horowitz, 1994). Superseding regionalised 'folk cultures' of earlier times, mass culture may be said to have begun with the late 18th century's burgeoning public of readers and listeners. It was expanded by 20th century communications technology. And with regard to theatre, where is the division? Plays can appeal to all at once.

Certainly consideration of the arts phenomenon throws up questions and challenges. One is the issue of the relationship of work to its public. Looking at a whole range of examples, we see that work which is popular in its day does not last, or at any rate if it is not forgotten it finds its own place, perhaps at a subsidiary level. Shakespeare in his day was not regarded as the best of the Elizabethan and Jacobean dramatists, even though he was listed among the major writers of his day. Some works of art are completely neglected in their day, such as Moby-Dick, but rise to prominence and greatness later on. The popularity of different works will change over time.

Another challenge is that of boundaries. In this volume we consider among the performing arts jazz and popular music, drama in the forms of opera and theatre; and we address also film and the visual arts. (For a variety of reasons, including space, many of the arts and crafts have been omitted). Are there any themes or issues common to all? On the face of it, even the issue of profit does not seem particularly central. Most of the activities are not-for-profit, but by no means all. Film could be considered a strong profit making activity, yet there are plenty of filmmakers who try to work outside the Hollywood ethos where profit is considered first among equals. Even in the highest of high arts such as (arguably) sculpture or opera, there are private sector impresarios who even in today's competitive environment, present opera – admittedly under special conditions – free of any government or public sector subsidy. In fact, several authors have pointed to the blurring of the boundaries between profit and non-profit activities.

Arts genres tend to be considered as discrete sectors and categories. Some are clearly for-profit while others such as opera may never have passed the market test. They are in need of investment and/or subsidy from either private patrons or the taxpayer through government policies. Much is made of the importance of developing relationships with the customer or client and the use of volunteers or friends is considered an important resource.

While some arts organisations cannot function without them, others consider them an underused resource. Exploration of the background and underlying motivations of volunteers in the arts suggest that that they tend to be older, highly educated and have distinctive sets of values.

It is perhaps unsurprising that opera is perceived very differently from orchestral concerts or drama. This has a number of implications. There are many beliefs about the arts, for example that someone who likes theatre will never attend opera. Do these apparently different performing arts attract the same audiences? It is unclear how true this is when it comes to selling tickets. Marketing managers are aware of the crossover that exists. Evidence exists because few theatres are dedicated to one form of the performing arts. Many venues and organisations will host not just opera performances but ballet. This can be seen, for example, in London at Covent Garden and the Coliseum. In Copenhagen, the Royal Danish Opera is promoted alongside drama. The Marketing manager for Scottish Opera promotes also a mix of activities at their base the Theatre Royal, and talks of the strongest crossover being between opera and drama; others see a worthwhile overlap between ballet and opera audiences, seen widely.

Commonly, reading a book on theatre or drama will produce little or nothing in the way of references to opera. To take one example, Giesekam in writing about amateur and community theatre in Scotland, gives fleeting mention to musicals and light opera. 'Grand opera' or opera on the amateur level is mentioned only two or three times in passing (Giesekam, 2000: 57–8).

We tend to behave as though there are other clear divisions such as high culture versus low culture, or arts versus crafts or local versus global. Another is between the professional and the amateur. 'Amateur', originally meaning someone who simply did not take payment for their contribution, has now shifted to become closer to a pejorative term. If something is amateurish, it is perceived perhaps as slipshod but at any rate something that falls short of the desired or even ideal standard. One might be considered worthy of public subsidy, the other not. However, some themes are critical and the arts in general have some commonality. For these purposes it hardly seems to matter which particular art we are addressing.

We set out in this volume to make some attempt to explore international themes. There is tension here as however international a movement or influence may become, art arises from small-scale local interactions. Kolb makes the case that the management and purpose of cultural organisations tends to vary somewhat from country to country because they are affected by the local culture of the community. Nevertheless, she argues that the 'ambience of a museum may vary from the US to Japan but there is still an immediately recognisable similarity across national frontiers. The same can be said of theatre, classical music, opera and dance' (Kolb, 2000: 2).

A specific example of this is Germany where its culture has historically placed very high value on its arts and gone so far as to support them with levels of subsidy that are, by international standards, comparatively generous. Only now, in the early years of the 21st century, is Germany's economic position forcing a rethink. The loss of such high levels of state funding has forced arts organisations to turn to other sources of support. One German theatre has moved into the independent sector, has accepted state subsidy at its existing level, but supplemented this with sponsorship and embarked on a dramatic cost cutting and teambuilding exercise. Some would say that the resulting organisation is much healthier in every way even though the culture in which the organisation operated would have found this an approach that was alien and innovative. Germany state subsidies for the film industry were also criticised for not benefiting the indigenous film industry as American companies who were able to apply by identifying loopholes in the funding regulations were accessing them.

The chapters in this volume identify themes and issues particular to that art form, but there are also many issues, which are common across all these arts. What then are some of the key themes that have emerged from these chapters? Service element, technology, education, diversity and the nature of the arts in themselves are identified in this book as critical themes.

The primary commonality between these art forms is the service element where production is inseparable from consumption. Within the service sector, the arts are competing broadly with other forms of education and leisure. In this competitive environment, it is vital that arts managers look beyond their art form, or other art forms as sources of competition and try to understand why their customers are loyal to them and why others are not. It is encouraging to note that, as outlined in the earlier chapters in this volume, arts marketers are starting to look beyond obvious motivations in attending or supporting various art forms and events and trying to understand the level of involvement their customers have or would like to have with the arts experience. Questions also need to be asked about the role which consumption of the arts plays in forming individual identity. Research by Kottasz (2003) has shown that young affluent men in London prefer to donate to arts organisations rather than other charities due to the perceived and actual benefits that they receive as a result of this.

Technology presents new challenges for the arts organisation. It can supplement, enhance or even replace the service provided. There is huge potential for new presentation of exhibits. So, for example, the National Gallery in London can offer courtesy of its sponsors a digitised guide to its exhibits that helps visitors make that helps visitors make more of their experience. In film, satellite distribution of product is going to revolutionise distribution, at once increasing quality, speed, efficiency and reducing costs. In the performing arts, new box office technologies offer opportunities for tracking the purchase activity of purchasers and offering new opportunities for segmentation.

However, it also raises challenges. An organisation buying a new box office system may have little more input than a list of names and addresses. Yet the lack of resources available for marketing may mean that its development can only be slow, incremental and piecemeal. Building up a picture of purchasing behaviour in the longer term presents more problems. For example, some forms of arts consumption are clearly family oriented. To take a commercial example, going to a movie or a pantomime are key experiences in the life of many children and represent part of an educational process. Theatre going may be less measurable or predictable. The use of a credit card to buy three or four theatre tickets may be relatively easy to record and track, but some managements point out that the individuals accompanying the purchaser remain unknown and hence perhaps unreachable with promotion for other offerings.

As Phillips said, 'Every person who has ever thought about the arts must have wondered why it is that when almost all young children find it natural to sing, dance, paint and give free reign to their imagination, interest in these things, let alone active participation, has become such a comparative rarity by the mid-teens … '. However, he goes on to ascribe uneven artistic activity to the fact that 'the general public is indifferent to and unconcerned in the arts. To the man or woman in the streets the arts will almost certainly seem irrelevant, an occasional activity pursued by a small, clannish elite' (Phillips, 1977).

Arts cannot be looked at in isolation. What we see in our theatres and other outlets are the tip of the iceberg, professionals at the peak of their careers. What is happening elsewhere, when we look to amateur provision and school education? As the UK school curriculum becomes more and more prescriptive, arts education is receiving less and less attention. 'Creative industries', argues William Sieghart, 'are worth £67 billion a year to the economy and yet art teaching in schools is struggling' (Hill, 2003).

Whose responsibility is such education? Increasingly, organisations operating in the arts are investing considerable efforts in outreach programmes of various kinds. Such campaigns quite apart from their intrinsic value are more likely to make the organisation appealing to sponsors. Accordingly the funding is mixed, with some, coming from public sources, some from private. But some companies see outreach work as a danger (Giesekam, 2000: 81) if it contributes to the marketing and audience development work. Arts organisations can become confused about their goals. For survival, they need to recruit younger consumers. Yet are young people open to the messages conveyed by the arts organisations? There are examples where this does not seem to be the case. Schools in the UK at least seem to be more and more focused on government prescribed content. Music, particularly classical music, and the arts seem to be increasingly marginalised (Morrison, 2002). One solution might be to develop more substantial outreach programmes going into schools.

The previous chapters have all addressed the nature of the arts in terms of the individual, society, the arts and business and art for art's sake. Art for the individual can play a social role, an educative role as well as transformation, informing the expression of their identity. We have also shown how the arts have a role in society, as a means of empowerment, social inclusion and information giving. The business benefits of the arts are also evidenced in terms of profit accrued directly from the arts as well as indirectly through business use of artistic forms, such as the use of music and visual arts in advertising and in creating ambiance in business organisations. Finally there are many who believe in promoting the practice of various art forms for their own sake; art for art's sake.

There is a social aspect to the performing arts. At first sight, this is not applicable to film yet when we reflect on reasons why we should see a film on theatrical release, rather than obtaining a video, one of the issues relates to timing and access. We may not want to wait until the video is released or travel to an out-of-the-way cinema. However, the collective audience reaction plays a part, both positively and negatively.

While artists may create initially to satisfy themselves, the audience is integral to the experience. Hill et al. (1995: 27) set this out in three forms; the audience as 'arts receptors'; the audience as associates, including stakeholders who may not actually be present; and audiences as customers.

Audiences vary from art to art. At an art exhibition, for example, people may wander round in small groups, with some discussion taking place, but for many the experience is almost solitary. Certainly galleries and museums are places of relative peace and quiet. However, this is not true of large-scale theatrical events.

The interaction between performers and audience at live events, not restricted to opera or indeed classical music, provides a fascination which many have tried to unravel. Susan Tomes, pianist with the Florestan trio, is one of them. 'It still mystifies me that each audience has its own characteristic way of listening. My colleagues and I always discuss "what sort of an audience" it is, and we always agree. Some audiences are focused, some scattered; some are cold, some eager, and some mysteriously draw out one's best. Yet when I'm in the audience myself, I deprecate the idea that I'm part of a collective personality' (Tomes, 2002). Keller compared the audiences for a concert given by a string quartet with those for a professional soccer match and made the point that while the first audience is conventionally considered more sophisticated, probably 90 per cent of its members will never have had the experience of playing in a quartet. 'It would be an un-expert audience, listening entirely passively without really knowing what the musicians were doing.' By contrast, probably only 10 per cent of the members of a football crowd have not played football. 'You'd find fifty thousand real experts, who knew physically and felt what was going on down there' (Black, 1990: xx). What happens if the audience is restless? Gielgud once famously said, 'Never say it's a bad house – it's your job to make it a good one.'

One of the contributions to the experience made by an audience is its applause, a feature worth a book chapter on its own. The performance ends, the curtain comes down, the audience members perhaps suspend their disbelief and move towards a level of different consciousness, preparing to show their gratitude and discharge some emotion in applause. The artificial nature of the performance is recognised in the performers who may or may not take their curtain calls to an extent, in character. Its nature is primitive and it is clear that the actors who played evil or unattractive characters find their applause quite different. It is as though we as audience members have not yet got our primitive feelings under control and cannot yet separate out the part or the direction from the acting.

The management of arts organisations is recognised as a distinctive and complex skill. Certainly in the UK, as in other advanced economies, there are many signs of the increasing professionalisation of arts marketers and managers. One of the pieces of evidence lies in the creation and development of the Arts Marketing Association (AMA) in the UK. Founded in November 1993, it sprang out of two former groupings: the Society of Arts Publicists and the Society of Northern Arts Publicists. The organisational change reflected the growing knowledge that there was a difference between marketing and publicity, and that marketing was a much more descriptive title for the complex activity undertaken within arts organisations. AMA now has 1500 members, a creditable achievement. According to its website, AMA 'is for people who persuade the public to experience the arts'. Its active and diverse membership regularly participate in professional development opportunities to improve their working practices. The visual arts and crafts, museums, performing and combined arts, film, cinema and literature are all represented. The AMA has hosted a broad programme of events. Historically, the annual conference has been the main focus of activity. In Manchester, in 1995, the first conference attracted 80 delegates. In 1996 at Warwick, 'Desperate for Promotion' attracted 120 people. The conference now attracts well over 400 arts professionals from across the UK and from outside the UK. In addition, other events hosted include seminars, workshops, day events and network meetings.

At the organisational level, arts marketing has indeed embraced many mainstream marketing tools. However, these attempts have been strengthened by various public sector initiatives. Commissioned by the Arts Council of England and published by the AMA, 'Thinking Big!' is intended to equip readers to create a strategic marketing plan for their own organisation, that is to look at the big issues, usually the long term ones. Cashman (2003) stresses the need for strategic analysis, often ignored at the expense of tactics. For too long, most subsidised arts organisations had employed in a so-called 'marketing' function people who were uninvolved in the larger picture. They were considered to be underpaid, overworked and undertrained. But in recent years this seems to be changing, a fact not unconnected with the rapid growth of the AMA and similar bodies elsewhere as noted in the earlier chapters. Funders of the arts want to see targets for growth and strategies for bringing more people and widening access – 'for the many, not the few'. In fact, they want evidence of goals and strategies, they want to see marketing plans. In the 1990s, more and more people were asking about the effect of 50 years of government subsidy in the arts. Have audiences been increased? How can the effect be demonstrated? How can future subsidy best be directed? All this seemed to point to the need for greater strategic awareness, monitoring of the effectiveness of different promotional tactics and a greater strategic role for arts marketers.

Kotler famously advocated that for-profit organisations should strive to become 'market oriented' in other words they should proactively set out to identify needs, wants and demands and then devise the offering to meet them. However, he also described other types of orientation, some of which better describe many arts organisations. For example, the product oriented company would be the kind of organisation that offered the public what it believed to be good for them, perhaps without any evidence in the traditional meaning of the word, of need. From another perspective, an arts organisation might be considered to operate with a societal aim, not just determining the needs and wants of target markets but to adapt the organisation to delivering satisfactions that 'enhance the consumer's or society's well being'.

Of course an arts organisation perhaps more than many has multiple orientations and aims. So among its multiple publics can be found not just segments of the general public, but a range of funding bodies some of which have very specific needs, and needs furthermore that are different from each other. So for example companies offering sponsorship deals, the local government offering a grant, national arts funding bodies, charitable trusts, Friends' organisations, are none of them simply customers in the business sense of individuals who come along to an event and buy tickets. All this results in a much more complicated offering.

In the context of private sector marketing, Doyle (2000) highlighted some ways in which the ideal, as espoused through generations of marketing textbooks and indeed by marketing practitioners, differs from the reality. In essence, 'while marketing is regarded as paramount, marketing professionals are disregarded'. The solution, argues Doyle, must depend on ways of justifying such marketing strategies in relevant financial terms. Managers must show that marketing will increase returns to shareholders. The issue that flows from this of course is what is the meaning of shareholder value, particularly in the public and not-for-profit sectors? And what for example might growth mean? Normally, Doyle argues, it needs to develop 'options which will allow it to explore new growth opportunities' (Doyle 2000: 65). This approach seems to represent an entirely economic perspective. Taking a measure of the financial health of an operation is a necessary but surely not a sufficient condition. What happens when we begin to look at organisations whose outputs are not measurable and where economic terms represent only a part, and perhaps only a small part, of its activity?

What are some of the other issues key in all management activity yet not normally seen in marketing textbooks? The domain of marketing as offered in academic books and textbooks is almost universal in its extent, touching on almost all aspects of management activity from the management of the board downwards. What marketing officers in their departments actually do is often limited to promotional activity, the production of the brochures, promotion including advertising and the selling of the tickets. A marketing perspective therefore focuses almost entirely on relationships with consumers or potential members of the audience. If however we take the wider view of marketing as a process in which an organisation engages directly with a wider range of publics or stakeholders to increase its influence we can see that much of this activity is not one in which the marketing department is normally involved. Fundraising, for example, is normally the province on a separate committee or division, formed of those who have a lot of wealth themselves as well as the distinctive skills involved.

The marketing concept espouses the importance of understanding the needs and wants of the customer. However, in the arts environment, as in many high technology environments, the product is regarded as the brainchild of the producer, who through a belief in its intrinsic value seeks ways of bringing to an appreciative audience. Although there is evidence of the use of the broader marketing concept as audience research is now employed more widely, arts marketing practice will always have this further complex dimension.

Traditional marketing theory has given the marketing mix a central role. However, in common with other service sectors, arts marketing practice necessitates greater attention to processes and the broad concept of customer care over a concern for product, price, promotion and place. These can be seen as subservient to the processes and customer care element of service delivery in the arts. For example, Tusa has argued (2003), the role of marketing departments is largely that of promotion, to let people know that particular events are being held and to encourage them to participate.

There is plenty of evidence that arts managements are trying hard to advertise and promote their product imaginatively and aggressively. In the UK, Ellen Kent's 'Opera International' touring productions of works from the classic repertoire are well received. Their Rigoletto is promoted on flyers not just with glossy images of glamour but with the tagline 'the opera they tried to ban', a comment that being true, few could take exception with even though the attempted ban was over 100 years ago. Classical can however be promoted in ways that encourage accusations of 'dumbing down'. As Evelyn Glennie put it, criticising crossover acts such as Bond and the Opera Babes, 'I am not a huge fan of some of the marketing that goes on. I come more from the background of wanting to see some honest music making' (Morrison, 2002). Increasing efforts seem to be made to promote institutions as being sexy, laid-back, and attractive to a younger audience. In the UK, a complaint against advertising by Phoenix Dance Theatre was upheld by the Advertising Standards Authority (ASA). 'Phoenix had advertised its show with an image of two distinctly naked dancers; and attracted by them, the complainant had purchased a ticket – only to find himself watching a performance in which not a stitch came off. In its defence, Phoenix argued that the nude image was no more than an atmospheric idea of a work that, being brand new, couldn't actually be photographed for its own advance publicity. But the ASA was unimpressed: if a leaflet showed naked dancers, they said, the public was entitled to naked dancers' (O'Boulez, 2003: 12).

Internationally, the pricing of the arts has been of public concern. For example, Hoggard highlighted the efforts of a whole range of UK arts institutions to provide cheaper ticket prices (Hoggard, 2003). Many accept that price represents a serious barrier to arts attendance. How does attendance at arts events relate to those for comparable occasions elsewhere, for example, soccer matches? One of the issues is that admission price can represent only a proportion of total income from all sources.

There seems some scope for bringing into arts management ideas from the private sector. This has been the case in the US for some time now. Recently in the UK, managers from an airline and a premier league football club addressed the Association of British Orchestras, extolling the virtues of applying yield management techniques. In the arts sectors, the use of subscription tickets has for some time been common in the performing arts and has now been adopted in the visual and other arts, most notably for special exhibitions. This approach enables those who book early and make multiple purchase for a series the chance to obtain discounts as against unit purchase of the same experience. However, the more sophisticated approach used by airlines has been unavailable to arts organisations as until now they have lacked the sort of technology that makes this feasible. This sort of approach, now being trialled by the Chicago Symphony, would mean that arts organisations would have the opportunity for example to increase price as the number of available tickets diminishes. A latecomer who turns up on the day of performance would therefore pay significantly more than those who prebook well in advance (Ward, 2003). It has to be said that this approach could mark a dramatic change from most current situations. At present the tendency seems to favour the last-minute approach. In theatre there is a cut-price ticket booth in Central London where unsold tickets are sold off cheaply on the day of a performance. However, in film exhibition, public sector principles of marketing have always been in practice. The first cinemas were wholly commercial enterprises. This is another manifestation of diversity of the marketing issues in the arts sector.

Some of the most interesting questions about the arts are concerned with politics and power. The appointment of the artistic director, normally undertaken by the board and the administrator or senior manager could set the artistic policy for some years and this is a critically important step. Yet no one would expect that the marketing departments can or should have a contribution to make in such a decision. Sometimes this decision seems to have been made on anything but artistic grounds.

The contributors to this volume represent a considerable level of diversity, most obviously in terms of their sectors or national origin but also in terms of their experience and the perspectives they bring. Furthermore, they have drawn on an eclectic range of sources, moving from film to personal experience to newspapers to conversations, as well as more traditional academic sources such as academic journal articles and interview. An Anglocentric or Western European view of the high arts is the prevailing orientation. However, we believe that our volume offers further heterodox insights from the margins.

Most importantly, many of the chapters draw on recent experience and primary research by their authors and others. A personal perspective in the arts is appropriate and indeed inevitable given that tastes differ from person to person and over a lifetime as learning takes place. What is surprising perhaps is the sense that so many researchers tend to deny this in the stance they adopt. Obviously all authors write not just out of their experience as consumers of the arts, but from managerial perspectives and to varying extents from participant observation. For example, many have worked as consultants to arts organisations. Dorothea Noble is past chair of Jazz East, and Iain Fraser chair of the Whitehall Theatre, Dundee. The approaches adopted by individual authors vary from those which develop and exemplify the systems, model based view of marketing to more radical themes from feminist or complexity perspectives.

Questions around audience development and marketing as well as government subsidy and the complications of dealing with a variety of conflicting publics therefore have a significant influence in forming the chapter content and the views expressed therein. Furthermore, diversity seems to be crucial. There is much talk of the importance of creative clusters where practitioners both compete and collaborate. Dorothea Noble and Iain Fraser have experience as chairs of arts organisations.

This volume has dealt with many key issues in arts marketing. However, much still remains to be explored. Arts marketing is still a relatively new discipline, despite recent developments. The attention being paid to the practice of marketing within the arts by the academic and practitioner community is set to develop the arts marketing further.

References

Abdalla, Amr. et al. (2002). *Evaluation Report No. 2 Studio Ijmabo, for Search For Common Ground*.

Adams, S. (1997). *The Barbizon School and the Origins of Impressionism*. UK: Phaidon Press.

Ades, D. (1988). *Dali*. London: Thames and Hudson.

Ahlquist, K. (1997). *Democracy at the Opera: Music, Theatre, and Culture in New York City, 1815–60*. Urbana, IL: University of Illinois Press.

Alan, C. (1992). U2: *Wide Awake in America*. Boxtree.

Alberge, D. (2003). ENO's new director 'the man to rescue company'. *The Times*, London, 7.

Aldeburgh Productions (2003). *The History of Aldenburgh Productions*. Aldburgh Productions.

Ambrose, J. (2001). *The Violent World of Moshpit Culture*. Music Sales Ltd., London: Omnibus Press.

Anderson, P. (1991). Constructing the arts industry. *Culture and Policy*, **3** (2), 51–63.

Andreasen, A. R. (1985). Marketing or selling the arts: an organisational dilemma. *Journal of Arts Management and Law*, **15** (1), 9–20.

Annual reports for Art Gallery of New South Wales, Canterbury Museum, Museum of New Zealand Te Papa Tongarewa, Museum of Victoria, National Gallery of Victoria 1945–2002 (various).

Anon (1978). A night at t'Opera. *The Sunday Times Magazine*, London, 78.

Antaki, C. and Widdicombe, S. (eds.) (1998). *Identities in Talk*. Sage.

Arnould, Price and Zinkhan (2002). *Consumers*. New York: McGraw-Hill.

Arts Council of England (1996). *Policy Document for Support of Jazz in England*. London: Arts Council of England.

Atal, Y. et al. (eds.) (1997). Poverty and participation in civil society. *Proceedings of a UNESCO/CROP Round Table* organized at the World Summit for Social Development in March 1995, Copenhagen, Denmark.

Atkins, H. and Newman, A. (1978). *Beecham Stories: Anecdotes, Sayings and Impressions of Sir Thomas Beecham*. London: Robson Books.

Austin, B. (1981). Rating the movies. *Journal of Popular Film and Television*, **7** (4), 384–99.

Austin, B. A. (1983). Critics' and consumers' evaluation of motion pictures: a longitudinal test of the taste culture and elitist hypotheses. *Journal of Popular Film and Television*, **10**, 156–67.

Austin, B. A. (1989). *Immediate Seating: A Look at Movie Audiences*. Belmont, CA: Wadsworth.

Australia Council (1990). Museums, Art Museums and Public Galleries: Report of a Survey, 1988–89, *Research Paper No. 3*, May, Australia Council, Redfern.

Australia Council (1991). Museums 1990: Art Museums, Museums and Public Galleries in Australia and New Zealand. *Research Paper No. 6*, May, Australia Council, Redfern.

Australia Council (1992). Museums 1991: Art Museums, Museums and Public Galleries in Australia and New Zealand. *Research Paper No. 7*, July, Australia Council, Redfern.

Australia Council (1993). Museums 1992: Art Museums, Museums and Public Galleries in Australia and New Zealand. *Research Paper No. 9*, June, Australia Council, Redfern.

Australia Council (1994). Museums 1993: Art Museums, Museums and Public Galleries in Australia. *Research Paper No. 12*, May, Australia Council, Redfern.

Australia Council (1995). Museums 1994: Art Museums, Museums and Public Galleries in Australia. *Research Paper No. 14*, June, Australia Council, Redfern.

Australia Council (2001). Planning for the Future: Issues, Trends and Opportunities for the Arts in Australia, Discussion Paper – February 2001. www.ozco.gov.au

Baddeley, G. (2000). *Dissecting Marilyn Manson*. Medford, NJ: Plexus.

Bailey, M. (1990). *Young Vincent: The Story of Van Gogh's Years in London*. London: Allison and Busby.

Balio, T. (1976). *The American Film Industry*. Wisconsin: The University of Wisconsin Press.

Barker, C. (2000). *Cultural Studies: Theory and Practice*. London: Sage.

Barnbrook, J. (1998). *Young British Art: The Saatchi Decade*. UK: Booth-Clibborn Editions.

Barolsky, P. (1995). A very brief history of art from Narcissus to Picasso. *The Classical Journal*, **90** (3), 255–9.

Barrere, C. and Santagata, W. (1999). Defining art. From the Brancusi trial to the economics of artistic semiotic goods. *International Journal of Arts Management*, **1** (2), 28–38.

Barrett, F. J. (1998). Creativity and improvisation in Jazz and organisations: implications for management learning. *Organisation Science*, **9** (50), 605–22.

Bates, C. S. (1983). An unexplored international market: the art market. *Journal of the Academy of Marketing Science*, **11** (Summer), 240–9.

Baumol, W. J. (1986). Unnatural value: or art investment as floating crap game. *American Economic Review*, **76**, 10–14.

Becker, H. S. (1978). Arts and crafts. *American Journal of Sociology*, 83, January, 862–89.

Becker, H. S. (1982). *Art Worlds*. London: University of California Press.

Beer, M. et al. (1984). *Managing Human Assets*. New York: Free Press.

Belk, R. and Groves, R. (1999). Marketing and the multiple meanings of Australian aboriginal art. *Journal of Macromarketing*, **19** (1), 20–33.

Benedetti, J. (2001). *David Garrick and the Birth of Modern Theatre*. Methuen.

Bennett, T. (1994). *The Reluctant Museum Visitor: A Study of Non-Goers to History Museums and Art Galleries*. Sydney: Australia Council.

Bennett, A. (2000). *Popular Music and Youth Culture: Music, Identity and Place.* Palgrave.

Bennett, A. (2001). *Cultures of Popular Music.* Open University Press.

Bennett, R. (2002). Competitor Analysis Practices of Grant-aided Provincial UK Theatre Companies. *Second Annual Colloquium on Nonprofit, Social and Arts Marketing,* Henley Management College and London Metropolitan University.

Bennett, T. and Frow, J. (1991). *Art Galleries: Who Goes?* Sydney: Australia Council.

Bennett, R. and Kottasz, R. (2001). Lead user influence on new product development decisions of UK theatre companies: an empirical study. *International Journal of Arts Management,* **3** (2), 28–39.

Berry, L. L. (ed.) (1983). 'Relationship Marketing' in AMA. *Emerging Perspectives on Services Marketing.* Chicago: AMA.

Bertone, S., Keating, C. and Mullaly, J. (1998). *The Taxidriver, the Cook and the Greengrocer: The Representation of Non-English Background People in Theatre, Film and Television.* Sydney: Australia Council.

Besterman, T. (1998). Saying what museums are for – and why it matters. *Museums Journal,* April, 37.

Betts, E. (1973). *The Film Business, A History of British Cinema 1896–1972.* London: George Allen and Unwin.

Bhattacharya, C. B., Rao, H. and Glynn, M. A. (1995). Understanding the bond of identification: an investigation of its correlates among art museum members. *Journal of Marketing,* **59**, October, 46–57.

Bigglook (2001). Disiplinlerarası Eğitmen Atölyesi/Deneysel Çalışmalar Karma Sergisi and Aktuel (2001). Varos miniklerine müzisyen okulu [online]. Available from: http://www.bilgi.edu.tr

Black, L. (1990). Hans Keller (1919–1985). The Keller Column. R. Matthew-Walker. London, Alfred Lengnick & Company Ltd. for the Motor Neurone Disease Association.

Blenker, P. (2001). In search of an adequate marketing approach for small entrepreneurial firms. In *Research at the Marketing/Entrepreneurship Interface* (Hills, G. E., Hansen, D. J. and Merrilees, B., eds.), pp. 70–85. Chicago: University of Illinois.

Boden, D. (1994). *The Business of Talk: Organisations in Action.* Cambridge: Polity Press.

Bokina, J. (1979). *Opera and Politics.* Yale University Press.

Botti, S. (2000). What role for marketing in the arts? An analysis of arts consumption and artistic value. *International Journal of Arts Management,* **2** (3), 14–27.

Bouder-Pailer, D. (1999). A model for measuring the goals of theatre attendance. *International Journal of Arts Management,* **1** (2), 4–15.

Bourgeon-Renault, D. (2000). Evaluating consumer behaviour in the field of arts and culture marketing. *International Journal of Arts Management,* **3** (1), 4–18.

Bowditch, G. (2003). A bold arts experiment or a patronising gimmick? *The Scotsman,* Edinburgh, 16.

Bowser, E. (1990). *History of the American Cinema, Vol. 2, 1907–1915.* New York: Charles Scribner's Sons.

Boyett, J. H. and Boyettt, J. T. (1998). *The Guru Guide: The Best Ideas of the Top Management Thinkers*. New York: John Wiley.

Brehm, J. (1966). *A Theory Psychological Reactance*. New York: Academic Press.

Broomhead, S. (2003). *Interview*. Glasgow: Scottish Opera.

Broomhead, S. (2003). *Interview*. London: English Touring Opera.

Brown, S. (1993). Postmodern marketing? *European Journal of Marketing*, **27** (4).

Brown, S. and Patterson, A. (2000). Figments for sale: marketing, imagination and the artistic imperative. In *Imagining Marketing: Art, Aesthetics and The Avant Garde* (Brown, S. and Patterson, A., eds.), pp. 4–32. London: Routledge.

Brownlie, D., Saren, M., Wensley, R. and Whittington, R. (1999). *Rethinking Marketing*. Sage.

Buckley, J., Duane, O., Ellingham, M. and Spicer, A. (1999). *The Rough Guide to Rock*, 2nd edn. London: The Rough Guides.

Butler, P. (2000). By popular demand: marketing the arts. *Journal of Marketing Management*, **16**, 343–64.

Byron, S. (1981). Big bucks, big losers. *Rolling Stone*, **17**, 14 December, 44.

Calder, J. (2003). *Interview*. London: Calder bookshop.

Caldwell, M. (2001). Applying general living systems theory to learn consumers' sense making in attending performing arts. *Psychology and Marketing*, **18** (5), 497.

Cameron, S. (1995). On the role of critics in the cultural industry. *Journal of Cultural Economics*, **19** (4), 321–31.

Carson, D. J. (1985). The evolution of marketing in small firms, in marketing and small business (special issue). *European Journal of Marketing*, **19** (5), 7–9.

Carson, P. P. and Carson, K. D. (1998). Theoretically grounding management history as a relevant and valuable form of knowledge. *Journal of Management History*, **4** (1), 29–42.

Carson, D. and Coviello, N. (1996). Qualitative research issues at the marketing/entrepreneurship interface. *Marketing Intelligence and Planning*, **14** (6), 51–8.

Carson, D., Cromie, S., McGowan, P. and Hill, J. (1995). *Marketing and Entrepreneurship in SMEs. An Innovative Approach*. UK: Prentice Hall.

Cashman, (2003). *Thinking Big! A Guide to Strategic Marketing Planning for Arts Organisations*. Arts Marketing Association.

Castells, M. (1996). The information age: economy, society, and culture. *The Rise of the Network Society*, 1. Cornwall: Blackwell.

Caust, J. (1999). Is the Audience more important than the art? The impact of economic rationalist policies on government intervention in the cultural sector with particular reference to Australia from 1993–1999, *AIMAC Conference*. Finland: Helsinki School of Economics and Business Administration.

Cavicchi, D. (1999). *Tramps Like Us: Music and Meaning Among Springsteen Fans*. Oxford: Oxford University Press.

Caws, M. A. (2001). *Manifesto: A Century of ISMS*. London: University of Nebraska Press.

Chambers, R. (1947). The need for statistical research. *Annals of the American Academy of Political and Social Science*, **254**, 169–72.

Chanan, M. (1980). *The Dream that Kicks, The Prehistory and Early Years of Cinema in Britain*. London: Routledge & Keegan Paul.

Chartrand, H. H. (1984). An economic impact assessment of the fine arts. *Third International Conference on Cultural Economics and Planning*, Akron, Ohio.

Chartrand, H. H. (1990). Creativity and competitiveness: art in the information economy. *Arts Bulletin*, **15** (1).

Citron, M. J. (2000). *Opera on Screen*. New Haven and London: Yale University Press.

Clancy, P. (1997). *From Maestro to Manager* (Fitzgibbon, M. and Kelly, A., eds.). Dublin: Oak Tree Press.

Clark, R. (1996). *Art Education: Issues in Postmodernist Pedagogy*. Canadian Society for Education Through Arts and National Art Education Association.

Clawson, H. J. and Coolbaugh, K. (2001). The YouthARTS Development Project (OJJDP Juvenile Justice Bulletin No. NCJ186668). Rockville, MD: Juvenile Justice Clearinghouse.

Cleary, P. and Murphy, C. (2002). Census mirrors real Australia. *The Australian Financial Review*, 18 June, 1–8.

Colbert, F. (2001). *Marketing Culture and the Arts*. Montreal: Presses HEC.

Colegrave, S. and Sullivan, C. (2001). *Punk. A Life Apart*. London: Cassell & Co.

Collier, L. C. (1978). *The Making of Jazz*. London: Macmillan.

Collins, J. (2002). *Separated Out*. Helter Skelter.

Committee of Inquiry on Museums and National Collections (1975). Museums in Australia 1975. Report of the Committee of Inquiry on Museums and National Collections including the Report of the Planning Committee on the Gallery of Aboriginal Australia ('The Piggott Report'), AGPS, Canberra.

Commonwealth of Australia (1994). *Creative Nation*. Canberra: Australian Government Printing Service.

Condon, P. and Sangster, J. (1999). *The Complete Hitchcock*. UK: Virgin Publishing.

Cook, J. (1995). *The Golden Age of the English Theatre*. Simon and Schuster.

Cornia, G. et al. (1987). *Adjustment with a Human Face*, Vol. 1. Oxford: Clarendon.

Cornwell, T. (2003). Actors' union urges sale of Theatre Royal. *The Scotsman*. Edinburgh: 16.

Cowen, T. and Tabarrok, A. (2000). An economic theory of avant-garde and popular art, or high and low culture. *Southern Economic Journal*, **67** (2), 232–53.

Crozier, W. (1997). *Music and Social Influence. The Social Psychology of Music*. Hargreaves and North. Oxford: Oxford University Press.

Culshaw, J. (1976). *Reflections on Wagner's Ring*. London: Martin Secker and Warburg Limited.

Culturelink 2001. www.culturelink.org

Currie, G. and Hobart, C. (1994). Can opera be brought to the masses? A case study of Carmen the Opera. *Marketing Intelligence & Planning*, **12**, 13–18.

D'Astous, A. and Colbert, F. (2002). Moviegoers' consultation of critical reviews: psychological antecedents and consequences. *International Journal of Arts Management*, Fall edition.

D'Astous, A. and Touil, N. (1999). Consumer evaluations of movies on the basis of critics. *Judgements, Psychology and Marketing*, **16** (8), 677–94.

Dale, M. (1997). *The Movie Game, The Film Business in Britain, Europe and America*. London: Cassell.

Dali, S. (1993). *The Secret Life of Salvador Dali*, translated by H. M. Chevalier. London: Alkin Books.

Davies, I. (1995). *Cultural Studies and Beyond: Fragments of Empire*. London and New York: Routledge.

DCITA (2003). See Department of Communications, Information Technology and the Arts.

Deakin University (2002). *A Study into the Key Needs of Collecting Institutions in the Heritage Sector*. Final Report, Deakin University, Faculty of Arts, Cultural Heritage Centre for Asia and the Pacific, Melbourne.

De Krester, H. (2002). U Tlkin 2 Me – a text book case. *Journal of Arts Marketing*, July 2002, Issue 6, 18–9.

DeNora, T. (1999). Music as a technology of the self. *Poetics*, **27**, 31–56.

Department of Communications, Information Technology and the Arts (2003). *Review of the National Museum of Australia, its Exhibitions and Public Programs*. A Report to the Council of the National Museum of Australia. AGPS, Canberra. www.nma.gov.au/aboutus/council_and_committees/review [Accessed 29 September].

Department of Culture, Media and Sport (1998). *Comprehensive Spending Review: A New Approach to Investment in Culture*: Consultation Paper. London, Department of Culture, Media and Sport.

Department of the Environment, Transport and the Regions (1999). *Local Government Act 1999: Part 1 Implementing Best Value: Circular 10/99*. London: Department of the Environment, Transport and the Regions.

De Silva, I. (1998). Consumer selection of motion pictures. In *The Motion Picture Mega-Industry* (Litman, B. R., ed.), Needham Heights, MA: Allyn and Bacon.

De Vany and Walls (1996). Bose-Einstein dynamics and adaptive contracting in the motion picture industry. *The Economic Journal*, **106**, 1493–514.

De Vany, A. and Walls, W. D. (1997). The marketing for motion pictures: rank, revenue and survival. *Economic Inquiry*, **35** (4), 783–97.

De Vany, A. and Walls, W. D. (1999). Uncertainty in the movie industry: does star power reduce the terror of the box office? *Journal of Cultural Economics*, **23** (4), 285–318.

Dibb, S., Simkin, L., Pride, W. M. and Ferrell, O. C. (2001). *Marketing Concepts and Strategies*. Boston, MA: Houghton Mifflin.

DiMaggio, P., Useem, M. and Brown, P. (1978). *Audience Studies of the Performing Arts and Museums: A Critical Review*. Washington, DC: National Endowment for the Arts.

Doyle, P. (2000). *Value Based Marketing*. London: John Wiley and Sons Ltd.

Drummond, J. (2000). *Tainted by Experience*. London: Faber and Faber.

Durie, J., Pham, A. and Watson, N. (eds.) (1993). *The Film Marketing Handbook: A Practical Guide to Marketing Strategies for Independent Films*. Madrid: MEDIA Business School.

Durie, J., Pham, A. and Watson, N. (2000). *Marketing and Selling Your Film Around the World*, Los Angeles: Silman-James Press.

Dyer McCann, R. (1987). *The First Tycoons*. New York: The Scarecrow Press, Inc.

European Audiovisual Observatory (2003). *Focus 2003, World Film Market Trends*, Strasbourg. http://www.obs.coe.int/medium/film.html.en

Ebert, P. (1999). *In This Theatre of Man's Life*, pp. 238. Lewes Sussex: The Book Guild Ltd.

Eco, U. (1977). *Das offene Kunstwerk*. Wiesbaden, Gabler.

Ehrenzweig, A. (1970). *The Hidden Order of Art. A Study in the Psychology of Artistic Imagination*. London: Paladin.

Elias, N. (1983). *The Court Society*. Oxford: Blackwell.

Eliashberg, J. and Shugan, S. M. (1997). Film critics: influencers or predictors? *Journal of Marketing*, **61**, 68–78.

Eliot, T. S. (1919). *Tradition and the Individual Talent* in Selected Essays. London: Faber and Faber [republished 1999].

Elliott, R. (1994). Exploring the symbolic meaning of brands. *British Journal of Management*, 5, June.

Elliott, R. and Wattanasuwan, K. (1998). Brands as symbolic resources for the construction of identity. *International Journal of Advertising*, **17** (2), 131–44.

Ellis, J. C. (1995). *A History of Film*, 4th edn. Boston: Allyn and Bacon.

Erdogan, B. (1999). Celebrity endorsement: a literature review. *Journal of Marketing Management*, **15**, 291–314.

European Commission (1992). *MEDIA Programme*. Brussels: DGX.

Evans, P. W. (1995). *The Films of Luis Bunuel: Subjectivity and Desire*. Oxford: Clarendon Press.

Evans, P. (1996). Government action, social capital and development: reviewing the evidence on synergy. *World Development*, **24** (6), 1119–32.

Evrard, Y. (1991). Culture et marketing: incompatibilite ou reconciliation? In *Proceedings of the 1st International Conference on Arts Management* (Colbert. F. and Mitchell, C., eds.). Montreal, Ecole des HEC. University of Waterloo, pp. 37–50.

Falk, J. H. and Dierking, L. D. (1992). *The Museum Experience*. Washington, DC: Whalesback Books.

Fawkes, R. (2000). *Opera on Film*. London: Gerald Duckworth & Company.

Feintuch, B. (ed.) (2003). *Eight Words for the Study of Expressive Culture*. Urbana-Champain: University of Illinois Press.

Feist, A. (1997). *From Maestro to Manager* (Fitzgibbon, M. and Kelly, A., eds.). Dublin: Oak Tree Press.

Feist, A. (1997). Consumption in the arts and cultural industries: recent trends in the UK. In *From Maestro to Manager* (Fitzgibbon, M. and Kelly, A., eds.). Dublin: Oak Tree Press.

Fenton, J. (2003). Defenders of lost causes. *The Guardian*, London, 24.

Fillis, I. (1993). *An exploratory examination concerning the use of marketing's promotional mix in visual art organisations*. Unpublished Masters Thesis, University of Ulster.

Fillis, I. (2000a). *An examination of the internationalisation process of the smaller craft firm in the United Kingdom and the Republic of Ireland*. Unpublished Doctoral Thesis, University of Stirling.

Fillis, I. (2000b). Being creative at the marketing/entrepreneurship interface: lessons from the art industry. *Journal of Research in Marketing and Entrepreneurship*, 2 (2), 125–37.

Fillis, I. (2001). Small firm internationalisation: an investigative survey and future research directions. *Management Decision*, **39** (9), 767–83.

Fillis, I. (2002a). Creativity, marketing and the arts organisation: what can the artist offer? *International Journal of Nonprofit and Voluntary Sector Marketing*, **7** (2), 131–45.

Fillis, I. (2002b). An Andalusian dog or a rising star: creativity and the marketing/entrepreneurship interface. *Journal of Marketing Management*, **18** (3/4), 379–95.

Fillis, I. and Herman, R. (2003). A biographical study of Isambard Kingdom Brunel as insight into entrepreneurial marketing endeavour. *Proceedings of the 8th Annual Academy of Marketing Symposium on the Marketing/Entrepreneurship Interface*, University of Gloucestershire, Cheltenham, January 8–10.

Fillis, I. and McAuley, A. (2000). Modelling and measuring creativity at the interface. *Journal of Marketing Theory and Practice*, **8** (2), 8–17.

Finney, A. (1996). *The State of European Cinema, A New Dose of Reality*. London: Cassell.

Fisher, T. C. G. and Preece, S. B. (2002). Evaluating performing arts overlap. *International Journal Of Arts Management*, **4** (3), 20–32.

Fox, D. M. (1963). *Engines of Culture: Philanthropy and Arts Museums*. Ann Arbor: Edwards Brothers.

Fraser, I. (1998). Friends' societies in British theatres: underdeveloped marketing devices? *1998 Annual Conference of The Academy of Marketing*. Sheffield: Sheffield Business School.

Fraser, I. (1998). Customer Development: a neglected technique?

Fraser, P. J. (2003). With the slight exception of money' and other stories. *Academy of Marketing/AMA/UIC Special Interest Group Research Symposium on the Marketing and Entrepreneurship Interface*, University of Gloucestershire, Cheltenham.

Fraser, I. S. and Fraser, P. J. (2003). Fund raising for the performing arts: life after the lottery – how can we adapt? Marketing Paper 18. University of Hertfordshire, 15.

Frith, S. (1996). *Performing Rites: On the Value of Popular Music*. Harvard University Press.

Furlong, W. et al. (eds.) (2000). *Issues in Art and Education: The Dynamics of Now*. London: Tate Gallery Publishing and Wimbledon School of Art.

Gainer, B. (1995). Ritual and relationships: interpersonal influences on shared consumption. *Journal of Business Research*, **32**, 253–60.

Gainer, B. and Padanyi, P. (2002). Applying the marketing concept to cultural organisations: an empirical study of the relationship between market orientation and performance. *International Journal of Nonprofit and Voluntary Sector Marketing*, **7** (2), 182–94.

Galbraith, J. K. (1973). *Economics and the Public Purpose*. Toronto: New American Library.

Gander, P. (1998). Playing to the Gallery. *Marketing Business*, June, 10–13.

Garbarino, E. and Johnson, M. S. (1999). The different roles of satisfaction, trust, and commitment in customer relationships. *Journal of Marketing*, **63** (April), 70–87.

Garratt, S. (1998). *Adventures in Wonderland: A Decade of Club Culture*. Headline.

Gelder, K. and Thornton, S. (eds.) (1997). *The Subcultures Reader*. Routledge.

Gibson, I. (1997). *The Shameful Life of Salvador Dali*. London: Faber and Faber.

Giddens, A. (1990). *The Consequences of Modernity*. Cornwall: Polity Press.

Giesekam, G. (2000). *Luvvies and Rude Mechanicals? Amateur and Community Theatre in Scotland*. Edinburgh: Scottish Arts Council.

Gill, A. (2001). *Peggy Guggenheim. The Life of an Art Addict*. London: HarperCollins.

Gill, J. and Johnson, P. (1991). *Research Methods for Managers*. London: Paul Chapman Publishing.

Goa, D. (2001). Communities and Museums: Building Lasting Relationships. Canadian Museums Association. www.museums.ca/diversity/pubrelationships.htm

Goldberg, F. (1991). *Motion Picture Marketing and Distribution*. Boston/London: Focal Press.

Goodall, H. (2001). *Big Bangs: The Story of Five Discoveries that Changed Musical History*. London: Vintage.

Goodridge, M. (1995). A dead cert? *Marketing Business Journal*, November 1995.

Gorn, G. J. (1982). The effects of music in advertising on choice behaviour: a classical conditioning approach. *Journal of Marketing*, **46** (Winter), 94–101.

Graham, G. (1997). *Philosophy of the Arts. An Introduction to Aesthetics*. London: Routledge.

Grampp, W. D. (1989). *Pricing the Priceless. Arts, Artists and Economics*. New York: Basic Books.

Gregory, A. (1997). The roles of music in society: the ethnomusicological perspective. In *The Social Psychology of Music* (Hargreaves, D. and North, A., eds.). Oxford: Oxford University Press.

Greig, D. (2003). *Interview*. Glasgow: Scottish Opera.

Gummesson, E. (2002). Practical value of adequate marketing management theory. *European Journal of Marketing*, **36** (3), 325–49.

Guthrie, T. (1961). *A Life in the Theatre*. London: Hamish Hamilton.

Hackley, C. (1998). Social constructionism and research in marketing and advertising. *Qualitative Market Research*, **1** (3).

Hackley, C. E. and Mumby-Croft, R. (1999). Marketing entrepreneurs as creative agents in a social matrix: towards a theoretical framework for marketing entrepreneurship. In *Proceedings of the Academy of Marketing UIC/MEIG-AMA Symposia on the Marketing and Entrepreneurship Interface* (Hulbert, B., Day, J. and Shaw, E., eds.), 1996–1998, pp. 505–14. Northampton: Nene University College.

Hagoort, G. (2000). *Art Management: Entrepreneurial Style*, 3e Eburon.

Hall, S. (ed.) (1997). *Representation: Cultural Representations and Signifying Practices*. Sage.

Hancocks, A. (1987). Museum exhibition as a tool for social awareness. *Curator: The Museums Journal*, **30** (3), 181–92.

Hanson, L. and Hanson, E. (1955). *Passionate Pilgrim. The Life of Vincent Van Gogh*. New York: Random House.

Harewood, G. L. (1972). Foreword. *Scottish Opera: The First Ten Years* (Wilson, C., ed.), p. 1. London: Collins.

Hargreaves, D. J. and North, A. C. (eds.) (1997). *The Social Psychology of Music*. Oxford: Oxford University Press.

Harland, J. and Kinder, K. (1999). *Crossing the Line*. Calouste Gulbenkian Foundation.

Harland, J., Kinder, K. et al. (1995). Arts in their view: a study of youth participation in the arts. Slough, National Foundation for Educational Research in England and Wales.

Harris, C. and Alexander, A. (eds.) (1998). *Theorizing Fandom: Fans, Subculture and Identity*. Hampton Press.

Harrison, A. (2000). *Music The Business: The Essential Guide to the Law and the Deals*. Virgin Publishing.

Harrison, C. and Wood, P. (2000). *Art in Theory 1900–1990: An Anthology of Changing Ideas*. Oxford: Blackwell Publishers.

Harrison, C., Wood, P. and Gaiger, J. (1998). *Art in Theory 1815–1900: An Anthology of Changing Ideas*. Oxford: Blackwell Publishers.

Haslam, D. (1999). *Manchester England: The Story of the Pop Cult City*. Fourth Estate.

Hayes, D. and Slater, A. (2003). Making friendships work – a strategic marketing framework for Friends and membership schemes in the cultural sector, based on dimensions of loyalty: friends and membership schemes – definitions and characteristics. *Annual Conference of the Academy of Marketing*. Birmingham: Aston Business School.

Heart of the Nation Project Team (2000). *Heart of the Nation: A Cultural Strategy for Aotearoa New Zealand*. Wellington: McDermott Miller.

Hebdige, D. (1979). *Subculture: The Meaning of Style*. Routledge.

Heilbrun, J. and Gray, C. M. (2001). *The Economics of Art and Culture*, 2nd edn. Cambridge University Press.

Hendon, W. S. (1979). *Analysing an Art Museum*. USA: Praeger.

Herman, G. and Leyens, J. Ph. (1977). Ratings films on TV. *Journal of Communication*, **27**, 48–53.

Herrman, A., Franken, B., Huber, F., Ohlwein, M. and Schellhase, R. (1999). The conjoint analysis as an instrument for marketing controlling, taking a public theatre as an example. *International Journal of Arts Management*, **1** (3), 59–69.

Hewitt, P. (2003). Opening address. *Arts Marketing Association Conference*, Poole, Dorset.

Higgins, C. (2002). For a few pennies more. *The Guardian*, London, 11.

Higgins, C. (2003). Raymond Gubbay's new opera house will bring cheap classics to the West End – and could spell disaster for ENO. *The Guardian*, London, 9.

Hills, M. (2002). *Fan Cultures*. Routledge.

Hill, A. (2003). Schools schedules sideline the arts. *The Observer*, London, 12.

Hill, E., O'Sullivan, C. et al. (1995). *Creative Arts Marketing*. London: Butterworth-Heinemann.

Hirschman, E. (1980). Comprehending symbolic consumption: three theoritical issues. In *Symbolic Consumer Behavior, Advances in Consumer Research* (Hirschman, E. C. and Holbrook, M. B. eds.). Ann Arbor.

Hirschman, E. C. (1983). Aesthetics, ideologies and the limits of the marketing concept. *Journal of Marketing*, **47** (Summer), 45–55.

Hirschman, E. and Holbrook, M. (1982). Hedonic consumption: emerging concepts, methods and propositions. *Journal of Marketing*, **46** (Summer), 92–101.

Hodkinson, P. (2002). *Goth: Identity, Style and Subculture*. Berg.

Hogg, M. and Banister, E. (1999). The structure and transfer of cultural meaning: a study of young consumers and pop music. *Advances in Consumer Research*.

Hoggard, L. (2003). Arts on the cheap. *The Observer*, London, 6–7.

Holbrook, M. (1986). I'm Hip: an autobiographical account of some musical consumption experiences. *Advances in Consumer Research*, **13**, 614–18.

Holbrook, M. (1987). An audiovisual inventory of some fanatic consumer behaviour: the 25 cent tour of a Jazz collectors home. *Advances in Consumer Research*, **14**, 144–9.

Holbrook, M. B. (1980). Introduction: the esthetic imperative in consumer research. In *Symbolic Consumer Behavior, Proceedings of the Association for Consumer Research Conference on Consumer Esthetics and Symbolic Consumption*, pp. 36–7.

Holbrook, M. B. (1981). Introduction: the esthetic imperative in consumer research. In *Symbolic Consumer Behavior* (Hirschman, E. C. and Holbrook, M. B., eds.). Ann Arbor, MI: Association for Consumer Research.

Holbrook, M. B. (1999). Popular appeal versus expert judgements of motion pictures. *Journal of Consumer Research*, **26**, 144–55.

Holbrook, M. B. and Zirlin, R. B. (1983). Artistic creation, artworks and aesthetic appreciation: some philosophical contributions to nonprofit marketing. In *Nonprofit Marketing* (Belk, R., ed.), Vol. 1. Greenwich, CT: JAI Press.

Holland, D. K. (2002). Cause and effect: why now, more than ever, the non-profit world needs design and vice versa. *Communication Arts*, **44** (1), March–April.

Honig, E. A. (1998). *Painting and the Market in Early Modern Antwerp*. London: Yale University Press.

Hopkins, J. and Sugerman, D. (1980). *No One Here Gets Out Alive*. London: Plexus.

Horner, B. and Swiss, T. (eds.) (1999). *Key Terms in Popular Music and Culture*. Oxford: Blackwell Publishers.

Horowitz, J. (1994). *Understanding Toscanini*. University of California Press.

Howard, U. (1982). *Artistry: The Work of Artists*. Indianapolis: Hackett.

Hubhard, G. and Taylor, D. (eds.) (1976). Challenge and change in art education. *Bulletin of the School of Education*, Indiana University, **52** (3), May 1976.

Huettig, M. D. (1944). *Economic Control of the Motion Picture Industry*. M.Phil. dissertation, University of Pennsylvania.

Hunt, S. D. (1976). The nature and scope of marketing. *Journal of Marketing*, **40**, 17–28.

Hutcheon, L. and Hutcheon, M. (1999). *Opera: Desire, Disease, Death*. University of Nebraska Press.

Hutchinson, D. (1977). *The Modern Scottish Theatre*. Glasgow: The Molendinar Press.

Hytner, N. (2003). To hell with targets. *Observer Review*, 12 January, 6.

Ikavälko, M. (2003). Relational exchange and commitment in art sponsorship. Case: finnish national Opera and Sampo. *International Conference on Arts and Cultural Management*, Milan, Italy: Universitá Commerciale Luigi Bocconi.

Ilott, T. (1996). *Budgets and Markets, a Study of the Budgeting of European Film*. London: Routledge.

International Council of Museums (1995). Statutes: Code of Professional Ethics, ICOM, Paris.

International Council of Museums (1997). Museums and Cultural Diversity: Policy Statement: Report of the Working Group on Cross Cultural Issues of the International Council of Museums, Paris.

Iverne, J. (2000). *The Impresarios*. Oberon Books.

Jacobs, L. (1968). *The Rise of the American Film.* New York: Teachers College.

Jedidi, K., Krider, R. E. and Weinberg, C. B. (1998). Clustering at the Movies. *Marketing Letters*, **9** (4), 393–405.

Jobber, D. (2001). *Principles and Practice of Marketing*, 3rd edn. McGraw-Hill.

Johanson, K. and Rentschler, R. (2002). The new arts leader: Australia Council and cultural policy change. *International Journal of Cultural Policy*, **8** (2), 167–80.

Johnson, B. (2002). Unsound insights, in looking back, looking ahead: popular music studies 20 years later. *Proceedings of the Eleventh Biannual IASPM Conference* (Kimi Karki, Rebecca Leydon and Henri Terho, eds.), pp. 704–12, July 6–10, 2001, Turku Finland: IASPM-Norden.

Johnson, M. S. and Garbarino, E. (1999). Customers of performing arts organisations: are subscribers different from nonsubscribers? *International Journal of Nonprofit and Voluntary Sector Marketing*, **6** (1), 61–77.

Johnson, G. and Scholes, K. (2001). *Exploring Public Sector Strategy*. London: Prentice Hall.

Jones, J. M. and Ritz, C. J. (1991). Incorporating distribution into new product diffusion models. *International Journal of Research in Marketing*, **8**, 91–112.

Jordon, N. (1997). Public Interview at Galway Arts Festival, Galway.

Judovitz, D. (1993). Art and economics: Duchamp's postmodern returns. *Criticism: A Quarterly for Literature and the Arts*, **35** (2), 193–218.

Jowett, G. S. (1985). Giving them what they want: movie audience research before 1950. *Current Research in film, Audiences, Economics and Law*, **1**, 19–35.

Jyrama, A. (2002). Contemporary art markets – structure and actors: a study of art galleries in Finland, Sweden, France and Great Britain. *International Journal of Arts Management*, **4** (2), 50–65.

Kahan, R. (1998). Using database marketing techniques to enhance your one-to-one marketing initiatives. *Journal of Consumer Marketing*, **15** (5), 491–93.

Kapferer, J.-N. (1997). *Strategic Brand Management: New Approaches to Creating and Evaluating Brand Equity*. Kogan Page.

Katz, E. and Lazarsfeld, P. E. (1955). *Personal Influence: The Part Played by People in the Flow of Mass Communication*. Glencoe, IL: Free Press.

Kawashima, N. (1998). Knowing the public: a review of museum marketing literature and research. *Museum Management and Curatorship*, **17** (1), 17–40.

Kay, G. (2002). Counting on Opera. *Opera*, **53**, 1447–53.

Kelly, M. (1826). *Reminscences*. London: Oxford University Press.

Kelly, L. and Sas, J. (1998). Separate or inseparable? marketing and visitor studies. Paper presented at *ICOM Conference Marketing and Public Relations*. Melbourne, Australia: 12–14 October.

Kerrigan, F. (2001). The good, the bad and the ugly: the role of trust in marketing films. *Academy of Marketing Annual Conference*, Cardiff Business School.

Kerrigan, F. (2002). Does structure matter? an analysis of the interplay between company structure and the marketing process in the film industry. *Academy of Marketing Conference*, University of Nottingham Business School.

Kerrigan, F. and Ozbilgin, M. (2003). Film marketing in Europe – policy and practice. *AIMAC Conference*, Boconni University, Milan.

Klein, N. (2000). *No Logo*. Flamingo.

Kolb, B. M. (2000). *Marketing Cultural Organisations: New Strategies for Attracting Audiences to Classical Music, Dance, Museums, Theatre and Opera*. Dublin: Oak Tree Press.

Kotler, P. (1979). Strategies for introducing marketing into nonprofit organisations. *Journal of Marketing*, **43**, 37–44.

Kotler, N. and Kotler, P. (1998). *Museum Strategy and Marketing: Designing Missions, Building Audiences and Generating Revenue and Resources*. San Francisco: Jossey-Bass.

Kotler, P. and Levy, S. J. (1969). Broadening the concept of marketing. *Journal of Marketing*, 33, January, 10–15.

Kotler, P. and Scheff, J. (1997). *Standing Room Only: Strategies for Marketing the Performing Arts*. Boston, MA: Harvard Business School Press.

Kotler, P. et al. (2002). *Social Marketing: Improving the Quality of Life*. Thousand Oaks, London, New Delhi: Sage.

Kottasz, R. (2003). Motivating the affluent young male to donate to non-profit arts organisations. Paper presented at the *AIMAC Conference*, Boconni University, Milan.

Lacher, K. T. (1989). Hedonic consumption: music as a product. *Advances in Consumer Research*, **16**, 367–73.

Lacher, K. T. and Mizerski, R. (1994). An exploratory study of the responses and relationships involved in the evaluation of, and in the intention to purchase new rock music. *Journal of Consumer Research*, **21**, September, 366–80.

Laine, C. (2000). Sounding off: a home fit for heroes, unless you play jazz. *Observer Review*, 6 August, 6.

Lancaster, G. and Williams, I. (2000). Consumer segmentation in the grey market relative to rehabilitation products. *Studies in Social Marketing Working Paper Series No. 4*. London: University of North London, 25.

Larson, R. (1995). Secrets in the bedroom: adolescents' private use of media. *Journal of Youth and Adolescence*, **24**, 535–50.

Lebrecht, N. (2001). *Covent Garden the Untold Story: Dispatches from the English Culture War 1945–2001*. London: Pocket Books.

Leftwich, A. (1994). Governance, the state and the politics of development. *Development and Change*, **25** (2), 363–86.

Lendt, C. K. (1997). Kiss and sell: the making of a supergroup. New York: Billboard.

Levin, D. J. (ed.) (1994). *Opera through other eyes*. Stanford: Stanford University Press.

Lewis, G. (1992). Museums and their precursors: a brief world survey. In *Manual of Curatorship: A Guide to Museum Practice* (Thompson, J. M. A., ed.), 2nd edn., pp. 5–21. Oxford: Butterworth-Heinemann.

Lewis, L. (ed.) (1992). *Adoring Audiences: Fan Culture and Popular Media*. Routledge.

Levy, S. (1959). Symbols for sale, *Harvard Business Review*, July/August, 117–24.

Lipietz, A. (1994). Post-Fordism and democracy. In *Post-Fordism – A Reader* (Amin, A. et al. eds.). Bodmin: Blackwell.

Litman, B. R. (1983). Predicting success of theatrical movies: an empirical study. *Journal of Popular Culture*, **16**, 159–75.

Litman, B. R. and Ahn, H. (1998). Predicting financial Success of Motion Pictures. In *The Motion Picture Mega Industry* (Litman, B. R., ed.). Needham Heights, MA: Allyn and Bacon.

Litman, B. R. and Kohl, L. (1989). Predicting financial success of motion pictures: the 80s experience. *Journal of Media Economics*, **2**, 35–49.

Littlewood, J. (2003). *Joan's Book: The Autobiography of Joan Littlewood*. London: Methuen.

Longhurst, B. (1995). *Popular Music and Society*. Cambridge, UK: Polity Press.

Loock, F. (1988). *Kuntsponsoring*. Wiesbaden: Deutscher Universitats-Verlag.

Lowe, A. (1995). The basic social processes of entrepreneurial innovation. *International Journal of Entrepreneurial Behaviour and Research*, **2**, 37–53.

Lukk, T. (1997). *Movie Marketing, Opening the Picture and Giving it Legs*. Los Angeles: Silman James Press.

MacDonald, M. (1999). Strategic marketing planning: theory and practice. In *The Marketing Book*, 4th edn. (Baker, M. J., ed.), pp. 50–77. Oxford: Butterworth-Heinemann.

Maitland, H. (1997). *A Guide to Audience Development*. The Arts Council of England.

Malbon, B. (1999). *Clubbing: Dancing, Ecstasy and Vitality*. Routledge.

Marceau, J. et al. (1998). *Art: A World of History*. New York: DK Publishing.

Marcus, C. (1998). A practical yet meaningful approach to customer segmentation. *Journal of Consumer Marketing*, **15** (5), 494–504.

Martin, G. (1970). *The Opera Companion*. London: John Murray.

McCracken, G. (1988). *Culture and Consumption: New Approaches to the Symbolic Character of Consumer Goods and Activities*. Indiana University Press.

McDonald, H. and Harrison, P. (2002). The marketing and public relations practices of Australian performing arts presenters. *International Journal of Nonprofit and Voluntary Sector Marketing*, **7** (2), 105–17.

McGuffog, T. (1997). *Managing the Supply Chain with Speed and Certainty*. London: The Article Number Association.

McKinley Douglas Ltd. (1995a). *A Framework for Funding and Performance Measurement of Museums in New Zealand*. Wellington, New Zealand: Museum Directors' Federation.

McKinley Douglas Ltd. (1995b). *Resource Guide Developing Performance Indicators in New Zealand Museums*. A resource guide for museums, their boards, funders and stakeholders developed by Peter Ames and participants during four one-day workshops. Wellington, New Zealand: Museum Directors Federation.

McLean, F. (1994). Services marketing: The case of museums. *The Service Industries Journal*, **14** (2), April, 190–9.

McLean, F. (1995). Future directions for marketing in museums. *European Journal of Cultural Policy*, **1** (2), 355–68.

McLean, F. and Cooke, S. (1999). Museums and cultural identity: shaping the image of nations. In *Heritage and Museums: Shaping National Identity* (Fladmark, M., ed.), pp. 147–60. Shaftesbury: Donhead.

Mehegan, S. (1995). Sweet Charity. *Restaurant Business*, **94** (12), 32–4.

Meyer, J.-A. and Even, R. (1998). Marketing and the fine arts – inventory of a controversial relationship. *Journal of Cultural Economics*, **22**, 271–83.

Mick, D. (1986). Consumer research and semiotics: exploring the morphology of signs, symbols, and significance. *Journal of Consumer Research*. September, **13** (2), 196.

Middleton, R. (1990). *Studying Popular Music*. Open University Press.

Middleton, R. (ed.) (2000). *Reading Pop: Approaches to Textual Analysis in Popular Music*. Oxford: Oxford University Press.

Milliman, R. E. (1982). Using background music to affect the behaviour of supermarket shoppers. *Journal of Marketing*, **46** (Summer), 86–91.

Milliman, R. E. (1986). The influence of background music on the behaviour of restaurant Patrons. *Journal of Consumer Research*, **13**, September, 286–9.

Mixer, J. R. (1993). *Principles of Professional Fundraising: Useful Foundations for Successful Practice*. San Francisco: Jossey-Bass Publisher.

Mokwa, M. P., Dawson, W. M. et al. (eds.) (1980). *Marketing the Arts*. Praeger Series in Public and Nonprofit Sector Marketing. Englewood Cliffs, NJ: Praeger.

Montias, J. M. (1994). The sovereign consumer. The adaptation of works of art to demand in the Netherlands in the early modern period. In *Artists, Dealers, Consumers. On the Social World of Art* (Bevers, T., ed.), pp. 57–76. Hilversum: Veloren.

Morris Hargreaves McIntyre (2002). Unpublished document.

Morrison, J. (2002). Classical stars rail at musical 'illiteracy'. *The Independent on Sunday*, London, 15.

Morrison, J. (2003). ENO to reduce performances and cut 70 jobs. *The Independent on Sunday*, London, 7.

Morrison, R. (2003). Irish maverick will offer flair – and need savvy. *The Times*, London, 7.

Morton, A. (2001). *Madonna*. Michael O'Mara Books.

Murphy, B. (1993). *Museum of Contemporary Art: Vision and Context*. Museum of Contemporary Art, Sydney.

Murphy, A. (1999). *Jean-Francois Millet*. USA: Yale University Press.

Museums Association UK (2003). Museum definition. www.city.ac.uk/artspol/mus-def [Accessed 29 September].

Neelamegham, R. and Chintagunta, P. (1999). A Bayesian model to forecast new product performance in domestic and international markets. *Marketing Science*, **18** (2), 115–36.

Negus, K. (1992). *Producing Pop: Culture and Conflict in the Popular Music Industry*. Edward Arnold.

Negus, K. (1996). *Popular Music in Theory: An Introduction*. Polity Press.

Negus, K. (1999). *Music Genres and Corporate Cultures*. Routledge.

Noble, J. V. (1970). Museum manifesto. *Museum News*, April, 17–20.

Noble, D. (2000). Improvisation and emergence: jamming and managing. *Complexity and Management Centre Working Paper*, University of Hertfordshire Business School.

Norris, D. O. (2003). *Clappers: A History of Applause*. London: BBC Radio 4.

O'Boulez, L. (2003). *Music and Musicians*. Private Eye: 12.

O'Shaughnessy, J. and Holbrook, M. (1988). Understanding consumer behaviour: the linguistic turn in marketing research. *Journal of the Market Research Society*, **30** (2), 197–223.

O'Riordan, B. (2002). Advertisers home in on their targets. *The Australian Financial Review*, 18 June, 8.

Outhwaite, W. et al. (eds.) (1996). *Social Thought*. Oxford: Blackwell, p. 136.

PACT/MMC Report (1994). *Factors Influencing the Production, Supply and Exhibition of Independent Films in the UK Market*.

Padmore, E. (2002). Experiences in Opera Management. London: Talk at Calder Bookshop.

Pallin, G. (2003). *Stage Management: The Essential Handbook*. London: Nick Hern Books.

Panofsky, E. (1940). Meaning in the visual arts: views from the outside. In *The Meaning of the Humanities* (Greene, T. M., ed.). Princetown: Princetown University Press.

Park, C. and Young, S. (1986). Consumer response to television commercials: the impact of involvement and background music on brand attitude formation. *Journal of Marketing Research*, **23**, February, 11–24.

Parsons, P. (1987). *Shooting the Pianist: The Role of Government in the Arts*. Sydney: Currency Press.

Perren, A. (2001). Sex, lies and marketing: miramax and the development of the quality indie blockbuster. *Film Quarterly*, Winter.

Phillips, A. (1977). *The Arts in the Scottish Regions*. Edinburgh: Scottish Arts Council.

Pick, J. (1986). *The State and the Arts City Arts*. The Arts Council.

Piggott Report, The (1975). See Committee of Inquiry on Museums and National Collections.

Pine, J. and Gilmore, J. (1999). *Experience Economy: Work is Theatre and Every Business a Stage*. Harvard Business School Press.

Pucely, M. J., Mizerski, R. et al. (1988). A comparison of involvement measures for the purchase and consumption of pre-recorded music. *Advances in Consumer Research*, 15, pp. 37–42.

Puttnam, R. (1993). *Making Democracy Work*. Princeton, NJ: Princeton University.

Puttnam, D. (1997). *The Undeclared War, The Struggle for Control for the World's Film Industry*. London: Harper Collins Publishers.

Radbourne, J. (1998). The role of government in marketing the arts. *Journal of Arts Management*, Law and Society, **28** (1), Spring, 67–82.

Radbourne, J. and Fraser, M. (1996). *Arts Management: A Practical Guide*. Sydney: Allen and Unwin.

Ramos, F. (2002). *The FotoDialogo Method: Using Pictures and Storytelling as Learning Tools*, American University.

Ravid, S. A. (1999). Information, blockbusters, and stars: a study of the film industry. *The Journal of Business*, **72** (4), 463–92.

Raymond, C. (1992). *Members Matter*. Arts Council of England.

Raymond, C. (1999). *Essential Theatre*. Arts Council of England.

Rentschler, R. (1998). Museum and performing arts marketing: a climate of change. *Journal of Arts Management, Law and Society*, **28** (1), 83–96.

Rentschler, R. (2001). Entrepreneurship: from denial to discovery in nonprofit art museums? *Research at the Marketing/Entrepreneurship Interface* (Hills, G. E., Hansen, D. J. and Merrilees, B., eds.), pp. 582–94. Chicago: University of Illinois.

Rentschler, R. (2002). Arts marketing: the age of discovery. *Journal of Arts Management, Law and Society*, **32** (1), 7–14.

Rentschler, R. and Gilmore, A. (2002). Services marketing in museums. *International Journal of Arts Management*, **5** (1), 62–73.

Rentschler, R. and Wood, G. (2001). Cause related marketing: can the arts afford not to participate? *Services Marketing Quarterly*, **22** (1), 57–69.

Rentschler, R., Radbourne, J., Carr, R. and Rickard, J. (2002). Relationship marketing, audience retention and performing arts organization viability. *International Journal of Nonprofit and Voluntary Sector Marketing*, **7** (2), 118–30.

Reussner, E. (2002). Strategic management for visitor-oriented museums: a change of focus. *International Journal of Cultural Policy*, **9** (1).

Riccio, L., Rollins, J. and Riccio, A. (2003). *The SAIL Effect*. Washington, DC: WVSA Arts Connection.

Ro, R. (1998). *Have Gun Will Travel: The Spectacular Rise and Fall of Death Row Records*. Quartet Books.

Robertson, H. and Miglorino, P. (1996). *Open Up! Guidelines for Cultural Diversity*. Visitor Studies Australia Council, Sydney.

Robinson, D. (1996). *From Peep Show to Palace, The Birth of American Film*. New York: Columbia University Press.

Robinson, K. (2000). Arts education's place in a knowledge-based global economy. In *Learning and the Arts: Crossing Boundaries, Proceedings from an Invitational Meeting for Education, Arts and Youth Funders*. Held January 12–14, 2000, Los Angeles.

Robinson, K. (2001). *Out of Our Minds: Learning to Be Creative*. Oxford: Capstone.

Røine, E. (1997). *Psychodrama: Group Psychotherapy as Experimental Theatre*. London: Jessica Kingsley Publishers.

Rollins, J. A. and Riccio, L. L. (2002). Art is the heART: a palette of possibilities for Hospice care. *Pediatric Nursing*, **28** (4).

Roskill, M. (1967). *The Letters of Vincent Van Gogh*. Glasgow: The Fontana Library, Collins.

Roth, E. (1969). *The Business of Music: Reflections of a Music Publisher*. London: Cassell.

Rouget, G. (1985). *Music and Trance: A Theory of the Relations between Music and Possession*. University of Chicago Press.

Routh, C. (1996). The Genre Survey. *Development Digest*.

Sandford, C. (1997). *Bowie: Loving the Alien*. Warner Books.

Sargeant, A. (1999). *Marketing Management for Non-profit Organizations.* Oxford University Press.

Sawhney, M. S. and Eliashberg, J. (1996). A parsimoinious model for forecasting gross box-office revenues of motion pictures. *Marketing Science*, **15** (2), 113–31.

Scatena, D. (1997). *Kylie: An Unauthorised Biography*. Penguin Books.

Schmitt, B. (2000). *Experiential Marketing*. Free Press.

Schroeder, J. E. (1997). Andy Warhol: Consumer Researcher. In *Advances in Consumer Research* (Brucks, M. and MacInnis D. J. eds.), 24, UT, Provo, 476–82.

Schroeder, J. E. (2000). Edouard Manet, Calvin Klein and the strategic use of scandal. In *Imagining Marketing: Art, Aesthetics and the Avant Garde* (Brown, S. and Patterson, A., eds.), pp. 36–51. London: Routledge.

Schulze, G. (1992). *Die Erlebnis-Gesellschaft. Kultursoziologie der Gegenwart*. Frankfurt, New York.

Selwood, S. (ed.) (2001). *The UK Cultural Sector: Profile and Policy Issues*. Policy Studies Institute.

Sen, A. (2002). *How Does Culture Matter?* Cambridge: Trinity College.

Sewell, S. (2002). *The secret death of Salvador Dali.* London, Riverside Studios, 29th August to 18th September.

Shankar, A. (2000). Lost in music? Subjective personal introspection and popular music consumption. *Qualitative Market Research*, **3** (1), 27–37.

Shapiro, B. (1973). Marketing for nonprofit organisations. *Harvard Business Review*, September/October.

Shipton, A. (2001). *A New History of Jazz.* London: Continuum Books.

Shuker, R. (1998). *Key Concepts in Popular Music.* Routledge.

Shuker, R. (2001). *Understanding Popular Music*, 2nd edn. Routledge.

Silverman, G. (2001). *The Secrets of Word-of-Mouth Marketing: How to Trigger Exponential Sales Through Runaway Word of Mouth.* New York: American Management Association.

Şişmanyazıcı, N. (1998). *Discussing the Impact of Globalization on Intra-Firm Human Resources Management and Development: A Turkish Private Sector Perspective.* Unpublished M.Sc. dissertation, Development Studies Institute, The London School of Economics and Political Science.

Smith, G. (2000). *Lost in Music: A Pop Odyssey.* Picador.

Sochay, S. (1994). Predicting the performance of motion pictures. *Journal of Media Economics*, **7** (4), 1–20.

Somogyi, D. (2001). *Mapping the Music and Plotting a Course: a survey of music making provision for young people in the eastern region.* Cambridge: JazzAce.

Speller, S. (2001). The best value initiative. In *Exploring Public Sector Strategy* (Johnson, G. and Scholes, K., eds.), pp. 111–27. London: Prentice Hall.

Spybey, T. (1996). *Globalization and World Society.* Hong Kong: Polity Press.

Stacey, R. (2001). *Complex Responsive Processes in Organizations: Learning and Knowledge Creation.* London: Routledge.

Stacey, R. D. (2003). *Strategic Management and Organisational Dynamics: the challenge of complexity.* London: Prentice Hall.

Standing Committee on Canadian Heritage (1999). *A Sense of Place, a Sense of Being: The Evolving Role of the Federal Government in the Support of Culture in Canada.* Ninth Report of the Standing Committee on Canadian Heritage, Ottawa. www.pch.gc.ca (no page numbers).

Statistics New Zealand (1995). *New Zealand Cultural Statistics.* Wellington: Ministry of Cultural Affairs.

Stockdale, F. (1998). *Emperors of Song: Three Great Impresarios.* London: John Murray (Publishers) Ltd.

Stokes, D. and Lomax, W. (2002). Taking control of word of mouth marketing: the case of an entrepreneurial hotelier. *Journal of Small Business and Enterprise Development*, **9** (4), 349–57.

Sweetman, D. (1990). *The Love of Many Things: A Life of Vincent Van Gogh.* London: Hodder and Stoughton.

Tambling, P. (1990). *Performing Arts in the Primary School.* Oxford: Blackwell.

Tambling, P. (1999). Opera, education and the role of arts organisations. *British Journal of Music Education*, **16** (2), 130–56.

Tapp, A. (1998). *Principles of Direct and Database Marketing.* Financial Times Professional.

Taraborrelli, R. (2002). *Madonna: An Intimate Biography*. Pan Books.

Thomas, E. G. and Cutler, B. D. (1993). Marketing the fine and performing arts: What has marketing done for the arts lately? *Journal of Professional Services Marketing*, **10**, 181–99.

Thompson, G. D. (1998). Performance measurement in museums and New Zealand's service performance reporting model, paper presented at the *Accounting Association of Australia and New Zealand Conference*, Adelaide, 6–8 July.

Throsby, D. (1994). The production and consumption of the arts: a view of cultural economics. *Journal of Economic Literature*, **32**, 1–29.

Throsby, D. and Mills, D. (1989). *When Are You Going To Get A Real Job? An Economic Study of Australian Artists*. Sydney: Australia Council.

Titon, J. T. (1995). Text. *Journal of American Folklore*.

Titon, J. T. (2003). Text. In *Eight Words for the Study of Expressive Culture* (Feintuch, B., ed.), University of Illinois Press.

Tomes, S. (2002). Ceaselessly active in Irish airs and classic graces. *The Guardian*. London.

Tomlinson, R. (1993). *Boxing Clever*. London: Arts Council of England.

Tomlinson, R. (1998). *Box Office Marketing Guides*. London: Arts Council of England.

Towse, R. (2001). Quis Custodiet? or managing the management: the case of the Royal Opera House, Covent Garden. *International Journal of Arts Management*, **3** (3), 38–50.

Tucker, V. (eds.) (1997). *Cultural Perspectives on Development*. London and Portland, Frank Cass.

Tusa, J. (1999). *Art Matters: Reflecting on Culture*. London: Methuen.

Tusa, J. (2003). *On Creativity: Interviews Exploring the Process*. London: Methuen.

UNDP (2002). *Deepening Democracy in a Fragmented World in Human Development Report*. New York, Oxford: Oxford University Press.

United Nations Development Programme (2003). The global challenge: Goals and targets [online]. Available from: http://www.undp.org/mdg/ [Accessed February 2003].

Vasari, G. (1998). *The Lives of the Artists,* translation by J. C. Bondanella and P. Bondanella. Oxford: Oxford Paperbacks.

Volkerling, M. (2001). From cool britannia to hot nation: creative industries policies in Europe, Canada and New Zealand. *International Journal of Cultural Policy*, **7** (3), 437–55.

Waldman, M. (2003). *Operatunity*. L. Hausman. London: Channel 4.

Ward, D. (2003). Orchestra get airs on selling seats. *The Guardian*, London, 7.

Warhol, A. (1975). *The philosophy of Andy Warhol. From a to b and back again*. San Diego: Harcourt Brace and Company.

Weaver, W. (1977). *Verdi: a Documentary Study*. London: Thames and Hudson.

Weil, S. E. (1990). Rethinking the museum: an emerging new paradigm. In *Rethinking the Museum and Other Meditations*, pp. 57–65. Washington, DC: Smithsonian Institution Press.

Weil, S. E. (1994). Forum: creampuffs and hardball. *Museum News*, American Association of Museums, September–October, **73** (5), pp. 42–3, 60, 62.

Weise, M. (1989). *Film and Video Marketing.* Studio City, CA: Michael Wiese Productions.

Wensley, R. (1999). The basics of marketing strategy. In *The Marketing Book* (Baker, M. J., ed.), (4th edn.), pp. 16–49. Oxford: Butterworth-Heinemann.

Weppler, N. R. and Silvers, R. (2001). A museum vision. Canadian Museums Association. www.museums.ca/diversity/pubrelationships.htm

West, S. (1996). *The Bulfinch Guide to Art History: A Comprehensive Survey and Dictionary of Western Art and Architecture.* London: Bloomsbury.

White, T. (2000). *Catch a Fire: The Life of Bob Marley.* Omnibus Press.

Widdicombe, S. and Wooffitt, R. (1995). *The Language of Youth Subcultures: Social Identity in Action.* Harvester Wheatsheaf.

Wiggins, J. (2003). Motivation, ability and opportunity to participate: a reconceptualization of the RAND model of audience development. *Proceedings of the 7th International Conference on Arts and Culture*, Milan, Italy, 29 June–2 July.

Withers, G. (1985). Artists' subsidy of the arts. *Australian Economic Papers*, **24** (45), 290–5.

Witts, R. (1998). *Artist Unknown: an Alternative History of the Arts Council.* London: Warner Books.

Wolf, M. (2000). *The Entertainment Economy.* Three Rivers Press.

Wright, N. (2002). *Vincent in Brixton.* London: Nick Hern Books.

Zillmann, D. and Gan, S.-I. (1997). Musical tastes in adolescence. *The Social Psychology of Music*, (Hargreaves, D. and North, A., eds.), pp. 161–87. Oxford: Oxford University Press.

Zufryden, F. S. (1996). Linking advertising to box office performance of new film releases: a marketing planning model. *Journal of Advertising Research*, July–August, 29–41.

Zukor, A. (1954). *The Public is Never Wrong.* London: Cassell and Company Limited.

Index